CREATIVE CHURCH

HANDBOOK

Releasing *the* POWER *of the* ARTS *in* Your Congregation

J. SCOTT McELROY

IVP Books

An imprint of InterVarsity Press
Downers Grove, Illinois

InterVarsity Press
P.O. Box 1400, Downers Grove, IL 60515-1426
ivpress.com
email@ivpress.com

InterVarsity Press® is the book-publishing division of InterVarsity Christian Fellowship/USA®, a movement of students and faculty active on campus at hundreds of universities, colleges and schools of nursing in the United States of America, and a member movement of the International Fellowship of Evangelical Students. For information about local and regional activities, visit intervarsity.org.

All Scripture quotations, unless otherwise indicated, are taken from THE HOLY BIBLE, NEW INTERNATIONAL VERSION®, NIV® Copyright © 1973, 1978, 1984, 2011 by Biblica, Inc.™ Used by permission. All rights reserved worldwide.

While any stories in this book are true, some names and identifying information may have been changed to protect the privacy of individuals.

Cover design: David Fassett
Interior design: Beth McGill
Images: © agsandrew/iStockphoto

ISBN 978-0-8308-4120-2 (print)
ISBN 978-0-8308-9759-9 (digital)

Printed in the United States of America ∞

 As a member of the Green Press Initiative, InterVarsity Press is committed to protecting the environment and to the responsible use of natural resources. To learn more, visit greenpressinitiative.org.

Library of Congress Cataloging-in-Publication Data
McElroy, J. Scott.
 Creative church handbook : releasing the power of the arts in your
congregation / J. Scott McElroy.
   pages cm
 Includes bibliographical references.
 ISBN 978-0-8308-4120-2 (pbk. : alk. paper)—ISBN 978-0-8308-9759-9
(digital)
 1. Christianity and the arts. 2. Creative ability—Religious
aspects—Christianity. I. Title.
 BR115.A8M397 2015
 246—dc23
 2015006643

P 25 24 23 22 21 20 19 18 17 16 15 14 13 12 11 10 9 8 7 6 5 4 3 2 1
Y 36 35 34 33 32 31 30 29 28 27 26 25 24 23 22 21 20 19 18 17 16 15

father,

man who

ty-five years

th and

Contents

Preface

THE BOOK YOU ARE HOLDING is not complete.

That is because it's not possible to *completely* cover the broad topic of the arts and creativity in the church in the limited number of pages a book allows. So I had to make choices about this manuscript's content, which led to two things: first, a focus on the art forms that have been *underdeveloped* in churches—which I'll explain in a moment—and second, a decision to make available online a plethora of content that wouldn't physically fit in the book.

In addition to this print book, I'm excited to provide you with the complimentary "*Creative Church Handbook* Resources and Extras," an extensive online cache of related materials and ideas. At JScottMcElroy.com/CCHand bookextras you'll find worksheets, sample documents, advice and recommendations, many additional detailed projects, color versions of all the pictures in the book, dozens of extra photos and much more. These resources and extras are exclusively for *Creative Church Handbook* readers: they won't come up in Internet searches, and are only accessible through the special web address. You'll see the online resources and extras referenced throughout these pages and the special web address at the end of every chapter.

But even the online resources and extras can only go so far. This new renaissance of the arts and creativity in the church is continuing to develop. New ideas, materials and inspiration will become available. New leaders will join the movement. This is why the nonprofit organization The New Renaissance Arts Movement (TheNewR.org) was created: to provide updated information on all the concepts associated with this book, and to connect you with others who are working them out. Make sure you join the New Renaissance email list, check in on the blog or follow its social media sites for the latest on what is happening with the arts in the church.

Since the priority of this book is to focus on the many art forms that have been underdeveloped in churches, some of the more developed art forms—particularly music and the technical arts—have taken a back seat. That's not because they are less important. In fact, it's clear that music is one of the most powerful and effective expressions of the arts and creativity in the church. Musicians and their music can create an atmosphere of worship, lead us into God's presence, allow us to make art in community (congregational singing), and so much more. Plus, recorded music is portable, enabling us to recreate worship experiences wherever we are, or to add a worship soundtrack to the moments of life. Most of the art forms in this book can be paired with music or incorporate music in some way. But the choice was made to not explore the creation and execution of music in the church here simply because the majority of churches already incorporate music in their services and programs. To a large extent, the modern church understands the impact and appeal of music. It's the other fields of the arts that we need help with.

Another area I don't fully explore is the realm of the technical arts—all the wonderful tools that can be used to mix and enhance sound, create lighting effects, project images and more. These of course require and add a great deal of creativity. They are often essential in the modern church experience and profoundly enhance how the congregation connects with the service and the message. But in-depth technical advice is a topic for another book, although I do include some thoughts here in this book, as well as recommendations and links in the online resources and extras. You can also find more information on the New Renaissance website.

One thing you *will* find here and in the online resources and extras is a thorough discussion of arts ministry: how to develop it and how to maintain it. This is because I believe arts ministry—sharing God's love through any and all mediums of the arts—plays an essential role in cultivating a church community where creativity can thrive. It can be part of the foundation of a creative church. Because it's rare to find in-depth guidance and information about arts ministry, the publisher and I have endeavored to provide a comprehensive overview here.

It's my hope that book this will become a treasured handbook for you. It's my prayer that God will use it and the resources associated with it to further his kingdom work in your life and in your church.

Introduction

WE LIVE AT AN EXTRAORDINARY TIME in history. Powerful, creative tools, unimaginable even a hundred years ago, are available to grade-school children. Instantaneous global connection is commonplace. Images and ideas packaged with the power of the arts can spread around the world in seconds. We're experiencing the greatest technological, communication and creative advances humans have ever seen.

Believers can detect God's presence in these advances. Our inadequate conceptions of him are frequently challenged by creative technology like the Hubble Telescope, which gives us new insight into his exquisite and boundless imagination. New scientific revelations about the complexities and processes of life and organisms give us a glimpse of his omnipotence.

The church is benefiting from technological innovations as well, realizing more ways to connect and communicate God's love, share the gospel and inspire revival. Quite a few congregations, especially larger ones, are actively using creative new media. However, for many churches, expanding their creativity beyond technology and music has been a challenge. (There are a number of reasons for this, which I'll discuss later.) These applications are just the tip of the iceberg; there is so much more creativity that God wants his church to enjoy and benefit from. In fact, many Christian leaders sense that he is inviting his people into higher levels of creativity and collaboration with him in all the art forms, from ancient art practices to cutting-edge technology to public art installations, from fine art to film to finger-painting. There is a sense that God is awakening the arts and creativity as natural expressions of worship, life and outreach for his bride, and that he is calling us to explore how we might more fully reflect his love and his character to humanity through these powerful mediums. Many are realizing that God wants to activate the creativity *inherent in us all* and actually collaborate with us in it. If we accept this invitation, creativity can thrive in our lives and churches, bringing us to a new level of effectiveness in the world.

At this unique time in history, I believe God is inviting the church on an incredible journey of better understanding his character and personality through the marvelous gifts of creativity. He is drawing us into the joy of creative collaboration with him and with our congregations, so *all* the gifts may operate in the body of Christ. Then the world may know him and feel his love through the creativity that is inseparable from his—and, as his children, *our own*—nature. He wants to show the world his love in creative, authentic and thrilling ways (Ps 36:5; 1 Jn 3:1; Eph 5:1, 25-27).

Still, many continue to question why we need the arts and creative expression in the church when teaching and preaching can convey God's will and ways to us. Many church leaders have felt this way since the Protestant Reformation, viewing the arts as nonessential, a waste of time and money, or even carnal or evil. This book seeks to offer answers to *why* the arts and creativity are *essential* for the church, how they can affect the church's growth and maturity, and how the arts' presence in churches will create a more accurate representation of God's personality in the world. You'll also find a treasure trove of ideas for *how* to successfully integrate the power of the arts into churches, with many practical projects and examples as well as wisdom from those successfully employing the arts and creativity in enhancing their church's mission and message. As the why and how of the arts in the church are examined, related themes like building an arts ministry, drawing out the creativity inherent in every Christian, supporting spiritual formation in artists and much more will be explored.

God is calling individual Christians and churches to operate boldly in the realms of imagination, innovation, beauty and creativity for his glory. He is calling us to help him rescue these powerful means of communication and expression from the jurisdiction of selfishness and evil. They've come to reside there largely because of our neglect of them. He wants to put them to work in the roles they were designed for—reconciliation, redemption and love. He is offering us an opportunity to lead a new renaissance, centered in the church, which will change the world.

May he, through his creative Spirit, revive and renew our hearts, our congregations, our communities and our planet!

······ **1** ······

A Renewal of the Arts and Creativity in the Church

Creative experience foreshadows
a new Heaven and a new Earth.

NIKOLAI BERDYAEV,
Dream and Reality

For we are God's handiwork,
created in Christ Jesus to do good works,
which God prepared in advance for us to do.

EPHESIANS 2:10

IMAGINE IF THE LOCAL CHURCH became the place in culture to experience creativity, beauty and transcendence.

It is possible.

Hundreds of years ago, churches were in many ways centers for these experiences, leading millions to experience God's presence through art and architecture. After the Reformation, Protestants largely abdicated that role. Now many churches are once again moving in that direction and beginning to develop creative arts programs that foster connection with the Creator.

Interaction with the arts and creativity is unavoidable in our culture. The average person encounters performances, music, and visual and media arts daily, even hourly. Most churches would like to become more fluent in the use of the arts in order to communicate truths about God more effectively. That's a worthy goal. God designed the arts to hurdle our barriers, slip past our intellect, and penetrate our hearts and souls with truth and insight. But he values the arts and creativity for reasons beyond their usefulness. He loves them because he *is* beauty and creativity (Ps 19:1; 96:6). Whether his beauty and creativity are expressed in nature or through the arts, embracing them enables us to more fully appreciate his personality and enjoy his presence.

A NEW RENAISSANCE

Throughout Christianity there are signs that a sort of new renaissance is rising, a Holy Spirit–initiated movement to integrate the arts and creativity into churches. This movement has the real potential to revive and rejuvenate our congregations, enhance our understanding of God and bring the body of Christ closer to maturity. And, looking outward, the movement is finding new and creative ways to engage the culture with spiritual art—not as propaganda but as an authentic expression of faith, love, truth and identity.

Christians of all traditions are noticing that God is sparking a renewed interest in the arts in their communities. Pope Benedict held a historic art summit with hundreds of world-renowned artists in the Sistine Chapel as part of a goal to "rekindle the special historical relationship between faith and art," saying it was the first of many arts initiatives.[1] Major evangelical organizations like Youth With a Mission (YWAM), Operation Mobilization (OM), Campus Crusade for Christ (CRU), the Navigators and InterVarsity Christian Fellowship have recognized the ability of the arts to communicate across barriers and have developed arts training and outreaches.[2] The international Lausanne Movement (founded by Billy Graham) produced a brilliant manifesto on the arts called "Redeeming the Arts."[3] The explosion in the use of music, electronic media and drama in Protestant and evangelical churches has been quite significant, and now more churches than ever before have added visual arts galleries to their buildings.[4] Many charismatics are using the arts as vehicles for encouragement, teaching and prophetic messages during their services and outreaches.[5]

The first substantial wave of this movement lapped into many churches in the mid-1980s in the form of contemporary worship music, swelling into a flood in the 1990s and 2000s. Within twenty years, music in many churches completely changed, and the majority now have at least one service where contemporary worship music is featured. Whether you prefer hymns or newer music, you must admit that this shift has enabled new generations to find relevance in their worship experience and opened the door for thousands of musical artists to create and play for God's glory.

This renewed interest in the arts goes beyond the church's attempts to stay relevant or find creative ways to win converts. In fact, many see it as a key ingredient to the foretold preparation of the body and bride of Christ (Eph 5:26), as well as a shift in the way the church influences the world as an agent of redemption and a force for good.

> *"I don't want you to think of art as a little frill or whipped cream on the cake of life. It's more like steak and potatoes."*
> Dallas Willard,
> address at Biola University,
> March 31, 1987

THE ESSENTIAL ROLE OF THE ARTS AND CREATIVITY IN THE CHURCH

There are a number of reasons for the emergence of this new renaissance, but I believe all of them point to one conclusion: the arts and creativity are meant to play an essential role in the church.

I wasn't always so passionate about that conclusion. Honestly, as I thought and prayed about this book, discouragement set in at the prospect of trying to build a case for the arts and creativity in the church. It was hard to find an argument that might persuade the leaders who see little need for the arts to think differently.

Then, one Saturday as I sat at a church retreat quieting myself in God's presence, he quite unexpectedly whispered a question: "What if integrating the arts into the church is more than just a nice idea (more than just for decoration or relevance)? *What if that integration is necessary for the maturity of the body of Christ?*" For me, it was an electrifying thought, and I was immediately filled with hope and purpose. *What if the arts and creativity are designed to play a key role in the maturing of Christ's bride? What if we need them in the church?* The more I prayed, studied, researched and posed that question to pastors and leaders, the more I became convinced of the truth of that concept.

Most will agree that God designed Christian community as a place where every believer's gifting, large or small, can be discovered, nurtured and developed for the benefit of the believers themselves, the members of the body of Christ and the wider world. Romans 12:4-6 says,

> For just as each of us has one body with many members, and these members
> do not all have the same function, so in Christ we, though many, form one
> body, and each member belongs to all the others. We have different gifts,
> according to the grace given to each of us.

So what happens when some of the intended gifts are simply missing? Can the
body properly function?

Artists carry the gifts of intuition, insight, imagination, creativity and more—
gifts designed by the Creator to ignite the heart and engage the whole person.
But these giftings also fit in with the traditional gifts listed in Ephesians 4:11-13.
The Amplified version sheds some interesting light on the passage:

> And His gifts were [varied; He Himself appointed and gave men to us]
> some to be apostles (special messengers), some prophets (inspired
> preachers and expounders), some evangelists (preachers of the Gospel,
> traveling missionaries), some pastors (shepherds of His flock) and teachers.
>
> His intention was the perfecting and the full equipping of the saints (His
> consecrated people), [that they should do] the work of ministering toward
> building up Christ's body (the church),
>
> [That it might develop] until we all attain oneness in the faith and in the
> comprehension of the [full and accurate] knowledge of the Son of God, that
> [we might arrive] at really mature manhood (the completeness of person-
> ality which is nothing less than the standard height of Christ's own per-
> fection), the measure of the stature of the fullness of the Christ and the
> completeness found in Him.

Of course, this is not an exhaustive list of spiritual gifts. Wayne Grudem
says, "A spiritual gift is any ability that is empowered by the Holy Spirit and
used in ministry of the church."[6] But even if this list were complete, we can see
how artists operate in several of the gifts Paul mentions here, such as prophets.
The arts are designed to reveal hidden meanings and truths to individuals and
groups. The prophets of the Old Testament often used performance or crafted
objects to convey God's messages. For example, Ezekiel was instructed to
make drawings and models, lie on his side a certain way and cook with dung
as fuel—all to illustrate what God was saying to his people (Ezek 4:1-16).

Prophetic lyrics and music were also a constant part of Jewish life. The tabernacle was adorned with maximum beauty to proclaim the past, present and future magnificence of God (Ex 25). Of course, God's artists today may not be oracles like the Old Testament prophets were, but as they learn to collaborate with him, he will use them in prophetic ways to bring truth and understanding to our churches, communities and culture.

As for the evangelistic gift, the arts speak across language barriers like few other forms of communication, using the universality of story, sound and symbol to convey the gospel. With the pastoral gift, worship pastors and (in the churches that have them) arts pastors lead congregations to connect with God in rich and heartfelt ways. The arts are excellent for teaching as well, especially in our visual society, because of their ability to bypass mental understanding and plant truth deep in the heart.

The gifts were given "so that the body of Christ may be built up until we all reach unity in the faith and in the knowledge of the Son of God" (Eph 4:12-13). How can we really be one unless we are sharing our gifts, functioning as God designed us? And how can we have a full and accurate knowledge of the Son of God without approaching a comprehension of his inherent beauty and creativity or his unending grace?

The rest of verse 13 answers the question about why we should seek to pursue these things: that we might "become mature, attaining to the whole measure of the fullness of Christ." We will never reach maturity or be the complete body of Christ without cultivating the gifts of the arts and creativity in the church.

> "The arts are not the pretty but irrelevant bits around the border of reality. They are highways into the center of a reality which cannot be glimpsed, let alone grasped, any other way."
>
> N. T. Wright, *Simply Christian*

If artists are not encouraged to contribute their gifts, observations, personalities and visions to the body of Christ, congregations and the universal church will continue to miss one of God's key traits—his astounding creativity. And without that, imagination and joy are blocked, and faith, which requires imagination (Heb 11:1), will not fully flower. Without the integration of the arts and artists into the church, the body of Christ might be physically, emotionally and mentally challenged. And we will continue to be far from Jesus' prayer that we would be one.

WHAT CAN BE DONE?

So what can pastors and leaders, churches, artists and supporters do to welcome this renewal of the arts and help the body of Christ mature? Practically speaking, pastors and leaders can look for ways to encourage creativity, integrate the arts into services and disciple artists. Churches can pursue and support artists and start art galleries. Artists can get training, grow in their craft, become part of a Christian community and look for opportunities to spark creativity in local congregations. Supporters can advocate for the arts in their church, donate time and money, and help educate congregations. The New Renaissance Arts Movement, a nonprofit organization I'm part of that connects churches with the arts, offers many resources on these topics at the website TheNewR.org.

But in the end, all this activity will not be enough to achieve a true integration of creativity and the arts into the church. Bono, lead singer from the band U2, said in a *USA Today* interview that his band tries "to write songs that raise the temperature of the room and find words for feelings you can't express. And then, as Quincy Jones says, you wait for God to walk through the door. Because in the end, craft isn't enough."[7] Impressive works of art, ingenious education and brilliant proposals—though all these things and more are needed—aren't enough for a new spiritual renaissance in the arts.

We must have divine inspiration. We must seek ideas from God, connecting and collaborating with him in our creativity on the projects he planned for us before we were born. We must pursue his guidance for how he would want to integrate the arts in our local churches.

Of course, this starts by learning to hear God's voice in prayer and in our everyday lives. Artists—or any Christian—will experience their greatest spiritual growth when they develop that aptitude. If you are a pastor or leader, fostering this deep, conversational relationship with God in your congregation is no doubt one of your heart's desires. When artists learn how to do this, they will naturally impart it to others through their work and personalities. Chapter five touches on teaching artists—and congregations—to hear God's voice and collaborate with him.

As local churches take the initiative to encourage creativity, they'll experience rich benefits in their services and community life. Just as pastors have specific messages from God for their congregations at specific times in history, so it is with the artists he has planted in church fellowships. As they are trained to hear God's voice, they will bring powerful messages that enhance what he is doing in congregations. And we are not talking about only master artists, but artists of various skill levels, extending even to the average churchgoers who have little idea of the creativity God has placed in them. Later chapters will look at ways to integrate all creative skill levels into our churches in order to promote spiritual growth and cultivate community.

The worldwide church stands at a unique time in history, in a position that no other institution can fill. Its decision to actively encourage the arts and creativity, to embrace and disciple artists, will benefit individuals, communities and the body of Christ in profound ways. It will enable the church to better fulfill its mission of offering God's love to the world.

But even if we do nothing in response to this moment in history, the power of the arts will continue to affect the world. As Bob Briner said, "Art has not lost its power because of our neglect of it. Its power is still there, but it's not being used for good."[8] It's time for the church to embrace the power of the arts and creativity, and join it with the power of the Holy Spirit to see lives transformed. The following chapters will provide practical tools to help that become a reality in your church.

See the online resources and extras for this chapter at JScottMcElroy.com/ CCHandbookextras.

NOTES

[1]Sarah Delaney, "Pope to Meet Artists in Sistine Chapel to Rekindle Faith-Art Dialogue," Catholic News Service, September 10, 2009, www.catholicnews.com/data/stories /cns/0904049.htm.

[2]J. Scott McElroy, "Lausanne Capetown 2010 Reaffirms Global Commitment to the Arts," *The New Renaissance Blog*, October 20, 2010, http://thenewr.wordpress.com/2010/10/20 /lusanne-capetown-2010-reaffirms-global-commitment-to-the-arts.

[3]The excellent "Redeeming the Arts" paper is available at http://stoneworks-arts.org /stoneworks/archives/658. For more on the Lausanne Movement, see www.lausanne.org /en/about.html.

[4]Letter from the executive director, CIVA (Christians in the Visual Arts), November 2008.

[5]Julie Meyer, "God's Media Army Is Arising in Movies, Music, Art, Games and More," *The Elijah List*, January 26, 2009, www.elijahlist.com/words/display_word/7760; Patricia King, "A Prophetic Word from Patricia King: 'Body of Christ Will Establish New Entertainment Ministry,'" *The Elijah List*, July 20, 2009, www.elijahlist.com/words/display_word/7834.

[6]Wayne Grudem, *Systematic Theology* (Grand Rapids: Zondervan, 1994), p. 1016.

[7]Bono, quoted in Edna Gundersen, "U2: Rock Giants Leave '90s Behind to Break Out of Zoo of Pop, Rap," *USA Today*, October 30, 2000, p. 2D.

[8]Bob Briner, *Roaring Lambs* (Grand Rapids: Zondervan, 1993), p. 28.

Ten Ways the Arts and Creativity
Support the Church's Mission

Make friends with the artist. Let him
rip off the veils of habit that obscure the beauty of
Christ in the faces we look at day after day. Let her restore
color and texture and smell to the salvation that has
become disembodied in a fog of abstraction.

EUGENE PETERSON,
For the Beauty of the Church

IN ADDITION TO THE IDEA THAT THE ARTS and creativity are *key to the growth and maturity of the church*, there are at least two other core benefits of the arts in the church. They enable us to *convey God's love to people more effectively* and *to worship God more fully*. I'll expand on each of these in the pages ahead. A host of other benefits fall under these big three, and ten of them are highlighted in this chapter.

Of course, these ten points are certainly not an exhaustive list of the arts' and creativity's benefits for the church; in fact, I doubt there's an area of the church's ministry and mission where the arts couldn't be of some service. Also, please note that these points are not in order of importance. That would be very difficult to determine since different churches will have varying priorities. They are simply listed here in an order that seems to flow.[1]

1. RELEASING CREATIVITY IN GOD'S PEOPLE

Most Christians would agree that God is the most creative being in the universe. From the mind-bogglingly beautiful celestial formations seen through the Hubble Telescope to the impossibly complex and equally exquisite universe inside a single cell, his creativity and ingenuity leave us in awe. And he never stops creating. He paints a million constantly changing masterpieces in pastel sunsets, majestic cloud formations and glistening ocean waves every day. His brilliance in conceiving, designing and sustaining living beings like humans and animals will never be eclipsed.

This supreme Creator is our *Father,* and we are his children. So, as they say about family traits, creativity is in our blood. Jesus, our brother if you will (Heb 2:11), said we would do even greater creative acts and miracles than he did while he was on the earth (Jn 14:12). For most of us that is hard to imagine, let alone achieve.

There seem to be several reasons why Christians feel we don't or can't live up to the family legacy of creativity. First, there is the misunderstanding of what creativity is. Many who think they aren't "creative" or "artists" don't feel they can access a lifestyle of creativity. Actually, a major part of creativity is problem solving and decision making—things we each do every day. How we respond to people and situations also requires creativity. Prayer led by the Holy Spirit is incredibly creative, regularly calling things into existence that are only seen in the mind's eye (Heb 11:1). The Holy Spirit is present and involved in each of these activities, and he loves to whisper and nudge and partner with us in them. When we listen and respond, that is flowing in creativity.

> "The glory of our future is continuing creativity in the life of God."
> Dallas Willard, address at the Talbot School of Theology faculty retreat on September 16, 2011

That leads to another misunderstanding: believing creativity is all up to us. The real joy in creativity is found in collaboration with God. Jesus claimed that he didn't do anything on his own, but only what he heard the Father speak to him (Jn 5:19). In other words, the only way that he did all the creative miracles and came up with all the creative answers and stories that stumped the learned men of the day was through collaborating with his (and our) Father in every situation. That creativity is also available to us when we learn to listen for God's voice.

The fact is we are *all* wired for creative collaboration. We cannot live without human collaboration on the natural level—it is essential for everything, from the conception of life to relationships to work. Even something as passive as watching a TV show requires creative collaboration. The actors and writers and producers could not continue to do what they do without someone to read or watch or hear. And our Christian life is full of collaborative experiences. We collaborate at the moment of salvation when we give our life to Christ and he takes our sin. When we turn our mind and heart to reading the Word, the Holy Spirit collaborates with us and brings understanding. In fact, collaboration is at the core of faith.[2]

When Christians realize that God—who knows every iota of our potential and truly cherishes us unconditionally—*loves* to collaborate with us, it unveils the opportunity for the most fulfilling and productive flow of creativity imaginable, even in the most basic things. God beckons us to get to know his intimate voice and then partner with him wherever we happen to be, collaborating to bring his kingdom and redemptive creative solutions into the world often in simple, ordinary ways. And while we partner with him, he reveals more of his incredible design and loving intentions for us.

Imagine if everyone in your church *expected* to collaborate with God in their average daily creative decisions, in their businesses and interactions. How the kingdom of God might flourish in your community!

> "Art is the signature of civilizations."
> Beverly Sills,
> *The Beacon Book of Quotations by Women*

An integration of creativity and the arts in your church will draw out the family trait of creativity inherent in each person. Those who operate in additional levels of creativity—the artists—can be a key to releasing this. God has brought specific artists to specific churches to be a blessing not just for what they can do but for who they are. These artists and "makers" in a fellowship will add texture, depth and meaning to everything God is doing in a church as their gifts for story, sound, symbol and movement are consecrated and released. The many examples and affirmations of this in the Bible make it clear that God designed the Christian experience to be rich and all-encompassing.[3] Properly discipled and empowered, the artists will lead your whole congregation into discovering and releasing God's dynamic creative flow.

2. Enabling Churches to Speak the Language of the Culture

The proliferation of the arts in our society is undeniable. Music, film, graphics, performance, public and visual art are the language of the culture. A revolution in worship music has taken place. An integration of visual, performance and the other arts into the church is the next logical step.

The arts speak to people by using language and symbolism that is familiar or meaningful to them. Creative expression provides connecting points for people who are unfamiliar with church culture and enables us to convey Christ's essence by showing, instead of always preaching. The world is looking for something real, something immediate and something truly creative. God is the

> *"Our culture is full of high-speed visual images and information, meanwhile our churches are still speaking on the level of words."*
> James Tughan

ultimate source of renewal, reality and creativity, and he is inviting us to collaborate with him so that the world may know him. And creative works can take on a life of their own and can plant God's seeds deep in hearts. They can make an impact far into the future.

The message of the gospel is timeless, but Jesus, Paul and the prophets regularly spoke in the vernacular of their culture. As we look for ways to speak the language of our culture, we might talk to young adults in our congregation about new trends and consult local artists and designers about creative ways to convey the messages God gives us. This doesn't have to be some desperate attempt to be "relevant." God's love is always relevant. But our culture's language is art and creativity.

3. Revealing the Gospel Message

Romans 1:20 says, "Since the creation of the world God's invisible qualities—his eternal power and divine nature—have been clearly seen, being understood from what has been made [the inconceivable artistry of his creation], so that people are without excuse." Long before Jesus came to redeem us from sin, God was openly revealing his loving intentions toward the world through his creativity. From the beginning, beauty, creativity and the arts were designed to convey God's love. They have not lost their power to do that, even though over the millennia humans have often turned them into idols, worshiping the creation instead of the Creator. God knew that could happen but deemed the benefits of lavish creativity to be greater than the danger of its misuse, even endowing his often wayward children with an enormous capacity for creativity in our own realm. It certainly seems that God would want to us to follow his lead, use what he has given us, and continue developing beauty, creativity and the arts as witnesses for him (Jn 14:12; Eph 2:10).

Whether you define the gospel story as the sweeping redemption of all of creation, the story of Jesus' incarnation and sacrifice, or the good news of a new way of life in Christ, the arts have and will continue to illustrate it very eloquently.

God designed the Hebrew tabernacle and then Solomon's temple using art and materials of dazzling beauty as a reminder of his glory, his people's preciousness to him, and their unique story of how he miraculously provided for and repeatedly rescued them. A thousand years later, after having been de-

Figure 2.1. The beauty of Solomon's Temple is reimagined in this model. Image: Shay Levy / PhotoStock -Israel.com

stroyed and rebuilt, the temple's beauty still astounded Jesus' disciples (Mk 13:1). And the redemptive story it told was still clear to those who would listen.

Jesus drew our attention to artistic symbols to punctuate his message, including how he would be lifted up like Moses' serpent sculpture (his crucifixion, Jn 3:14) and how he would rebuild the "temple" in three days (his resurrection, Jn 2:19). In his ministry, he consistently shared the good news using story and parable, inviting people to use their imaginations to allow the images he presented to come alive and to find meaning within those imaginings. Jesus recognized that words or commands (alone) were insufficient. In order for people to make changes, they must first be able to imagine what is possible.[4]

During medieval times, when the illiteracy rate in Europe was as high as 98 percent, the arts played a very practical role in teaching the gospel. Stained-glass windows, sculptures, paintings and more illuminated the redemption story for those who could not read.[5]

"Redeeming the Arts" offers an eye-opening breakdown of the role of creativity in the biblical narrative:

> As the biblical narrative unfolds, it does so in stories and poetry. In fact, approximately 75 percent of scripture consists of story, 15 percent is expressed in poetic forms, and only 10 percent is propositional and overtly instructional. In our retelling of the same story, we have reversed this biblical pattern. Today an estimated 10 percent of our communication is designed to capture the imagination of the listener, while 90 percent is purely instructive.[6]

Most churches on this earth wouldn't go as far as flipping that 10/90 equation around, and this book isn't necessarily advocating such a radical shift. But even a small percentage increase of using the arts and creativity to engage the imagination and illustrate the gospel could have an impact on the effectiveness of the church's mission. And it would put us more in line with the communication style used to recount the biblical story for thousands of years.

> "Art is . . . putting a frame around a moment."
> **Frederick Buechner,**
> **Beyond Words**

4. Leading in Worship

For many Christians, music and song is the art form that we usually associate with worship, and indeed, it is an extremely powerful vehicle to transport us into communion with God and our fellow believers. In the Old Testament, God designated a whole tribe of musicians, the Levites, who would do nothing but lead the people in glorifying God. But music certainly isn't the *only* art form designed for worship. He created *all* of the arts to facilitate, enhance and draw us into adoration of him.

Not only did the rich symbolism of the art crafted for the Hebrew temple tell the story of God's love for his people, it was also perfectly designed to lead his people into the highest worship. Every utensil, every sculpture, all the precious materials—gold, bronze, jewels—every angle, size and position of every element of the building, not to mention the specific way the ceremonies and rituals were done, were all designed to turn the people's hearts and minds toward God. "He conceived an interactive worship service for the Hebrew pilgrims that appealed to and engaged all their senses: sight, smell, taste and sound. For them worship in the Temple of the Lord was a total body experience."[7] Even the inhabitants of heaven embrace the arts as part of their full worship of God before the throne, employing color, movement, sculpture, song and story (Rev 4:3, 10; 5:8-10).

In later chapters, especially chapters eight and ten, we explore projects that facilitate worship through the arts, connecting people, their senses, and their imaginations to God and worship of him in ways that music alone can't.

5. CONNECTING IN OUTREACH

"Preach the gospel at all times, and when necessary, use words."
Francis of Assisi

The arts have the ability to bypass the filters of the mind and speak directly to the heart and emotions, often without words. This makes them an excellent instrument for the work of church outreach when the crossing of cultural, language, educational or other barriers is needed.

Because of their unique abilities, the arts can also be a tremendous help in missions. They play a strategic role in every culture, and every people group reinforces and passes on its story through the arts, so most cultures can relate to the good news story conveyed this way. This is one of the reasons why a number of missions organizations are using the arts in overseas outreach. They can often gain access where traditional missionaries or evangelists cannot.

For many years a group from YWAM (Youth with a Mission) led by Colin Harbinson toured the world with the musical dance production *The Masterpiece*, an allegorical take on the redemption story. They performed in over sixty countries on all continents. They were featured at international sporting events like the Olympics, in command performances for world leaders and in improbable situations like inaccessible communist China in the mid-eighties.[8] The show's dramatic format transcended language and cultural barriers. Thousands who would never go to a church or listen to a preacher saw the gospel through those performances, including presidents and dignitaries, and many were led to Christ.

Closer to home, there is no shortage of opportunities to engage people with the arts through local church outreach.

It should be clear to all how important it is for the faith community to have its voice present in the culture of which it is a part. The gospel comes as an alternative to the agenda of the society; it offers a different understanding of what it means to be human. Art is able to express this in subtle and meaningful ways and to do so in a "language" those outside the church will understand. In this way the art of the Christian can be what [Calvin Seervald] has called "redemptive art":

Figure 2.2. Scene from "The Masterpiece," an adaptation of "Toymaker & Son," written and choreographed by Colin Harbinson. Photo © Impact Productions.

"By 'redemptive artistry' I mean something much closer to what the dove did for Noah in the ark. Noah was wondering whether the punishing flood had receded and the earth was now habitable again. The dove came back bearing fresh olive leaves (Gen. 8:11), a token that the faithful Lord was giving new life on earth after the awful judgment on world sin. Maybe we could consider artistry by the redeemed for their neighbor as simply giving a metaphoric promise of life and hope at the gracious Rule of Jesus Christ on earth.... Redemptive artistry will be bearing fresh olive leaves."[9]

Some churches have seen great results when they've carried these fresh olive leaves into nursing homes, hospices and Alzheimer's care centers. Church-associated arts ministries like Vine Hearts in Boise, Idaho, have brightened the lives of scores of shut-ins through simple arts activities and lessons. And by consistently showing up and sharing their talents, they have led patients and staffers to Christ. They agree to not evangelize when they go into a facility, but the love of Christ invariably shines through. Questions are asked and answered, and lonely lives are changed.

At the first nursing home where Sherri Coffield, the Vine Hearts director, offered her art services, the facility director was very wary, even antagonistic. She didn't want any evangelistic "funny business." But as Sherri showed up consistently, carrying God's love in her smile and art supplies in her hands, the residents and the facilities director began to trust and appreciate her. When the director suffered a stroke, Sherri visited her in the hospital. Through tears, she told Sherri that she wanted the "glow" that she had. Sherri was able to lead her to the Lord, and when the director returned to work, she opened the doors wide to Vine Hearts, offering to host worship services in addition to the arts activities. These are doors that may never have opened through traditional outreach methods.

There are plenty of scientific confirmations for the healing effects of the arts.[10] They can connect the disabled or mentally incapacitated to memories, aid in lucidity or bring them joy. According to the Alzheimer's Association, the ability to express and connect through art in a safe and social environment can help bridge communication gaps and increase self-esteem for persons with dementia. In these cases, "the creative process is as important and meaningful as the artwork itself."[11] Alzheimer's patients who might not be able to communicate verbally may experience an awakening when a paintbrush is put in their hand. Others who were unresponsive have dramatically "come to life" upon being exposed to music.[12] Relatives who have watched their loved ones become a shadow of their former selves are overcome with joy when their family member unexpectedly creates a watercolor or acrylic painting with the help of an artist. That little painting will continue to bring a ray of hope while hanging on the patient's bedroom wall or attached to their family's refrigerator. It would seem to make sense for churches, which are called to minister to the infirm and forgotten, to train and commission artists to share Christ's love and light in this unique way.

Similar concepts and results apply to arts outreach programs focused on troubled teens, abused women, those with eating disorders, addicts and others. The arts can provide an avenue of healing and connection, and can open the door to share deeper levels of God's love to those who are hurting.

Music, drama, dance or visual art can provide extremely effective centerpieces for community outreaches like festivals or picnics, appealing to people who may never step into a church. Children will flock to hands-on art projects that your church might offer in the neighborhood. Artists sent from your church may be able to present their work or perform in schools, shopping malls, social organizations and other places that wouldn't consider giving your teaching pastor a platform. And the arts can become a real asset in connecting with groups in your community who don't speak English. They may not understand the words but they can see the visual or feel the music, and grasp the emotional or spiritual meaning.

The entirety of chapter seventeen is dedicated to exploring the possibilities of the arts in outreach.

6. ASSISTING IN PRAYER

Art has been intertwined with prayer for thousands of years. The builders of the medieval cathedrals took a lesson from the Hebrew temple and fashioned architecture that can be seen as a prayer in itself, pointing the viewer toward heaven on the inside and out. In recent decades, it seems the vision for sacred architecture as an assistance in prayer has been neglected by many Protestants, especially evangelicals, although there are signs that it's coming back.[13]

The use of the visual arts as an aid in prayer is also gaining more momentum. Starting with King David's continual celebration of the Ark of the Covenant in the tabernacle at Jerusalem around 1000 B.C. (1 Chron 16:37), there have been a number of continual 24/7 (around the clock) prayer movements over the millennia—from the monastic "vigil prayers" in the fifth century[14] to the Moravians, who prayed uninterrupted from 1727 to 1827 in the town of Herrnhut, in what is now Germany.[15]

In the 1990s a contemporary movement of 24/7 prayer sprung up in places around the world, and now it's not uncommon for churches to organize 24/7 prayer periods that last for several weeks. Singing or music is a central part of this movement, but expression with visual arts is also common. Many of these churches have a dedicated prayer room that often overflows with art during prayer weeks as pray-ers discover that picking up an artistic implement to express themselves to God is a joyful, freeing experience. Anyone can discover a wonderful freedom in making prayer-room art. It can be made anonymously with no need to feel inhibited or to judge the work on technical merit. It's all an acceptable prayer. (More about art in the prayer room in chapter eleven and prayer rooms in chapter sixteen.) Sometimes leaders will show these prayer pictures during a service and use them as illustrations of what God might be saying to their congregations.

Another concept is "praying in color," a loosely guided form of using colors and shapes to pray that was popularized by the book series of the same name.

Author Sybil MacBeth developed this style of relating names or prayer requests to her doodles after finding it difficult to focus in prayer due to her antsy personality. She says it's "an active, meditative, playful practice. It is both process and product. The process involves a re-entry into the childlike world of coloring and improvising. The product is a colorful design or drawing that is a visual reminder of the time spent in prayer."[16] "Many have found these kinesthetic/interactive practices of making art as prayer to be very meaningful, and a 'way in' to God's healing, loving presence."[17]

Some churches have begun using the arts as a form of praying or blessing people in individual prayer times, calling it "personal prayer art." This exciting practice is detailed in chapter ten, but in a nutshell, it is simply this: an artist prayerfully asks God for a picture or word for a person, takes a risk and draws it, then offers it to the person as a prayer, always with the qualification to "test it" for accuracy. This is amazingly effective in conveying God's love to individuals. When they take the picture with them, God can continue to speak to them through it, sometimes for years.

One of the oldest uses of visual art as prayer is with painted or mosaic icons, first mentioned in historical documents about two hundred years after Christ. The Greek word *eikon* means "an image or likeness that represents something else." Iconography is rooted in the theology of the incarnation (Christ being the *eikon* of God).[18]

Orthodox icons are typically egg tempura paintings on wood, often small. There are rich patterns of religious symbolism associated with them.[19] Icons have engendered controversy over the centuries, with reported instances of worship of the icon itself (idolatry), leading to the smashing of icons (iconoclasm) during the Reformation. This history sometimes makes Protestants wary of icons, but most Orthodox churches, many Anglican, Episcopalian and Catholic, and some other traditions use them in prayer and meditation today. They'll tell you they are not worshiping the icon but instead see it as a window into the eternal and a legitimate way to connect with God in prayer. These thoughts were backed up by the Second Council of Nicaea in A.D. 787.

Most iconographers consider making (or writing) icons a very holy practice and continually bathe it in prayer. One author explains, "Icons change you from within because they are a prayer. They will at times create an atmosphere inside you to receive something new from God. They will plow the field or prepare the ground, so that you can receive what God is doing next."[20]

The incarnational nature of the arts and creativity—making the invisible visible—can provide wonderful assistance in focusing our prayers and building our faith.

Figure 2.3. Modern icon *Descent into Hades,* by Fr. Leo Arrowsmith. 4′ x 3′ acrylic on MDF. Modern iconographers follow the same canons of the gospel as ancient practitioners, but often interpret them in their own style. See more of Fr. Arrowsmith's icons at dovetaleicons.blogspot.com. Image: Stan Martins.

7. HELPING RELEASE BEAUTY IN THE LOCAL CHURCH

"When an artist pursues the beautiful, he or she opens a channel between God and humanity. It is an extension of the revelation that occurs through the beauty of creation."[21]

God cares about beauty. It is an inherent aspect of his character; he loves and creates beauty just because it is part of who he is (Ps 19:1). If God values the kind of wild, mind-boggling beauty we see through the Hubble Telescope, shouldn't we?

We can cultivate beauty in our worship through music, visual art, performance such as dance or drama or multimedia, in our worship spaces through design and architecture, visual art and lighting, and so many other ways—even through our landscaping.

> "The Lord God was playful enough to make lobsters and gingko trees, quartz crystals and red-haired girls with freckles. God wants us to laugh and enjoy the imaginative riches smiling and crying everywhere."
>
> Calvin Seerveld, *Rainbows for a Fallen World*

Beautiful design or architecture can be a beacon of light and hope in a community and can quietly and persistently reaffirm that message for decades and even centuries. How long have many churches lived with a dearth of beauty in their worship spaces? The answer might be "about five hundred years"—that is, since the Reformation. Catholic churches have struggled with this as well. When he announced the Vatican's November '09 Arts Summit, the president of the Pontifical Council for Culture said that the art and architecture of many modern churches "do not offer beauty, but rather ugliness."[22]

It's time for the church to tap into and portray the multifaceted personality of this awesome and beautiful God through the use of the arts, so that the world may know him.[23]

8. Returning Imagination and Creativity to the Church

The concept of imagination has been neglected in some Protestant circles, for a number of possible reasons. It could be because of the negative use of the word in the Bible, as in "vain imaginings," or the idea that intellect is the primary way of knowing God while the heart, emotions and imagination are less important, or even dangerous.

But faith requires the use of imagination. Jesus encourages people to use their imaginations to understand his parables, and God intended the gift of imagination to be a great benefit to us. "Imagination is what enables us to think with the heart and feel with the mind, a task Jesus seems intent on our learning to do."[24] Although creativity and imagination are not a destination in themselves, they exist to point us to the glorious love of God. Opportunities to positively exercise creativity and imagination are woven into all aspects of human life and do not belong to the arts alone.

> The role of the imagination is not to take us away from reality, but to expose us to new ways of seeing things. That is why the parables of Jesus are so powerful—they invite us to imagine things we have not thought before. The gospel comes to us as a living word and draws us to think imaginatively of how things could be different. Imagination is capable of moving us closer to the truth about the world as we look through the lens of scripture. As an imaginative activity, art too can open our eyes to see old things in new ways.[25]

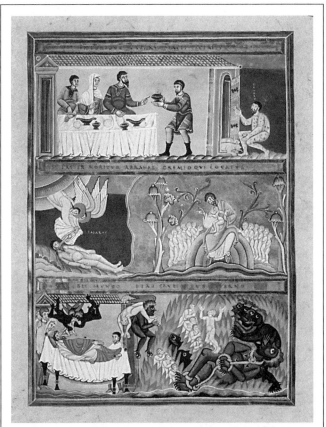

Figure 2.4. *Lazarus and Dives,* an imaginative illustration of Jesus' parable of Lazarus and the rich man from Luke 16:19-31. This illumination is from the Codex Aureus of Echternach, produced at the Abbey of Echternach between 1030 and 1050. Image is in the public domain.

Our longings for transcendence, beauty and truth can be addressed through engaging the imagination. While the church has sometimes shown little interest in speaking to the human imagination, the world has made prolific attempts to fulfill those God-given longings, using the arts and creativity, movies, music and story. What if God's people and his church were leaders in working with the arts to address the longings he designed us with? Imagine that!

> "By means of art we are sometimes sent—dimly—briefly—revelation unattainable by reason."
>
> Alexander Solzhenitsyn

9. Bringing Healing and Illumination in Unique Ways

The ways that the arts and creativity communicate to our emotions and senses make them particularly effective for the Holy Spirit's use in sort of "ambushing" us—getting past our defenses to heal and illuminate in surprising ways.

One recent example of this came during a creativity workshop I led at a Midwestern church. A woman had decided to attend, even though she didn't consider herself "creative," just to have fun and to be with her friends. At a break we did a creative exercise to loosen up and engage our bodies: a "silly walk" (inspired by Monty Python's "Ministry of Silly Walks") where people were encouraged, one at a time, to do their silliest walk across the sanctuary while everyone else cheered them on. This lovely woman is very outgoing and a joyful, mature believer, but when her turn came she was overcome with dread. She forced herself to limp through the exercise then stood to the side asking God what was happening; why did she feel this way? He quickly began to speak to her about a subtle fear that had developed—a fear of what people thought of her. As she received prayer from other attendees, God brought healing to places in her heart that had been broken for years. She prayed throughout the following week for a complete healing from this fear and by the next weekend she felt like a different person, free from that self-conscious weight. That following weekend she was to have a leadership role in a women's retreat, but didn't realize until the day of that it would require speaking in front of a group, something that would have caused her to freeze up before. Because of the healing that God had initiated through the "silly walk" she was able to speak confidently and step into her calling as a leader, which in turn affected dozens of women at that conference.

We might be amazed at the healing we'd see in our churches if we ask God to give us out-of-the-box ways to illustrate the truths he wants to convey.

10. Reconciling Artists to God

I recently spoke with an artist named Corinna who came to Christ through the arts program at her local church. She decided to attend church one day just out of curiosity and was surprised to see art tables (see chapter ten) stocked with art supplies in the sanctuary and available during the worship part of the service. She was fascinated by the idea that her creativity could have a place in church, and started attending regularly, always creating a little art at the art tables during worship. She officially gave her life to Christ at one of our Creative Church conferences, saw it transformed to become full of purpose and joy, and has become an active part of the church's arts ministry.

> "That the arts are corrupt does not mean that Christians can abandon them. On the contrary, the corruption of the arts means that Christians dare not abandon them any longer."
>
> **Gene Veith,** *State of the Arts*

For centuries, millions of artists like Corinna have been disconnected from their true Source, wandering in search of elusive creative fulfillment. Most have known that there is a spiritual aspect to the creative process, but God is calling them to the joy of true collaboration with him. They were designed to be conduits of his joy and messages here on the earth. Their purpose is to observe the world and receive messages from God, then translate and express them to their fellow humans. Most artists long to collaborate with a force larger than themselves, in work greater than what they're capable of alone. We can lead them to it. We can lead them to their richest and most fulfilling lives when we teach them to converse with God and partner with the Holy Spirit. And the church can offer them a support system that no other institution can. More about that in chapters five, six and eighteen.

Again, this is not an exhaustive list of the benefits of the arts and creativity in the church, and in fact the ten on this short list could each be expanded to fill its own chapter, and in some cases a whole book. You'll find more in-depth discussion on many of them in later chapters.

See the online resources and extras for this chapter at JScottMcElroy.com/ CCHandbookextras.

NOTES

[1]You may notice that in this chapter I quote several times from "Redeeming the Arts," the excellent paper published by the Lausanne organization in 2004. It's an eloquent statement about the increasing importance of the arts in Christianity. The full version of that document is available in PDF form at http://stoneworks-arts.org/stoneworks/archives/658.

[2]J. Scott McElroy, *Finding Divine Inspiration* (Shippensburg, PA: Destiny Image, 2008), p. 30.

[3]Colin Harbinson, ed., "Redeeming the Arts," *The Creative Spirit* (Jackson, MS: Belhaven College, 2005), p. 23.

[4]Harbinson, "Redeeming the Arts," p. 6.

[5]Michael Streich, "Medieval Religious Art as Education," June 17, 2009, http://suite.io/michael-streich/1wvw2nv.

[6]Harbinson, "Redeeming the Arts," p. 23.

[7]Robert Mock, "Gold in the Temple of Solomon, the Garden of Eden, the Margolit, Almugim, Golden Tables and Industrial Gemstones," March 2003, www.biblesearchers.com/temples/jeremiah7.shtml.

[8]See http://colinharbinson.com/toymakerandson/history.html to read more about this ministry.

[9]Harbinson, "Redeeming the Arts," p. 40; quoting Calvin Seerveld, *Bearing Fresh Olive Leaves* (Toronto, ON: Tuppence Press, 2000), p. 112.

[10]Heather L. Stuckey and Jeremy Nobel, "The Connection Between Art, Healing and Public Health: A Review of Current Literature," *American Journal of Public Health* 100, no. 2 (2010): 254-63. Available online at www.ncbi.nlm.nih.gov/pmc/articles/PMC2804629.

[11]Marie Marley, "Connecting with Alzheimer's Patients—Even in the Latest Stages of the Disease," *Huffington Post*, September 9, 2014, www.huffingtonpost.com/marie-marley/alzheimers_b_1244155.html.

[12]See www.youtube.com/watch?feature=player_embedded&v=fyZQfop73QM#!.

[13]Visit the AIA (American Institute of Architects) Interfaith Forum on Religion, Art and Architecture at http://network.aia.org/interfaithforumonreligionartarchitecture/home.

[14]See "Continual Prayer," *Wikipedia*, http://en.wikipedia.org/wiki/Continual_prayer.

[15]See a history of 24/7 prayer at www.ihopkc.org/prayerroom/history.

[16]Sybil MacBeth, *Praying in Color* (Brewster, MA: Paraclete, 2007), p. 5.

[17]Lynn Penney, "Praying in Color," *Presence: An International Journal of Spiritual Direction* 13, no. 4 (2007): 12.

[18]See "Icon," *Wikipedia*, http://en.wikipedia.org/wiki/Icon.

[19]See www.religionfacts.com/christianity/things/icons.htm.

[20]W. McNichols, "Praying with Icons," *America*, November 4, 1995, p. 24.

[21]Barbara Nicolosi, "The Artist: What Exactly Is an Artist and How Do We Shepherd Them?" in *For the Beauty of the Church*, ed. W. David O. Taylor (Grand Rapids: Baker, 2010), p. 106.

[22]Quoted in Sarah Delaney, "Pope to Meet Artists in Sistine Chapel to Rekindle Faith-Art Dialogue," *Catholic News Service*, September 10, 2009, www.catholicnews.com/data/stories/cns/0904049.htm.

[23]For an in-depth discussion on the subject of beauty in the church, see W. David O. Taylor, ed., *For the Beauty of the Church* (Grand Rapids: Baker, 2010).

[24]Michael Card, *Scribbling in the Sand* (Downers Grove, IL: InterVarsity Press, 2002), p. 103.

[25]Harbinson, "Redeeming the Arts," p. 11.

3

Envisioning the Arts and Creativity in Your Church

Write down the revelation and make it plain on tablets so that a herald may run with it.

HABAKKUK 2:2

IT'S TIME TO THINK ABOUT how specific creative applications may work in your church. For most, that means you are on your way to starting an arts ministry, if you don't already have one. The precursor to that launch is to cast a vision and/or decide on a mission for the ministry. This will most likely be refined and revised as the ministry takes shape, and because of that, whatever you come up with here shouldn't yet be set in stone. Simply use it as a guideline at this point, but an important guideline that is informed by the overall vision of your church and one that will give you a direction to pray and walk.

In the 1990s and 2000s the use of media and technology grew in churches and became a creative staple. Today this mix of music, lighting, tech, media, stage design, drama and graphics is often called "worship arts." Many churches have a highly developed worship arts team that is responsible for bringing these artful elements to bear in Sunday-morning services. Some even have a specialized creative "design team" within worship arts that is responsible for crafting the elements of a series, service or message into a cohesive package.[1] And Sundays just keep coming, so the worship arts process or design team can develop into an efficient machine, in some cases producing services on par with professional mainstream events.

When I talk about arts ministry, I'm generally talking about something in addition to the worship arts team, although arts ministry should intersect with worship arts and inform it. In other words, often the worship arts mission is to use music, technology, design and sometimes drama to engage people during the Sunday services, lead them into the presence of God, and illustrate the sermon. The arts ministry mission may include those goals, though it generally uses less music and technology and more of the visual, performance and language arts. But arts ministry can expand well beyond Sundays to facilitate creativity and community in members of the congregation during the week. Your arts ministry may include live painting and art on stage, or a gallery, art studio, artist community, arts outreach or many other applications we'll highlight in the coming chapters.

Churches like Mosaic in LA and Imago Dei in Portland have actively integrated creativity into their fellowships and also combined the leadership of the worship arts and arts ministry teams by designating a leader who oversees both. This helps the two teams share thoughts, experience community together and have a more unified approach to creativity in the church. I think this is a good model for the future. But in many other churches the idea of arts ministry outside of the Sunday worship arts team's efforts is just now gaining interest. As is the case with most ideas whose time has come, decades of dedicated work done mostly in anonymity by pioneering artists have prepared the way for this subject to become relevant. These pockets of arts advocates have practiced and promoted the arts in their local churches, believing passionately that the church should be a center for creativity. Many have burned out or given up in frustration because of the barriers they've encountered. (Chapter twenty addresses some of those barriers.) Their work was not in vain, because in many cases their efforts planted a seed or provided a foundation of what could be.

One church that illustrates the convergence of the work of the past and God's timing is Saddleback Church, in Lake Forest, California. It is known as one of the largest and most influential churches in America.[2] Led by Pastor Rick Warren, author of *The Purpose Driven Life*, Saddleback was established over thirty years ago and leads evangelical Christianity in many areas. But in recent years they've had to decide whether they would be content being an aging baby boomer congregation or somehow regenerate themselves to engage younger people. Jim Dobbs, a trained artist and professional communicator, found himself in the middle of that conversation.

Several years ago, Jim felt the call to establish an arts ministry. He didn't know if it would be in a church or independent, but he did all the required preparations to start a nonprofit and then waited for God's timing. Dobbs is a graduate of Biola University's art program and an advertising executive, and he'd always wanted to make a difference in the arts. The go-ahead from God never came for his nonprofit, so he moved on to work with communications in various churches, finally ending up at Saddleback. A number of artists had tried to bring the arts into Saddleback services and programs over the years with mixed results. When Jim arrived he got involved with and sometimes led arts projects around the church, some of which got the attention and approval of Pastor Rick, but a full-blown arts ministry never took off. He went to seminary while working at the church, and the dream of the seeing the arts flourish in churches was awakened in him again, so he wrote a paper about it, keeping it to himself. Later he was promoted to an executive steering team for the thirty-thousand-member church, finding himself working directly with Rick Warren. One of the topics their team tackled was how to make sure the younger generations were being engaged in a church full of baby boomers. One day Jim walked by Pastor Rick's office and heard Rick calling him to come in for a minute. He said, "Jim, what's missing?"

"What do you mean?" Jim asked.

"Well, what is your big passion?"

Jim said, "Do you really want me to tell you?"

"That's why I asked!" Jim says he heard a drum roll in his head right before he took a deep breath and said, "It's the visual arts."[3] Then he laid out the value for the arts in the church that he'd written in his seminary paper. Rick was intrigued and called a spontaneous meeting with the other leaders, giving Jim the floor. He laid out what they would need for success: a budget, a space and a full-time staff person. The consensus was, "Let's do this!" and an arts initiative, later named Ex Creatis, was born. Rick even came up with the vision statement himself: "To be the center for the arts in Orange County." At the time of this writing, Ex Creatis is a young initiative, but I expect it to become a model and a leader in arts ministry in the church, not only through Saddleback's worldwide influence but also because of the commitment of the church and the quality leadership of Jim Dobbs and the ministry director, Jason Leith. As I've talked to arts leaders around the country, many of whom have wondered if arts ministry in the church will ever take off, this story of God's timing at one of the world's most influential churches gives hope.

It may be time for you to start dreaming with God and praying for favor about the role the arts and creativity can play in your church. If so, the best advice I can give is to pray through every part of the process, asking God what he wants to do. Because the truth is, God wants to see these things flourish in your church more than you do. He can't help but express his love creatively, and he invites us to collaborate in doing that.

Be free to dream about your art ministry's focus and let your church's vision and mission inform your dreams. What does your church feel called to? Justice, compassion, missions, working with the poor, healing? Your arts ministry will most likely complement your church's calling. This is especially important to focus on if you don't yet have the support of church leadership.

Figure 3.1. Saddleback Ex Creatis logo.

A worksheet, "Envisioning the Arts and Creativity in Your Church," is provided in the online resources and extras for this chapter. The rest of this chapter is devoted to thoughts and tips that will help you think about crafting your mission/vision.

Envisioning Without the Support of Leadership

When you don't yet have church leadership support but you know (through prayer and confirmation) that God is calling you to envision an arts ministry, aligning it with what the church values is essential. When the leadership sees how arts ministry can practically enhance just one area of focus in a church community, it becomes more interesting to them. A coherent vision that serves the church's mission could be just the thing to convince leaders that arts ministry is a brilliant idea. But even if doesn't convince them, don't give up, and don't allow yourself to become bitter.

Pray about whether you should go through the exercise of creating a vision/mission statement for a future arts ministry or if you should put it aside for now and move on to something else. And look at the "When the Answer Is No" section in chapter four.

If you sense you are to go forward with creating a vision or mission statement, here are some suggestions to help you generate ideas.

1. *Ask God.* As you envision how creativity and the arts can flourish in your congregation, ask God for his unique ideas for your congregation, and then listen for his response. It really is amazing how he will inspire and spark our imaginations when we spend time in prayer, listening to him while alone or with others.

2. *Brainstorm.* Hold a good old-fashioned brainstorming session with a few people at the church who are interested in seeing the arts come to life. Write down ideas as they come. Remember the brainstorming rule that no idea is bad at this stage. The arts team at Rock Harbor Church in Orange, California (in Disneyland's backyard), often uses Disney's practice of "blue sky" brainstorming to come up with creative ideas, which is kind of like brainstorming on steroids. Basically, ask your brainstorm group members to come up with ideas that are fantastical, where the sky is the limit, and then write them down. Then, later, see if you can pare the idea down a bit, then a bit more, and keep going until you have something manageable that you could actually execute.

3. *Others' ideas.* This book is full of ideas for how to integrate the arts into your church. You might scan it before you fill out the worksheet.

4. *Look at who you have.* Who is currently in your church that is interested in arts ministry? Include them in your envisioning process and ask them what their passions are and what they would like to see materialize.

I should acknowledge that technically there is a difference between a vision and mission statement. Among other things, a vision statement "defines the optimal desired future state—the mental picture—of what an organization wants to achieve over time." A mission statement "defines the present state or purpose of an organization and answers three questions about why an organization exists—WHAT it does; WHO it does it for; and HOW it does what it does."[4]

Having pointed that out, it's certainly possible to have a vision statement and not necessarily feel the need for a mission statement in your arts ministry. Or to have a detailed mission statement that includes the vision. Or have the mission of the ministry serve the vision of the church. The bottom line: it's good to have *something* on paper so everyone is on the same page.

Jessie Nilo, director of VineArts Boise, shared these thoughts about envisioning art ministry:

> The night God gave me the vision for VineArts, I didn't know even one artist in our church yet, but I wrote down this vision:
>
> > To serve God, our local church, the community, and other artists by growing spiritually and artistically together.
>
> I didn't have the "how" yet, but I imagined painters, sculptors, writers, poets, photographers, and metalworkers hanging out to gather and pray and create. Today here's what our 4-fold vision looks like: We *serve God* by holding art exhibits and giving people the opportunity to worship him visually, and also by leading in worship and contemplation as people experience the gallery space individually. We *serve our church* by creating sanctuary backdrops, artwork for nights of worship, and other collaborations with our pastors. We *serve the community* by offering a writers' group, culinary group, filmmakers' group, and opening our art studio to the public Saturdays and Wednesdays, and by sending our artists into the community to minister through art. We *serve artists* by discipling them inside a safe, Christ-centered community, while challenging them to grow artistically.[5]

> "If there is one single change in approach I believe can transform Christian worship in the West, it is that each community of faith do the work of reframing and contextualizing rather than just copying what has worked somewhere else."
>
> Mark Pierson, *The Art of Curating Worship*

Also, make sure you see Dave Blakeslee's thoughts on working with leadership in chapter twenty.

> "One of the primary services the arts can render to theology is their integrative power, their ability to interrelate the intellect with the other facets of our human makeup."
>
> Jeremy Begbie, *New Insights Through Art*

For an analysis of seven arts ministries and their vision/mission statements see the online resources and extras for this chapter.

DEVELOPING A THEOLOGY FOR THE ARTS

Manuel Luz, author of *Imagine That* and worship pastor at Oak Hills Church in

Folsom, California, has done some good work on developing a theology of the arts. Understanding the biblical basis behind the arts can help in envisioning their place in your church and help leadership put them in the context of what the church believes.

I asked Manuel to contribute his thoughts on this as a "last word" to this chapter.

One of the reasons why the arts don't take hold in some churches may simply be an issue of misunderstanding. Church leaders and pastors often cannot connect the dots between the role of the church—worship, discipleship and evangelism—with the arts. But there is a rich and comprehensive rationale that we can draw from which can provide a biblical foundation for the arts in the local church.

Theology is simply what you believe as it relates to God. So a "theology of the arts" is what you believe about the arts as it relates to God.

A Brief Theology of the Arts

What we believe about the arts can be summarized in four sections: The nature of God, the nature of us, the nature of our calling as artists, and the nature of artists in community.

The Nature of God

God is by nature a Creative God (Gen 1:1–2:2). If you look at the first five words of the Bible, "In the beginning, God created, . . ." you see two very important aspects of God's character: he is timeless and he is creative. So God defines himself, right from the start, as the eternally Creative One. All of creation is a byproduct of the nature of our God.

And that's not all. All things were created through the person of Jesus (Jn 1:1-3; 1 Cor 8:6; Col 1:15-17). In the nothingness of the beginning of time, the creative muse of the triune Godhead flowed through the pre-incarnate person of Jesus.

When God surveyed all that he had made, he declared that it was good (Gen 1:31). To be "good" in a theological sense is more than a statement of approval. He said it was good because the beauty of creation perfectly reflected the attribute of goodness that is God.

So God is forever creative, forever joyful at his eternal acts of creation and is also glorified through the beauty of his creation. What does that imply for us?

The Nature of Us

We are made in God's image (Gen 1:26), and that means much more than we realize. We are creative beings—artists and engineers and builders and dreamers—because we are made in the image of a creative God.

God also equips us to act on our creativity. He gives us sentience, intellect, physicality (like opposable thumbs), passion and free will. In fact, creativity is a subset of free will. Theologically speaking, free will is the ability to make choices separate from (and sometimes in opposition to) our omnipotent God. When you understand what an amazing gift free will is, you begin to get a sense of how creativity is such an important part of what it is to be human.

That's not all. We are endowed with an innate, mysterious understanding of what is beautiful in God's eyes. Deep in our souls, we each have this inborn aesthetic (Rom 1:20), which is another aspect of being made in God's image. This is why we are universally drawn to the beauty of a starry night or a baby's laughter or a red rose. It is a sympathetic resonance to beauty that points us to God.

The Nature of Our Calling

Theologians describe a concept known as the cultural mandate—God's command to us to fill, subdue and rule over the earth. This includes acts of productivity and creativity—to be fruitful and multiply, to steward the earth, and even to form, create and imagine (Gen 1:26-28; 2:19-20). In fact, we would not have been able to fulfill God's command if humanity did not have creativity as a defining characteristic.

The arts are a part of the cultural mandate. So artists of faith have the very important job of expressing life in Christ, in authentic truth and beauty. We must steward our artistry for the good of the body (Mt 25; Lk 12:48; 1 Cor 12), for our talents do not belong to us, but to God. Which brings us to our last point.

The Nature of Community

Jesus called us to become a new kind of community that he called the church (Mt 16:18; Acts 2:42-47). This new kind of community is endowed with all manner of spiritual gifts and talents and abilities (1 Cor 12), and all of these are intended for one another. As such, artists of faith are not intended to live as individuals, cloistered in our workshops and art studios, but within the context of others (1 Chron 22–25). Thus, as artists, we have the need to create within the context of the church and share our art for the sake of the church (Phil 2:1-4).

This has implications. The church should be a place where artists are encouraged, nurtured, discipled, held accountable and appreciated for their essential role (Eph 2:19-22). And leaders and pastors of churches should create a safe and accepting place where artists of faith can serve and express their art fully. Artists of faith provide an essential expression of life in Christ, and the role of the church is to allow these expressions to encourage, challenge, prophesy, edify and point people to God.

Theology and Mission

The calling of the artist of faith and the mission of the local church must be compatible and complementary. But the arts should not exist in a church simply as a vehicle for a message. In the larger sense, the arts are an essential expression of life lived in Christ. If your church's mission is to worship God and grow disciples and reach out to the world, one of the best things a church can do is to empower and unleash the artists of faith in your congregations to simply be who God intended them to be.[6]

See the online resources and extras for this chapter at JScottMcElroy.com/CCHand bookextras.

Figure 3.2. *Beyond the Ruins: Business* by Bryn Gillette, from the Haiti—Beyond the Ruins series. Bryn's goal is to affect culture with this series by calling attention to Haiti's ongoing needs as well as its bright future. 32" x 80" oil on wood. Used with permission of the artist.

NOTES

[1]See more about design teams in the online resources and extras for this chapter.

[2]Kent Shaffer, "2013's Top Ranked Churches in America," *Church Relevance*, http://churchrelevance.com/resources/top-churches-in-america.

[3]Jim Dobbs, interview with the author, January 2014.

[4]Jennell Evans, "Vision and Mission: What's the Difference and Why Does It Matter?" *Psychology Today* (blog), April 24, 2010, www.psychologytoday.com/blog/smartwork/201004/vision-and-mission-whats-the-difference-and-why-does-it-matter.

[5]Written contribution from Jessie Nilo.

[6]Written contribution from Manuel Luz.

How to Launch an
Arts Ministry in Your Church

*As evangelical Christians, we have tended to relegate art
to the very fringe of life. We have misunderstood the concept of the
Lordship of Christ over the whole of man and the whole of the universe
and have not taken to us the riches that the Bible gives us
for ourselves, for our lives, and for our culture.*

FRANCIS SCHAEFFER,
Art & the Bible

*Start by doing what's necessary; then do what's possible;
and suddenly you are doing the impossible.*

FRANCIS OF ASSISI

IN THE LATE NINETIES, Cyndee Buck, an artist and Christian art educator, saw a need at her church, Lutheran Church of Hope in West Des
Moines, Iowa, that she thought the arts could fill. She noticed sixth- through
ninth-grade kids who were old enough to get into trouble but not old enough
to get a job or drive, and they needed something to keep themselves occupied
during the summer. So she and three others put a proposal together to start
a creative arts ministry for these kids, took it to the church leadership and,
after many weeks of discussion, got permission. They called it Express Your
Faith, and the plan was for adult artists to come and teach evening arts work-

shops to the kids. They would show them how to create artwork that visually reflected a Bible story or principle. The kids loved it. When the parents saw what their children were doing, they asked for similar classes. So the group started adult arts sessions that touched on a variety of artistic mediums. Through the adult classes they started a gallery. And soon they began hearing stories of people coming back to church because of the artwork on the walls. Now, many years later, the arts ministry at the church has grown to include several galleries, a studio, a number of affinity groups, regular workshops, a monthly artist gathering, arts support for a number of the church's ministries and three part-time staff to oversee it all. It all happened naturally in response to needs that presented themselves.

Around the same time that Cyndee Buck was cultivating the arts at her church in Iowa, another Cindy, Cindy West (now Limbrick) in Colorado Springs, was on a similar path. She was on staff at Woodman Valley Chapel as the worship arts director. At the time they were very strong in the performing arts but not doing anything with the visual arts. So she decided to start an arts ministry, calling it Imago Dei, and simply put an ad in the bulletin that said something like, "Interested in joining a new arts ministry? If you are a photographer, painter, graphic designer . . ." and she listed them out, instead of just saying "artist" because, she reasoned, that word can kind of scare people who think, *I'm kind of creative but I'm not an artist.* According to Cindy, twenty-four people came that first morning. "It just blew me away. They said, 'What does this look like? We don't know about being artists in the church.' I just said, 'We'll figure this out as we go along.' There was a lot of trial and error. That's when Rory Noland's book *Heart of the Artist* had come out, and we decided to meet once a month on a Saturday morning and go through the book." They started doing live painting on the stage—a new thing that nobody had seen done—and incorporating the arts into Sunday services. They created a large gallery on the blank hallway walls of the church. "It turned out to be such a God-breathed vision," Cindy says. The artists came to understand that God had a purpose in their art, that they could make a difference in someone's life.

Cindy has since started the nonprofit Awakening Artists, which builds on what she learned with the arts ministry at Woodman.[1]

Whether a church member proposes it or a staff member initiates it, there are a number of ways to launch an artist ministry in a church. It's preferable to have the support of senior leadership, as happened at Saddleback in starting Ex Creatis (see chapter three). But even in that case it took years of artists trying to get things started there before leadership recognized it was valuable. And that was through a set of divine circumstances. So, as with most things, we look for God's timing, a recognition of which comes through faithfulness and prayer.

There are many ways to start an arts ministry, and God will give you your own specific course of action if you seek him. Still, I think it's helpful to provide a step-by-step guideline that many have used as a foundation for their launch.[2] Take what you can from it. The rest of the chapter addresses some specific situations and offers additional recommendations.

GUIDELINES FOR BEGINNING AN ARTS MINISTRY

The following guidelines are designed for *artists* who want to start an arts ministry, program or outreach at their church. (Make sure to see the online resources and extras for chapter four designed for *pastors and leaders* who want to start an arts ministry, program or outreach at their church.)

1. Start praying now for God's guidance. First, it's important to take some time to pray through what role God would have you play in starting or facilitating an arts ministry. Ask him to check your motives, prepare your heart, and confirm if he is calling you personally to initiate or lead. It's good to be clear about this because there will be challenges ahead. You may encounter increased spiritual warfare, so you'll need prayer support. Ask someone else to pray with you and for God to open the doors. You want this to happen naturally, in God's timing, and to not be forced. God has a plan for the arts and creativity in your church, and if you listen and wait he'll share it with you and others.

2. Talk with someone in leadership about integrating the arts into your church. Your senior pastor may or may not be the person to approach to start this dialogue; it may be the worship pastor or an elder who "gets" you. It's common for churches to be cautious about embracing new ideas, so you need to be patient and respectful in your approach. You may have already created a mission/vision statement as recommended in chapter three, but if not, try to determine what is important to your church and its leadership (e.g., outreach, discipleship, justice, community, etc.) and imagine how an arts ministry can further that mission. Put that or your mission/vision statement into a presentation that makes sense to leadership. See if there is an official process for starting a ministry in your church. There may be an application you need to submit. If your church is more open to the arts, explore where the leadership would like to go with the arts in the future. Ask for dates when arts projects would fit in to services. Get permission to hold a meeting for artists, if that seems to be the next step.

On the other hand, if you run into a brick wall here and the answer is no, go to the heading in this chapter titled "When the Answer Is No."

3. *Invite artists to meet and pray.* See if you can put a notice in the church bulletin for an arts ministry meeting at the church or a nearby coffeehouse. Serve some dessert or snacks if you can. Open with prayer. Use the time to get to know each other, maybe ask everyone to introduce themselves and tell what kind of art they like to do. Perhaps share some inspirational ideas from this book or other sources. Another possibility is to have a spiritually mature guest artist speak who will inspire everyone with a ten-minute talk about his or her own journey of art and faith. Talk about possibly starting an arts ministry. If you've written up a vision, share it with them and ask their opinions. Or you could brainstorm ideas of what arts ministry could do. Don't commit to ideas yet, but listen carefully and write down suggestions. Gather contact information and circulate a survey.[3] If you have a large group, break up into groups of four people or so to pray for needs, for healing, for projects, for commissioning. Foster connection. You might invite people to an event, like an art workshop or a night of worship

Figure 4.1. Artists at Lincoln Berean Church study a book by Rory Noland. Photo: Jennie Prescott.

and the arts. Talk about dates for another meeting, possibly a repeating time once a month or once a quarter.

4. *Start off by doing a multi-week book study.* When you start meeting regularly, it's a good idea to build community and camaraderie among artists before launching into projects. One excellent way to do this is to start with a book study. This will help build relationships in the group; you'll learn and grow together and create a unified vision. See the online resources and extras for this chapter for a list of book studies.

5. Start to identify leaders. As you meet and get to know everyone, watch for people in your group who are passionate about arts ministry. Do they have an area they specialize in or can get excited about? Maybe God is calling them into a leadership role. Pray about this. Read the section on leadership skills in chapter five.

6. Initiate some projects. After you've built community and gotten to know each other for at least a few months, start exploring projects or ideas you might try as a group. It's good to give your growing group of artists a project to work toward. Go back to step two and think about how you can assist in the mission of the church. Take some time during the meeting to brainstorm and listen to God together, asking him how you can collaborate with him through the arts.[4] There are many project ideas that can get your artists, the congregation and the leadership involved and enhance the church's mission. Look at chapters seven, nine, fifteen and seventeen. You may need to start slowly with projects that are easy to grasp. In many cases you will be educating the congregation and/or leadership in how to engage with the arts in a church setting. After you develop some ideas, invite your pastor or a leader to a meeting to talk about how they might work.

Other things that will activate the talent and enthusiasm of your artists might include having some of them offer a workshop on their area of expertise to the congregation or starting an art gallery in the church (see chapter fifteen), or you might collaborate to put together a special mid-week arts service, or design holiday services. Even if no specific church projects are immediately available, you can still build momentum by continuing to meet or setting up monthly or quarterly "creative days" where artists eat, create and encourage one another in their creative callings.

> "The Holy Spirit speaks many languages; among them the languages of art in all its forms."
> **Frank Tracy Griswold**

7. Maintain community with your artists. See chapter six, "Crafting a Creative Arts Community," for more tips and direction.

IDEAS FOR THE EARLY STAGES OF ARTS MINISTRY—ARTS COMMUNITY FOUNDATIONS

As you get your monthly gatherings off the ground and build the foundation for arts ministry, you'll want to stay relaxed and let things evolve. Anyone can start an arts ministry if they are walking with God and he gives them a passion for it. A good indicator that you are on the right track will be the presence of moments of joy. There are few things quite as joy giving as collaborating with God in what he is doing.

The following are a few tips for the first year of arts ministry.

- Meet in a welcoming, cozy, artsy space, if you can, and one that is centrally located for church members. If you meet at the church, try to add some touches like lamps and rearrange chairs before the meeting.

- Make opening and closing prayer standard.

- Have someone who understands the thoughtful depth and sensitivity of artists set the tone of the gatherings.

- Share the vision/mission of the group regularly, but make it clear that it will evolve.

- Try to include food. Artists love food. (They don't call us starving artists for nothing.)

- You may have new people every time you meet, so make introductions a regular part of your meetings. It is fun to tie them in with an icebreaker. See the online resources and extras for this chapter for icebreaker ideas.

- As you get going, invite everyone to bring something creative that inspires them or that they are working on.

- Prepare something devotional in nature, but feel free to not share it if the meeting doesn't need it.

- Start a Facebook group and make it

Figure 4.2. Friends enjoy the paintings of fellow artist Bryn Gillette on display. Photo: Sheila Hudson.

closed so that everyone can share their work or ideas freely with group members without making them public to the whole world.

- Get everyone's contact information so you can email and Facebook meeting dates for information.

- Support each other's endeavors: gallery showings, events and so on.

- Try to go to movies or museums together outside of your regular gatherings. Have discussions afterward.

- Redirect conversations if one or two people tend to take over the discussion.

- You may want to steer clear of making art together at first because of the self-protective tendencies of artists who don't yet know each other.

- Avoid working on projects for the church for a while. Let the group get comfortable and realize you are not trying to get something from them.

- Don't appoint leaders or define roles too soon; rather, wait and see who rises naturally to leadership in your group, learning what their passions are. Jessie Nilo says, "I watched our participants and waited a full year. When the time seemed right, I asked individuals to pray about being on my arts leadership team. Specific job descriptions will evolve naturally as the ministry evolves." See more about raising up leaders in chapter five.

- Leave everyone wanting more. End events on time. Don't schedule art gatherings too frequently. Listen. Encourage. Follow through.

- Keep praying for the next step, asking God to daily fill you with his love for creative people. Ministering to creatives is alternately very fulfilling and draining. You cannot meet their needs; only God can.

You'll find more details on crafting arts community in chapter six.

AFTER THE FOUNDATION IS SET—WHAT DOES OUR ARTS MINISTRY DO?

After your community of artists has been gathering regularly for a few months to a year and you've gotten to know each other fairly well and had some fun times, the desire will naturally grow to start ministering to the church and/or the local community through the arts.

At this point, pull out your original vision/mission and assess where you are. Is your vision/mission still on track, considering the people you have in the group and the direction the community seems to be leaning? It will probably need some tweaking, and you can do that with the help of the group. Pastor Tri Robinson says, "Living things grow, and growing things change." Don't expect the culture and structure of your group to remain static if your ministry is truly alive. It's common for arts ministries to adjust what they do from year to year.

Some of the things you'll do at this stage of growth in your arts ministry include:

- raising up other arts leaders (chapter five).

- figuring out what types of outreach you'll do with the arts (chapter seventeen).

- deciding if you'll host a gallery (chapter fifteen).

- deciding if you are going to have a studio or workshops (chapter fourteen).

- deciding on how and when you'll produce arts projects for services (chapters four and eight).

- creating testing grounds for the arts. If someone wants to dance or paint live, present drama or spoken word, or any other art presentation, have them do it for the arts community first, then in an evening or casual service, before graduating to Sunday morning (chapter eleven). Of course, if they are a confident professional this can be circumvented, but often even professionals will benefit from this process of sharing their gift with their arts community first, before presenting it to the larger congregation.

All of these things can develop organically as the members of your arts community grow and God speaks to them about sharing their gifts, and as church leadership and the congregation become accustomed to what God is doing through the arts in your church.

Arts Ministry Wisdom

Finding balance. When Cindy West Limbrick started the nonprofit Awakening Artists she felt God encouraging her to base the ministry on three main tenets: call, community and compassion. To recognize and explore the artist's call to collaborate with God, to become part of a vibrant creative community and to give away what we have to those who need it: this creates a great balance for an arts ministry.

● ●

YOU MIGHT BE AN ARTS LEADER IF . . .

The following thoughts come from Jessie Nilo, director of VineArts Boise. She is one of the most passionate arts leaders you'll find.

You might be an arts leader if . . .

- You have a burden to extend God's love to artists.

- You have a holy discontent when you see a lack of creativity in spaces of worship and prayer.

- You long for all types of artists to have opportunities for glorifying God individually and corporately.

- You want to see pastors, artists, and church members understanding and supporting one another while learning from each other.

- You want to help empower artists to grow closer to Christ.

If this is you, pray for God's leading and don't be afraid to act on whatever he prompts you to do.

Read more about raising up other leaders in chapter five.

● ●

As you launch your ministry you'll go through seasons. You'll start with this season of inviting artists into their calling and then into community to share life and creativity. Eventually you'll move to helping them give away what they have and spark creativity around them. And as the arts ministry matures you'll see a balance of the three.

Start small. Where two or more are gathered, take it seriously. Jessie Nilo says, "Even ten years later, at its most basic level, VineArts is three artists praying for each other in someone's living room. Our arts ministry has grown strong, hundreds of lives have been touched through making and seeing art, and lots of new people have joined our church *because* of the arts ministry. But without the simplicity of a few hearts sharing small moments, the whole thing would fall apart."

Respect your church leaders. If there are currently artistic misunderstandings between you and the pastor, staff or congregation, don't despair.

God can work it out. If you are humble and respectful from the beginning, gentle education and prayer should take care of the rest. You can't expect people to embrace the unfamiliar right away. Give them frequent exposure to the arts and patient education, along with your cheerfulness and grace. They will most likely reciprocate with understanding and acceptance, eventually giving you their trust, and finally assigning value to what you do.

It can hurt. C. S. Lewis wrote in *The Four Loves*,

> To love at all is to be vulnerable. Love anything, and your heart will certainly be wrung and possibly be broken. If you want to make sure of keeping it intact you must give it to no one, not even to an animal. Wrap it carefully round with hobbies and little luxuries; avoid all entanglements. Lock it up safe in the casket or coffin of your selfishness. But in that casket—safe, dark, motionless, airless—it will change. It will not be broken; it will become unbreakable, impenetrable, irredeemable.[5]

You'll definitely get hurt leading arts ministry. Among other things, artists can be sensitive and easily hurt, and you will probably feel their pain. And occasionally you will be the target of their response to it. But here's the thing: can any ministry in God's kingdom promise you won't be hurt? Love artists, help them heal, teach them to love others, and give them opportunities to grow *through* their pain into deeper maturity in Christ.

Keep focused. God is about people, not about building cool ministries or programs. So focus this ministry on people; generally, those who want to be in creative community first, those who will be affected by arts ministry in the congregation second, and your local community third. Of course, God will give you the unique mix of the people you are to focus on, but the point is that people are the high priority and what you produce—artwork, events, programs and so on—are lower priority. Keeping this focus in mind is how the successful arts ministries profiled in this book have flourished. Artists need to first be accepted, loved, discipled and set on the path to healing; then you'll see them respond to that experience with gratitude and joy. From that place of wholeness and abundance some will want to serve the church with their talents and become the creative leaders God made them to be. They will lead the church toward a greater release of creativity in the congregation.

Invite other churches. After your arts ministry is up and running—the culture and structure of your gatherings are developed and you've started to establish what you do as a group and a ministry—you might think about inviting people from other churches to participate and collaborate artistically. Not every church has an arts ministry, after all. It's not a competition. Different churches are meant to perform different functions within the body of Christ. Maybe someday you'll help a sister church birth its own art ministry.

When you can't seem to sustain an arts ministry. Try going back through the how-to steps at the beginning of this chapter. As you read this book you may discover that you haven't taken the time to build artist community or that you've burned artists out. You may not yet have the right person to lead. If that's the case, ask people you know are interested in it to hold the whole idea of arts ministry in your church up in prayer for a time. Then revisit it with those people on a certain date, and see if God will reveal any answers.

WHEN THE ANSWER IS NO

If you're told no to starting an arts ministry, hang in there. It's okay. Ask again later. And, as is mentioned a number of times throughout the book, do not allow yourself to become bitter. Remember that a program (or the lack of one) cannot define or restrict humble serving in the name of Christ. If you feel that God has called you to remain at the church, you still have options. First, pray to discern God's plan in this. It simply may not be the right time, or maybe God is calling you to be the prayer catalyst and someone else should lead. Any way you slice it, you do not want to force an arts ministry into existence. Seek God and let it develop naturally. If, after prayer, you feel he's giving you the go-ahead to keep pursuing this, here are some ideas for what you *can* do:

- Connect with other artists in your church and get to know them. Spend time with them. You might support them financially or buy their art, offer encouragement, or pray for them regularly. If the "yes" for arts ministry comes in the future you'll have a head start on creating an arts community.

- Be a blessing to your pastors and staff and pray for them. They work hard, and the arts may be completely new to them.

- Meet with a friend on a regular basis and have your own little arts community. Do all the community things you'd like for an arts community to do together. Test out your ideas on a small scale.

- Connect with other arts leaders in your city or around the area and learn from them. Ask them to pray for you. Maybe get involved in their arts ministry, while still attending your home church.

- If you realize that anger, pride or a sense of entitlement has crept into your heart, stop everything and ask God to deal with it. Jessie Nilo says, "God is the only one who can demolish barriers and give other people epiphanies;

Figure 4.3. Artists from the Indy Vineyard Arts Community (IVAC) share dinner and creative ideas. Photo: JSM.

you can't. Cry out to him from your heart. I have seen real miracles happen in the of hearts church leaders. Sometimes they've been changed overnight."

- Read everything on the arts you can. See the online resources and extras for this chapter for a list of recommended books.

- Collect success stories and testimonies of your interactions with the arts and artists and the how the arts operate in other churches. You may be able to share them with your leadership when the time is right. You can find ideas for this at the New Renaissance Art Movement website and blog at TheNewR.org.

- Ask the Lord for creative ideas of how to spark the arts in your church.

- Research established traveling artists who can come to your church and do a professional presentation. This could open the door to more interest in the arts. Look for a list of these people on the Arts Links at TheNewR.org.

If you need to simply tuck your dream away for a while and pray for God to open a door, remain alert for opportunities. And remember, the fact that God has you in this church means he *is* doing something with the arts, right now, through your presence there. Just be yourself and humbly share what God has given you, and you may have more of an impact than you know.

See the online resources and extras for this chapter at JScottMcElroy.com/ CCHandbookextras.

NOTES

[1]Cindy also wrote *Saying Yes: Accepting God's Amazing Invitation to Artists and the Church* (Colorado Springs: David C. Cook, 2009).

[2]These guidelines were coauthored by Jessie Nilo.

[3]There is an arts survey available in the online resources and extras for this chapter.

[4]See the book *Finding Divine Inspiration* (http://FindingDivineInspiration.com) for more on leading artists to hear God's voice. J. Scott McElroy, *Finding Divine Inspiration: Working with the Holy Spirit in Your Creativity* (Shippensburg, PA: Destiny Image, 2008).

[5]C. S. Lewis, *The Four Loves* (New York: Harcourt, 1960), p. 121.

Inspiring, Empowering and Leading Artists in the Church

I see little of more importance to the future of our country and of civilization than full recognition of the place of the artist.

JOHN FITZGERALD KENNEDY,
Remarks at Amherst College, October 26, 1963

WHEN WE CHOOSE TO INSPIRE, disciple and empower the artists in our churches, guiding them into a collaborative relationship with God, they will help lead the rest of the congregation on the path to unlocking our inherent creativity. The result—a creative church—can change the world.

But as we pursue this path it's vital to remember that arts ministry and creativity in the church aren't ultimately about the artwork crafted or the level of creativity our church attains. At the core, the reasons we want to embrace the arts and creativity are *to love people more effectively, to worship God more completely* and *to facilitate the maturity of the body of Christ.*

For arts leaders this starts with loving and caring for our artists as individuals, helping them to grow spiritually and turning them to their true source. This chapter offers a few ideas of how to do that. I'll start with some thoughts on how to lead artists.

LEADING ARTISTS

The successful arts leaders I've talked to have several things in common:

- *They regularly seek God in prayer for direction and ideas.* James Kearny observes,

> Jesus said that he only did what he saw the Father doing; he only spoke as he heard the Father speak. We should not attempt to establish God's kingdom in our ways, with our wisdom, with our strength.[1]

- *They hold their arts ministries loosely,* understanding that approaches and ways of doing things can and will change. Nick Benoit of Willow Creek says,

> I feel like with creativity, you have to be constantly changing, and maneuvering how you get there. Also, the very natural tendency of artists is to be in for a season, and then to be out for three seasons. They might get a professional gig, or just be kind of generally flaky like artists sometimes are. In my experience, I have not had a lot of success with the strategizing and the standardizing [of arts ministry]. I've had a lot more success with pastoring of the artists. And I think that requires a level of personal investment in people and a constant sensitivity to changes within the ministry, and the changes within the church. And you flex to all of those, all of the time.[2]

- *They exhibit faithfulness.* Ann Willams of Visual of Voice says,

> Ministry, especially [our] visual arts ministry, is about the long haul. You have to be willing to be there for the long haul so the artists understand; we're not going anywhere anytime soon. And this is safe, and it's okay for you to come in, even if you wait three or four years, its okay, we'll still be here.[3]

- *They are patient.* Jessie Nilo of VineArts says,

> Take your impatience and urgency to God as an offering to him. Relax and get some training in spiritual leadership or take an art or music class for fun and watch how the instructor interacts with their students. Don't take on too much ministry too fast, whether informal, spontaneous ideas or official church projects. Do a little, and serve your people well. Be very intentional and pray about their needs.[4]

Ann Williams adds,

> When I first got on the [leadership] team, I was the young buck who
> came in and wanted to push everything and go fast. The gal who was
> leading just told me to be patient.
> And now I'm the one saying, "I think
> in God's timing this will happen." But
> you have to create a team for sustain-
> ability, otherwise you would go mad.
> We are seeing things now that we
> were hoping would happen but we
> didn't know they'd be happening the
> way they are. A lot of it is just getting on your knees and asking God,
> "Okay, what do we do next?"[5]

> "Artists to my mind are the real
> architects of change, and not
> the political legislators who
> implement change after the fact."
> William S. Burroughs, at the
> Walker Art Center

- *They exhibit empathy.* An arts leader should be able to understand where
  artists are coming from and be able to encourage and invest in them. Jessie
  Nilo says that when she first stepped into arts ministry,

  > I was completely unprepared for the emotional responses of artists.
  > Creative people began to approach me out of nowhere, people I had
  > no idea were artistic. Teenagers followed me in the church hallway
  > to read me a poem they'd written that morning. Office workers
  > poured out their jumbled-up frustrations about creative blocks. Pro-
  > fessional artists confessed creative paralysis due to perfectionism.
  > People shared their history, their dreams, their fears and their aspira-
  > tions. Nobody seemed to care what my background was or what
  > kind of art I did. They just wanted to be heard and embraced as an
  > *artist.* I saw hope on every face.
  >
  > My heart began to expand, not only for artists but for me; I began
  > to feel things more profoundly and see things more deeply, in ways
  > I never could before. Deepening my sensitivity has done me a world
  > of good.[6]

LEADERSHIP SKILLS

Many times arts leaders are simply artists who have little or no leadership
training but feel called to advocate for arts ministry in their church. They may

have a natural leadership gift but, like Moses in Exodus 3 and 4, they feel un-qualified to lead.

If you find yourself leading artists and learning about it as you go, it's a good idea to seek out some training. If an artist came to you and said they wanted to increase their skills in a certain medium, you'd suggest—among other things—taking some classes, reading some books and learning from those who've done it. Apply that advice to grow your skills in the art of leadership. If your church has a leadership training program, get involved in it. Go to a leadership conference. Ask a staff member who is a good leader to mentor you. Become a regular reader of leadership websites like those listed in the notes for this chapter.[7]

A word about balance: even though arts ministry is all about the people and the worship, it's important to retain the vision for where you believe God is taking you in the context of the church's vision. Jesus is possibly the best example of this. He could have walked around addressing every urgent thing he saw, healing everyone everywhere, because he was capable of it. This would have seemed to be a good thing, but it wouldn't have been the best thing. The best was that Jesus cut short his good work and was obedient to die a violent and (at the time) seemingly needless death. The good is often the enemy of the best.

> "The characteristic common to God and man is apparently that: the desire and ability to make things."
> Dorthy L. Sayers, *The Mind of the Maker*

All that to say, you can't please everyone in your arts ministry. Luann Jennings says,

> As arts leaders, "the people we lead" might well have very different agendas and needs. We can't—and don't have to—meet all of those needs. We can trust God to do that. It might be a hard conversation to have to say to someone, "I'm sorry, we don't do that" or even "No, we're not going to do that." If we work as leaders in churches, we might encounter an expectation that an individual church is supposed to meet all of someone's needs. But it can't, and wasn't designed to.[8]

So we are always praying for God's leading and for balance to remain loving and caring leaders while seeking God and moving toward the vision he is giving for the ministry.

CARING FOR YOUR SOUL

Leading artists is often fun and thrilling, but it can also be difficult and emotionally draining. Make sure to take care of yourself. Keep in regular contact with a spiritual mentor who understands what you are facing. Engage in community outside of the artist's group, with people who aren't necessarily artists. Keep up your spiritual disciplines and practices. Connect with artists or peers from outside your church. And make time for your own creative expression in a setting where there is no leadership responsibility and no pressure to excel.

• •

Arts leadership is worth every bit of struggle and sacrifice. Arts leader Lynn Westergren says that while she dreams of a simple solitary life of making art, she knows she wouldn't be satisfied, because as an arts leader,

> I've tasted the joy of nurturing creativity in others, leading an entire congregation into the unknown of where our collaborative efforts will take us, and coming out on the other side with art that exceeds even my expectations, injecting life and deeper meaning into our desire for knowing God. I've heard the sincere thank yous of artists given an opportunity to share their work as part of a well thought out framework. I've felt the rightness of art being a key component of church life.[9]

• •

INSPIRING AND EMPOWERING ARTISTS

What follows are some thoughts on enabling artists to step into the life that God has called them to: a joyful journey of creative collaboration with him.

Help artists understand who they are in Christ. It's so important for artists—and everyone—to live life and do the work God's called them to from a place of understanding how loved and accepted they are by their Father. Really knowing this changes everything and addresses the fears listed below.

In a seminar I'll sometimes show pictures of galaxies and nebulas and talk about God's brilliant creativity. These galactic pyrotechnics serve no known purpose to us and in many cases are simply gas and dust. This God is big—big enough to create things that are thousands of light years across. Then I may show them some pictures of the inside of a cell, which contains a universe of information, and remind them that God designed that and made it work. I may show a close-up of the eye of a gecko, stunningly beautiful and elegantly functional. I tell them God made these things for his pleasure. And he made you for

Figure 5.1. The Sombrero Galaxy is roughly eighty-two thousand light-years wide and is located approximately twenty-eight million light-years from earth. Photo: NASA and the Hubble Heritage Team (STScI/AURA).

his pleasure too. He had a specific purpose in mind when he thought you into existence, a way for you to collaborate with him that would bring both of you joy. But he loved you before you ever did anything for him, when you were still in the womb. And nothing will ever change the love of this amazing God for you. In fact, if you never did anything else for him from this moment on, how he feels about you would not change. You are his beloved; he is especially fond of you. If you did everything he ever asked of you from this moment on, it wouldn't make him love you any more than he already does. You would experience more of the joy that comes from collaboration with him, but he would not love you more. No matter what you do or don't do, no matter what you intended to do and didn't do, God will never love you any more or any less. You are loved, unconditionally by the greatest being in existence anywhere.[10]

Then I have them "soak" in worship music, inviting them to close their eyes and just ask God to speak to them about how he feels about them. This can be an incredibly moving experience, and there are often many tears shed.

I'm overwhelmed every time God reveals more about the depth of his uncon-
ditional love for me, whether through an exercise like this or some other
sweet way, and I imagine it's something I'll never stop learning about.

Helping artists connect with God in ways like this leads them to become
more empowered and inspired in their lives and work.

Help them intentionally listen for God's voice. One of the most important
things any believer can do is to learn how to hear God's voice. Of course there
are many ways that God speaks to us: through reading the Bible, preaching
and teaching, other believers, art, nature, circumstances or events, and in
waiting silently in prayer. In my experience the two most effective ways to
consistently hear God's voice are through meditating on the Bible and listening in prayer. We would do well to help the artists in our charge develop
these skills.

Walter Wangrin Jr. says prayer at its simplest should consist of this: we
speak, he listens, he speaks, we listen. We often miss that last part and don't
make the time or the effort to really stop and listen.[11]

Practices that will help artists hear God's voice regularly include:

- *Listening prayer.* Basically, listening prayer is expecting that God wants to
and will speak as we intentionally listen and then making time for that to
take place. What we hear can be recorded in a prayer journal.

- *Prayer journaling.* Unlike the kind of journal kept for high school English class
or one that recounts the details of a famous person's life, a prayer journal should
be private and personal. It's a space where we should feel safe to express deep
thoughts and cries of the heart and where we can learn to hear God's voice by
recording what we think he is saying without judging it. We can always come
back to test it later. Embracing the freedom of the prayer journal concept can
be life changing, deepening our dialogue with God and making faith real.[12]

- *Lectio divina. Lectio divina* is the ancient practice of mediating on Scripture
and then listening for what God may be saying to you through it. There are
different variations, but generally you chose a Scripture passage to mediate
on and then consider that passage in four steps: reading, meditation, prayer
and contemplation. First, you slowly read through the passage with a listening heart, inviting God to speak. Second, you reread and meditate on it,
spending some time with it, permitting God to connect the truths to your

life. Third, you pray through it, responding to what God has spoken to you. And fourth, you contemplate what God seems to be saying, while resting and listening in his presence.[13]

- *Corporate listening.* Corporate listening is listening prayer in a group. It's a great way for a leader to model listening in prayer for other believers, and it builds faith as listeners hear similar things or confirm what others have heard. See an example of this in chapter six as a part of the VineArts community description.

- *Personal prayer art.* Practicing personal prayer art is a wonderful way to listen for God's voice on behalf of others. See the complete description of how it is done in chapter ten.

If certain artists are not inclined to journal, meditate or even stand still, ask them how they have most often heard from God. Maybe it's walking in nature or listening to music. Then encourage them to put themselves in those situations and ask God to speak to them there.

A rule of thumb with listening for God's voice is that obedience enhances the listening process. The more you act on what you hear (after confirmation), the more you will hear.

Help them understand their calling. Many artists have never heard that God had a purpose in mind when he designed them with artistic abilities. Still others have trouble believing it, and many more have difficulty living in that truth.

God designed all humans with the ability to hear his voice, whether through intentional listening, like I just described, or by picking up his messages from the world around us as written about in Romans 1:19-20. But most humans would rather not take the time to listen. We fill up our lives with noise and media and distraction, making it hard to hear God communicating his purpose to us. The following suggestions will help artists better understand and live into their calling.

Artists are called to listen and translate.

But God, in his great mercy has not given up on getting through to humans. Of course, he has given us the Bible and wonderful preachers and teachers to share the truth in clear ways, but He has also placed among us people who share the truth in a more subtle, intuitive way. They are people who are wired to listen, who often find they are unhappy when they tune out the messages and observations they encounter. These people are the artists, the folks Ezra Pound calls "the antenna of the race." While the rest of society may be tuning out, the artist is still bringing messages from God, even if he doesn't realize it. And he is using his art to make sense of those messages. "Their art is both their tool of discovery and their means of transmitting their messages back to others."[14]

Encourage artists to grow in their calling to listen and translate by talking about the meanings and messages of the world around us, and help them discover new ways to convey those messages.

Artists are called to collaborate with God to bring his kingdom to the world. Our efforts in the mastery of matter often leave us wanting. For matter to achieve its highest form and us to become what we can as artists and Christians there needs to be a spiritual component, a collaboration with the Holy Spirit.

> The model for collaboration was set in Genesis 1:26 when it was revealed that the Trinity collaborated together to create. All of life involves and requires collaboration; between a man and woman for a child to be born, between a speaker and listener for a concept to be understood, and an infinite number of other examples. God gave all Christians the joyful privilege of collaborating with him to bring his kingdom to the world in myriad ways. And the artist has the honor of collaborating with God in fashioning material in ways that glorify him. There is nothing like the sensation of engaging our skills and abilities to collaborate creatively with the Creator. This partnership starts with learning to hear God's voice, and intentional listening intensifies it. Leading them into collaboration with God in their work is one of the greatest gifts you can give an artist.[15]

Artists are called to worship. We worship God in part through developing the skills and abilities he has given us, and art making is no exception. In fact, art making will often facilitate a worship experience for others (Ex 31:1-6).

Jamie Wells, founder of ArtWorship, says,

> If everything was created to give praise to God, then what we as artists are doing is completely worshipful. God created man in his image. God desires man to reflect the character traits God himself possesses. With art worship we humbly attempt to put on canvas a living creation that is spinning wildly within us just as the cosmos once spun into place so long ago.[16]

Individual calling. Beyond these general callings there is, of course, the specific individual calling. One way we can help an artist discern what that is—if they don't already know—is to spend time with them personally: praying, talking and doing ministry together.

Here are a few other things we can encourage artists to do in order to get a better handle on their specific calling.

- Get connected and stay connected with church community. Christians around you can help identify and support you in your calling. A small group that's walking with you can give great input and offer prayer support. And you can become less self-focused by interacting with and supporting them.

- Risk and obey. When you believe God is calling you in a certain direction, pray about taking a risk and moving on that call. Obey what he instructs you to do.

- Write down or record words, nudges, epiphanies, observations and so on. Taking note of these things will give perspective on what God has consistently been speaking to you. It can highlight themes and put pieces of the puzzle together.

- Take a spiritual gifts assessment and a personality test. There are a number of these kinds of tests available, many of which are free online. These can confirm leanings or directions you may be considering. If at all possible, ask someone who knows how the tests work to help you process the results.

- Find a spiritual director or mentor.

- Develop a prayer journal. See the comments on this earlier in the chapter.

- Ask your Christian friends to help you confirm and test words of prophecy, knowledge or advice people have given you.

Help them pursue spiritual formation. "Christian spiritual formation is the process of being conformed to the image of Christ for the sake of others. It is inspired by the Holy Spirit and grounded in Scripture and a faith community."[17] Showing artists how to be intentional about their spiritual formation will help them address many

> *"I'm called to be a Christian. And the best way I know to be a Christian is to be an artist."*
> **Chris Stoffel Overvoorde,**
> *Passing the Colors: Engaging Visual Culture in the 21st Century*

issues and questions about their calling as a Christian and an artist. They'll learn to use tried and true tools for growing and sustaining their faith and deepening their intimacy with God. And that will affect every area of their life.

Several tools already mentioned in the chapter can help artists along the path of spiritual formation, but some additional helpful practices include

- exploring the spiritual disciplines of prayer, Scripture reading, fasting and confession
- taking regular retreat time to connect with God
- focusing on developing consistently godly interactions with others in our everyday lives
- asking God how we can represent him or collaborate in what he is doing in all circumstances

Help them to identify lies and wounds in their lives and to overcome them. Artists can be sensitive souls. God designed them that way so that they would recognize and convey his messages to the world. But that often means that they have been hurt somewhere along the line. It also means they can be susceptible to the lies the enemy launches at them. Your church may have a program for identifying and dealing with lies and wounds, such as Celebrate Recovery, SOZO inner healing and deliverance, or others.[18] If so, encourage your artists to go through it, if that's appropriate. You can also initiate group book studies that will help identify and deal with wounds. Many times just recognizing and putting a name to a wound or a lie will begin to curtail its power and start the process of healing.

Show them what is possible. Nick Benoit, creative director at Willow Creek, talks about raising expectations:

> One of the things that I loved about my four years at Rock Harbor (Orange, California) was that everything we did in the arts was all volunteer driven, and to do that well you have to be constantly encouraging and pastoring people to understand their potential. Because I think a lot of artists in the church sell themselves short. They listen to what their . . . teachers . . . and their education and classes and critiques [have told them they are capable of]. And they have completely cut off the reality that whatever their talent level, when you combine that with what the Spirit of God is capable of, it will absolutely defy

Figure 5.2. *Three Cairns* by Andy Goldsworthy. Constructed of stacked prehistoric Iowa limestone. Goldsworthy's artwork is site specific, using natural materials from that location. Many of his sculptures are temporary and use things like ice, leaves, twigs or rocks, and are featured in the documentary *Rivers and Tides.* Photo: Phil Roeder/Flickr/Creative Commons. License information available at https://creativecommons.org/licenses/by/2.0.

your greatest imagination. We are capable of far more than we give ourselves credit for and far more than other people have given us credit for.[19]

Inspire artists with what other artists have done, bringing them regular examples of innovative and excellent art. Show an Andrew Goldsworthy documentary, a visual tour of a great cathedral and how it was built, or a video of Landfill Harmonic, a musical group that makes instruments from trash. Show them folk art and testimonies of healing and transformation through art from Bethel Arts. Encourage them to dream about how they can make a difference in the world by collaborating with God and using what he's given them.

Help them overcome fear and hindrances. In her TED talk on creativity, Elizabeth Gilbert raised the question "Is it logical that anybody should be expected to be afraid of the work that they feel they were put on this earth to do?" As an arts leader and an artist you may find yourself constantly repeating—to yourself and your artists—the words of God to Joshua, "Have I not commanded you? Be strong and courageous! Do not be afraid; do not be discouraged, for the LORD your God will be with you wherever you go" (Josh 1:9).

> "What separates artists from ex-artists is that those who challenge their fears, continue; those who don't, quit. Each step in the art making process puts that issue to the test."
>
> David Bayles, *Art and Fear*

It takes courage to make something and share it with others, courage to put your heart and your talent (or your self-perceived lack of it) out there for all to see. So for many artists, fear in its various forms is the greatest nemesis to creativity.

Fear may manifest as

- *Performance orientation.* Educator Dr. Gregory Schraw says: "Students with mastery orientation seek to *improve* their competence. Those with performance orientations seek to *prove* their competence."[20] The same applies to artists. Regularly exploring the concept of empowering that was mentioned earlier in this chapter and helping them understand who they are in Christ are the best ways to combat and overcome performance orientation.

- *Perfectionism.* "To require perfection is to invite paralysis. The pattern is predictable: as you see error in what you have done, you steer your work toward what you imagine you can do perfectly. You cling ever more tightly to what you already know you can do—away from risk and exploration, and possibly further from the work of your heart. You find reasons to procrastinate, since to not work is to not make mistakes."[21]

  One way to break perfectionism in visual artists is having them paint live on stage or during a service, which allows them to do what they can in a specific time frame and then entrust it to God. (Of course, in the case of painting on stage, this only works with an artist who is skilled and ready for that. Thrusting someone up there who is not ready in order to cure perfectionism could be like shock therapy.) For writers, try doing Morning Pages like Julia Cameron describes in *The Artists Way*.[22] For practitioners of other art forms, quick, sometimes spontaneous expressions of their art for individuals or small audiences can be helpful. Like the visual artist doing personal prayer art (chapter ten), the artist will see what an effect even a quick, imperfect creative presentation can have and how God can move through it to touch someone profoundly.[23]

- *Procrastination.* Procrastination is often closely related to perfectionism in that artists may put off doing something because they are afraid it will be inadequate. Therese Borchard writes,

  > You make good work by (among other things) making lots of work that isn't very good, and gradually weeding out the parts that aren't good, the parts that aren't yours. It's called feedback, and it's the most

direct route to learning about your own vision. It's also called doing your work. After all, someone has to do your work, and you're the closest person around.[24]

Of course fear comes in many other forms as well. The best blanket advice to help artists deal with this is to continue loving them and pointing them to God's love for them, because "perfect love drives out fear" (1 Jn 4:18).

- *Help them see their destiny.* Encourage your artists with these words:

> You have a place in history that no one else can fill. God planned good works (and work) for you to do even before you were born. Your destiny is to collaborate with God in the work he leads you to, and your willful collaboration ushers his Kingdom into the world. Don't worry about dreaming big dreams, he has that handled. Commit to living purely and to quietly listening for his voice every day and see where he takes you.[25]

- *Stay beside them as they walk it out.* One key way that we help artists walk out their destiny is by providing them with creative community: a group of artists to journey alongside them. The next chapter is completely devoted to that.

A large part of walking out a destiny is being obedient to take each individual step. Arts leaders can journey alongside artists, regularly reminding them to take a risk and obey God's direction, trusting that he will make a way as they go forward, even if it is

> "Art should be a form of play, rejoicing before the face of God."
>
> Hans Rookmaaker, *The Creative Gift*

with trembling steps. Nick Benoit talks about what obedience looks like:

> Obedience is huge for artists. I think I'm so big on this because before I came to Rock Harbor I'd never done spoken word in my life. One day God just started giving me some words and I started writing them down. I was terrified of what I had because I didn't know what it was. And I went to a meeting where we were planning our weekend services and I [knew] I was supposed to bring it up but didn't. At the very last second I said, "Okay, so there's this idea I have and I don't really know what it is," and they were just like, "Well read it." So I did. Everyone said, "Oh my gosh, our church has to hear this!" And that was the first time I ever did spoken word. Ever since then when I get

those little rhymes in my head, I recognize it because of that first act of obedience and the way I saw God use it in my life and the life of our church. I go, "Okay, this is going to require an act of obedience for me again." And that's one of the things—when we are talking about the hearts of our artists . . . I want them to recognize. Those little whispers they hear, those are some of the ways that God uniquely speaks to them as artists, and those are things that they have to be obedient with. It's not just their personality; it's not just their talents, their gifts; that's the voice of the Spirit calling them to give a gift to the church and to give a gift to the world.[26]

RAISING UP LEADERS

As an arts ministry grows, it will be natural to look for and identify others who can take on leadership roles. Of course, most of the time these leaders will be volunteers. At the time of this writing, not many churches pay their director of arts more than a stipend, few have full-time directors of arts, and still fewer have paid assistant leaders. So in many cases you'll be looking for volunteers who catch the vision for your arts ministry and who have time to invest in it.

God tends to orchestrate arts ministry in churches by slowly and organically aligning opportunities, desires and people. The process of raising up leaders is no exception to this trend, but it often requires some encouragement from the director of arts to help others step into the leadership roles God has for them. There is much joy in encouraging each other in our gifts and in working side by side in the fruitful work he has called us to do. This makes healthy, functioning community so much more fun than being "lone rangers."

> "He who works with his hands is a laborer,
> He who works with his hands and his head is a craftsman,
> He who works with his hands, his head, and his heart is an artist."
> St. Francis of Assisi

Ann Williams says her first step in identifying leaders for the Visual Voice ministry at Lincoln Berean Church is just getting on her knees and praying for God to point them out.

With us, that [seeking God] is really essentially what happened. There are just certain people that rise to the surface. They have a heart for the people and the ability to carry things through.

I have been able to spend time with all the leaders to know where their hearts are. Then it's just building that relationship, knowing when to ask and trusting they are going to pray about it to know that that's where God wants them.[27]

Jessie Nilo describes trying to identify leaders early on:

At our first meeting, I remember seeing some promising art leaders, and I remember my disappointment when I never saw them again. On the other hand, some of those whom I pegged as perplexing or insecure grew into my most valuable art leaders. Go figure!

That's why I recommend being slow to select team leaders. Eventually you'll need a team to help you, but for a while as you do things like open brainstorming meetings and small events, you can just see who comes. Watch who jumps in to help you, who prays for people, who encourages artists, who loves making and sharing artwork with strangers, and who asks about logistics or offers to bring supplies. Pay close attention to these people, learn what their artistic passions are, and invite them to help you brainstorm the next event. Ask God to show you their servant heart.[28]

If you took the advice in chapter four and circulated a survey in your first arts meeting, look over your surveys and see if people are excited to start specific groups for the arts such as writing, culinary, theater and so on.[29] After doing this, Jessie advises,

Don't commit to long-term groups yet. At this point I recommend scheduling one-time workshops or one special evening for a potential affinity group, not scheduling repeating monthly meetings in stone until you're absolutely sure that a fantastic, mature leader is in place for that group.

Meanwhile keep nurturing any organic groups and leaders that you see emerging, giving potential leaders opportunities to lead occasionally while not appointing any long-term positions yet. Do NOT keep doing this by yourself, or it may die! Pray for great leaders to emerge in the arts.[30]

Still, there will probably be times when you are working alone, especially in the beginning. If your volunteer leaders have not yet surfaced, you may have to recruit help from family, friends or artists you know. Luann Jennings says,

From my experience working with many arts leaders, and as an arts leader myself, I am convinced that the most challenging and important tasks we face are . . . recognizing when we need help, getting the right kind of help, then letting them do their jobs. Some tasks we do need to do ourselves. Some tasks should be done by others, particularly by others whose own work is doing that job. Our first question should be: Is this something I need to do myself? If so, we monitor our personal stamina and get the right kinds of support as soon as we need it. If it's not something we need to do ourselves, then, by all means, delegate. But remember Jethro's injunction to Moses to select "capable" and "trustworthy" people to serve under you (Exodus 18:21), then lead them well. "If you do this and God so commands, you will be able to stand the strain, and all these people [i.e., those being served by our work] will go home satisfied" (Exodus 18:23).[31]

Leading any group of Christians is an honor and a great privilege, and being invited to inspire, empower and lead artists has additional rewards. The work that God is doing in them is often expressed in their artwork, so you can see the tangible, material result of your leadership investment, which is gratifying and humbling. And the artists' expressions may also have an influence on others who view or experience their art, sometimes for years into the future. Your leadership of artists not only affects them individually, but also everyone who witnesses their work. This leadership of artists in the church is a high calling, and God will grant you grace, wisdom, courage and peace as you walk it out!

See the online resources and extras for this chapter at JScottMcElroy.com/ CCHandbookextras.

NOTES

[1]James D. Kearney, "The Gift of Leadership," *Christian Arts Entrepreneurs, Leaders and Advocates* (blog), June 23, 2011, http://churchandart.org/2011/06/23/the-gift-of-leadership.

[2]Interview with the author, January 2014.

[3]Interview with the author, January 2014.

[4]Written contribution from Jessie Nilo.

[5]Interview with the author, January 2014.

[6]Written contribution from Jessie Nilo.

[7]Luann Jennings, former director of arts at Redeemer Presbyterian Church, New York City, offers several recommendations: See Michael Hyatt's *Intentional Leadership* blog (michaelhyatt.com). Hyatt is the chairman of Thomas Nelson Publishers. Also see John Maxwell's leadership books. If possible, attend the Willow Creek Global Leadership Summit.

[8]Interview with the author, January 2014.

[9]Lynne Westergren, comment in response to the post "The Reluctant Leader," *Christian Arts Entrepreneurs, Leaders and Advocates* (blog), June 6, 2011, http://churchandart .org/2011/06/06/the-reluctant-leader.

[10]For a list of verses talking about our identity, see Ken Boa, "Who Does God Say I Am?" Bible.org, May 11, 2006, https://bible.org/article/who-does-god-say-i-am.

[11]We could spend a whole chapter on this point, and in fact, I wrote a complete book on it: *Finding Divine Inspiration: Working with the Holy Spirit in Your Creativity* (Shippensburg, PA: Destiny Image, 2008).

[12]*Finding Divine Inspiration* covers this concept in detail and directs readers in a proven way how to set one up.

[13]For more details on *lectio divina*, see Brian Hardin, "Lectio Divina: Divine Reading," *BibleGateway* (blog), September 6, 2012, www.biblegateway.com/blog/2012/09/lectio -divina-divine-reading.

[14]Steve Turner, *Imagine: A Vision for Christians in the Arts* (Downers Grove, IL: InterVarsity Press, 2000), p. 88.

[15]McElroy, *Finding Divine Inspiration*, p. 36.

[16]Jamie Wells, "Painting and Practicing the Image of God," *Relevant Magazine*, February 19, 2003, www.relevantmagazine.com/life/whole-life/features/1678-painting-and-prac ticing-the-image-of-god#lzAguom8KtQCOUpg.99.

[17]"Spiritual Formation," www.georgefox.edu/seminary/about/formation.html.

[18]*Sōzō* is the Greek word translated "saved," "healed," "delivered." SOZO ministry is a unique inner healing and deliverance ministry aimed to get to the root of things that hinder your personal connection with the Father, Son and Holy Spirit.

[19]Interview with the author, January 2014.

[20]Gregory Schraw, "Promoting General Metacognitive Awareness," *Instructional Science* 26 (1998): 113-25, emphasis added.

[21]David Bayles, *Art and Fear* (Eugene, OR: Image Continuum, 2001), p. 30.

[22]Julia Cameron, *The Artist's Way* (New York: J. P. Tarcher/Putnam, 2002).

[23]For more ideas on how to overcome perfectionism, see Therese J. Borchard, "10 Steps to Conquer Perfectionism," *PsychCentral*, September 13, 2014, http://psychcentral.com/ blog/archives/2011/05/31/10-steps-to-conquer-perfectionism-2/?all=1.

[24]Ibid., p. 26.

[25]McElroy, *Finding Divine Inspiration*, p. 73.

[26]Interview with the author, January 2014.

[27]Interview with the author, November 2013.

[28]Written contribution from Jessie Nilo.

[29]Available in the online resources and extras for this chapter.

[30]Written contribution from Jessie Nilo.

[31]Luann Jennings, "Arts Leadership and the Bible, Part 4," *Christian Arts Entrepreneurs, Leaders and Advocates* (blog), October 3, 2012, http://churchandart.org/2012/10/03/ arts-leadership-and-the-bible-part-4.

······ 6 ······

Crafting a Creative
Arts Community

*There can be no vulnerability without risk; there can be
no community without vulnerability; there can be no
peace, and ultimately no life, without community.*

M. SCOTT PECK,
The Different Drum: Community Making and Peace

*We have all known the long loneliness
and we have learned that the only solution is
love and that love comes with community.*

DOROTHY DAY,
*The Long Loneliness: The Autobiography of
the Legendary Catholic Social Activist*

AN ESSENTIAL INGREDIENT OF a creative church is a healthy creative community. In fact, it's difficult for arts ministry or congregational creativity to be sustained without developing a support community for them.

Many have observed that God lives in community, the Father, the Son and the Holy Spirit existing together and benefiting from each other. J. R. R. Tolkien thought that "the love of the Father and Son (who are infinite and equal) is a Person": the Holy Spirit.[1] To put it even more poetically:

Love must have an object, argued Richard of St Victor in the twelfth century.

If God is love and has always been love then he must always have had "another" upon whom to direct his love. Furthermore, argued Richard, love must have a third party otherwise it's self-indulgent. True love desires the beloved to be loved by another. So the Father and Son desire to share their love with another: the Holy Spirit.

But the Trinity is more than a community of love or a close family. It's a community of being. The persons of the Trinity share one being or one nature. In verse 21 [of Jn 17] Jesus prays that those who will believe in him will be one "just as you, Father, are in me, and I in you." In verse 23 he speaks of "you in me." Addressing the Father, he prays that his disciples may be one "even as we are one" (22). Father, Son and Spirit mutually indwell one another.[2]

While it's true that, as Miroslav Volf says, "the Christian God is not a lonely God,"[3] many of his children are. This seems to be because we neglect the model of community that God represents and invites us into. Many artists also experience isolation because their work requires them to spend long hours alone. Painters, poets, musicians, writers, sculptors and other artists often need singular concentration as they create. On top of that, many have introverted temperaments, preferring to limit their interactions with people. Even so, these artists still have a need for human connection and care. They should be able to find that in faith-based creative community.

As more churches begin to grasp the importance and impact the arts can have in their congregations, there is a danger that artists will be valued and used for what they can do and not receive what they need to thrive. There are many stories out there of artists who have been used, abused or misunderstood by the church over the years. Most artists who have been around the church for any length of time can tell you one. We certainly don't want to perpetuate that unfortunate story line. So if you really want to have a welcoming atmosphere for artists and see the arts and creativity thrive in your church, there needs to be a place for healthy artist community, a place where artists can be known and cared for before they ever do anything for the church.

> "... to build a community of artists who would collaborate to create moments of transcendence in church."
>
> Nancy Beach, *An Hour on Sunday*

Creating community for artists can be a difficult task. But when it happens organically, it can be simple and natural. Yes, artists can be elusive, introverted, isolated by work habits and hesitant to commit. There might be times when the phrase "like herding cats" comes to mind. But when they do gather, it can be magical. It's common for healthy groups to experience heartfelt, poetic sharing, stunningly beautiful vulnerability, empathetic, empowering prayer, much-needed connection with like-minded people or sudden, invigorating flashes of talent. And when these things happen, it's not unusual for the unini-tiated to think, "Oh my gosh, *this is what's been missing in my life!*"

At its basic level a sense of community can be developed by spending time together, connecting, experiencing joy and serving together, often around a common interest. We can't force community to happen, but we can create an environment where it is likely to thrive. That means first learning how to love people. In fact, if you can love people and be dependable in your commitment to them, you can start an arts community group.[4]

There are many ways to build artist community, and what you come up with may not look exactly like any of the models here. Like all other facets of arts ministry and creativity, if you seek God, he will show you the unique ex-pression that will work best in your church. Don't be afraid to try things, fail at them and then try again.

SOME ELEMENTS OF COMMUNITY GATHERINGS

You can refer back to the section "Ideas for the Early Stages of Arts Com-munity" in chapter four for some foundational thoughts on running your meetings, but below are some additional ideas for what your artist community might do when they get together. Of course, you wouldn't want to try too many of these in a particular meeting; that could be overwhelming. In fact, a common characteristic of all the groups profiled in this chapter is that they do not over-program; they don't try to do too much, and they expect what they do to be fluid, changing from meeting to meeting. If you have encouragement, laughter and prayer, then you have the foundation for a good group.

Prayer. It may sound clichéd or overly spiritual, but authentic, honest prayer together is the best thing you can do to build creative community. You'll see several examples of how this can work later in this chapter: pray for each other's lives, struggles and work as described in the Indy Vineyard ex-ample; pray, wait and listen for God's ideas as seen in the VineArts example;

pray for encouraging or prophetic words for each other or people that come to mind like Bethel Arts does. Invite God to have a voice in your community, and he will do some surprising things.

Worship. In community, simpler is generally better. Even one song on an acoustic guitar can help center people and add another refreshing artistic element to the mix. Have your group experiment with worshiping God through the members' particular art forms. It might take several times of getting used to this or relaxing so that they can worship, but this practice could open up new avenues of expression for the artists and the group as a whole.

Bible studies. You don't have to just study Bezalel or biblical creativity, although those are good topics. Ask God to highlight a biblical concept or Scripture passage, and see where the discussion goes.

Book studies. There are many books on the arts to study together that will benefit your community, giving them a shared experience and getting everyone on the same page. See the online resources and extras for this chapter for notes on important books.

Film clips. Show the latest incredibly creative YouTube video or play a movie clip about a creative topic from the Internet and discuss. Maybe even make a video together.

Field trips. Hit up an art fair, a play, museum, park or gallery opening—anything that stirs your group's creativity.

Eat together. There are many examples of people eating together in the Bible: Jesus' miraculous feeding of thousands, his mealtime visits to various disciples' and leaders' houses, and, of course, the Last Supper. Eating together with your arts group, at least occasionally, is a simple and enjoyable way to build healthy community.

Make things together. After your arts community has been meeting for a while and gotten comfortable with each other it can be wonderful to have times of creating together. This could be in a weekly open studio (see chapter fourteen), during workshops, as a creative retreat day or a short creative exercise. Creating in community is one of the things the Trinity models for us in Genesis.

Serve together. As your arts community matures, make serving together a regular part of your schedule. You'll find a number of examples of that in this chapter, including Lincoln Berean Church, whose photographers serve as a team and take pictures of church and community events together, or the writers at Lutheran Church of Hope who write greeting cards for the care and missions ministries together.

Figure 6.1. Artists at Mosaic Church in Los Angeles work together to design, fabricate and install sculptures that illustrate the church's core values. Photos: Josh Anderson.

Cultivate joy. As was said earlier, a good indicator that you are on the right track with your arts community will be the presence of joyful moments. When artists and creators get together with their tribe and feel like they are understood and fit in, it is life giving. This sets the group up to experience a kind of "unity of will"[5] that, especially when it intersects with collaborating with God in what he is doing, will bring joy.

Play together. Play, which is interconnected with cultivating joy, is something your group can experience regularly and can also facilitate in the congregation. Play in your arts community could look like experimenting with new artistic forms together, doing off-the-wall creative exercises, playing pranks, social time, and so on.

Ask God which areas you can focus on to build the unique arts community he has in mind.

> "I think what churches have sometimes done is mistakenly communicated to artists and creatives in the church—people who are probably the most sensitive and the most emotionally connected—'What we accomplish as a community is more important than the individuals of the community.'"
>
> **Roy Cochran, The Grove Center for the Arts & Media**

General Artist Community Meeting Models

I interviewed dozens of arts leaders for this book in an effort to give you a wide cross section of arts community practices. There isn't room to include all the wonderful information I collected, but here are some examples of churches and groups who are doing arts community well. You'll also find more examples in the online resources and extras for this chapter.

Creating a safe place for artists. The Grove Center for the Arts & Media is a Southern California-based nonprofit that cultivates the spiritual life and creative work of artists through Grove Gatherings, Getaway artist retreats, generosity and online resources for artists. The Grove is an independent nonprofit organization that welcomes artists from all streams of Christianity. They desire to create a safe place for all artists, whether they serve in the church, the entertainment industry, the public art sphere or university setting. Since many artists experience isolation in their work, The Grove provides the care and community they need, gathering artists on a monthly basis to create community, share a wonderful meal, music, prayer and laughs.

Most Grove Gatherings are

Figure 6.2. Roy Cochran leads an artists' gathering with Grove Center for the Arts & Media in Orange County, CA.
Photo: Joey O'Connor.

held in artists' homes—creative and inspiring places—and not in a church. The Grove hosts these gatherings on neutral ground because they draw artists from many churches and all walks of life.

Grove Gatherings typically host fifty people for dinner and drinks, inviting the community members to contribute to expenses. A musician will lead worship for 20 minutes or so, mixing storytelling and musicianship. Guest artists lead TED-like talks on the intersection of art, faith, creativity, community and craftsmanship. Small group conversation follows to discuss the evening's topic, followed by prayer for each other. With dessert and an after-party, many of the artists are just getting warmed up. The evening often lasts until midnight or later!

The Grove also offers free online resources, webinars and online classes designed to help artists in their spiritual lives and creative work. They help artists raise money for their art projects, events and professional development through the Creative Funding for Artists program.[6]

> "The colors we use to paint our own lives splash all over the souls of those closest to us."
> Erwin McManus,
> The Artisan Soul

Growing leaders in community. VineArts, the arts ministry at the Boise Vineyard, was established in 2004 by Jessie Nilo and has grown to involve many facets of the arts, over one hundred active artists and several community groups that meet regularly.

One of the VineArts community groups is specifically for the nineteen leaders of the various VineArts activities, and they get together once a month to encourage and update each other. This meeting is invitation only and the leaders involved represent ministries that include the art gallery, book study, writers and culinary groups, and more. Director Jessie Nilo talks about the leaders meetings:

> We always open with prayer and ask that we would be in tune with what God is doing. Sometimes, depending on the art events on the horizon, we'll have silent listening prayer and invite everyone present to sketch, scribble, and jot down any ideas or impressions that come to them. We invite the Lord to share his plans with us, then we just listen, usually for around ten minutes. Then we compare notes and find that two or three of us wrote down the same idea or phrase. When we first started doing this some members of my team had never experienced this type of corporate prayer,

and they were not sure of what to expect. I didn't try to make them more comfortable by interjecting small talk. Sure enough, God would reveal his plans through the most surprising people present. And he continues to do so when new team members join our times of corporate waiting prayer.

Sometimes these VineArts leaders meetings consist of comparing notes, talking about upcoming dates and events, and brainstorming future endeavors. Our team also unanimously agreed that we need some kind of agenda when we have a business-style or brainstorming meeting to avoid endlessly unfocused talking. As a team, we get the business out of the way first.

Sometimes our monthly meeting will be devoted to just having fun together, maybe in the form of a project or a field trip.

And then sometimes I am pressed by the Lord to just open it for prayer for each other and to share about challenges or victories people have had or are currently in.

> "Artists can help people to understand their Bibles better, to give expression to their spirituality and to help them grow spiritually."
>
> James Tughan

One rule that I uphold is to never make anyone feel coerced or pressured into attending a VineArts event or meeting, even leadership meetings. People are able to jump in and out of serving in leadership according to what season they're personally in. If they're taking a sabbatical from service, they are still encouraged to come to all of our leadership gatherings in order to remain solidly in community. Such freedom to serve brings a very high retention rate.[7]

Show and prayer. The Indy Vineyard has hosted a number of arts communities over the last twenty years. The current incarnation is called IVAC, Indy Vineyard Arts Community.

IVAC meets one Friday evening a month at 7 p.m. at a host home or in the special "home group" room at the church (it's very casual with couches and lamp lighting). Members get notices through the closed Facebook group or email.

The evening starts with socializing and snacks, then transitions to an opening prayer and a quick introduction from all in attendance. If there are new people (and there often are because group attendance fluctuates), members will go around the room and introduce themselves. Usually, the leader will ask for members to include what their preferred form of creative expression is or to answer an odd icebreaker like "What's your favorite tree and why?" or "What was your first bike, and how did it make you feel?"—something to get the group loosened up and laughing and help them learn more about each other.

Elements of the night change depending on God's leading but can include:

- *A featured artist.* Someone from the group or from the local arts community may be invited to give a twenty-minute presentation about their art. It could be anything from stand-up comedy to a visiting Disney artist describing his process to a chapter reading from an author's book in progress and more. Then they'll gather around the artist to pray for their life and work, speaking words and offering pictures of encouragement. Featured artists always leave feeling invigorated by this connection and personal prayer.

- *A reading.* Sometimes they'll have a reading from an inspirational book that sparks discussion about the creative process.

- *Show and prayer.* Often they'll invite everyone to bring something they are working on (any form of creativity), do a five-minute presentation on it, then let the group pray for them. This is a wonderful community builder.

Figure 6.3. Cathy Feeman leads an artist's discussion on live painting in the church.
Photo: JSM

- *Leader message.* Sometimes the leader will share a relatively short five- to ten-minute message of something on his heart, then open up a discussion about it.

- *Sharing inspiration.* Everyone may be invited to bring or share about something that is inspiring them creatively right now. This could be anything from a trip to the local art museum to the change of seasons to something they saw on the Internet. It's often an invitation to recognize how God's creativity is affecting them and to take time to express why that is.

- *Creative exercises.* The leader may find a simple and fun exercise to get creativity flowing or make one up. Sometimes God will give the leader something entirely new in prayer.[8] Exercises have included drawing an object with the non-dominate hand; playing a word association game; searching the house for an inspiring object, drawing it or writing about it, then presenting it to the group; and more.

The group always ends in prayer.

Once a quarter they'll have a creative day where everyone brings something they want to work on and gathers for a number of hours on a Saturday. They might start at 1 p.m., giving people the morning free, and then go until dinner when they have a meal together. People are encouraged to show what they are working on during or after the meal. This is always a great community builder and a lot of fun. They invite people to drop in as they can and stay however long they like.[9]

Building community through relationship. The arts ministry at Lincoln Berean Church in Lincoln, Nebraska, has operated in various forms since the mid-nineties, finally coming to be called Visual Voice a few years ago. They oversee five galleries, regular arts classes and forums, and have over two hundred people on their arts contact list. They feel God has called them foremost to build arts community.

There are classes and workshops on the arts going on as many as four nights a week, covering many interests and skill levels. (See more details about the Visual Voice classes and workshops in chapter fourteen.) These classes often introduce people to the ministry and allow the team to get to know them, listen to them and see where they fit best in the arts ministry. Director Ann Williams talks about their group:

> Another way we build community is to create special exhibits for the artists to participate in. We choose a theme and invite artists to make work specifically for that exhibit. We then gather the artists two to three times over a three-month period (or longer depending on the size of the project), and we share with one another, talk through creative struggles, life, and make art. We go wherever the Spirit takes us those evenings, and it's amazing what the people share.
>
> We've also built community by having artists come together around a larger project. For example, this fall we set up four teams of people to create four tables illustrating the idea of community to go in our new coffee shop

area. Through this time, participating artists had to struggle through the challenge of creating together (many of whom had never done that before).

Figure 6.4. Artists at Visual Voice arts ministry at Lincoln Berean Church work together on a mosaic project. Photo: Jennie Prescott.

It was awesome to see God move through this process. Some really great community-themed tables were created, and the people who were involved learned a little about biblical ways of working through conflict.

We stress team environments in the gallery too. Our two rotating spaces have one lead installer per space, and it is their job to communicate when help is needed to hang or dismantle the exhibits. During installation time, team members connect through serving together. Community is built around the task of hanging the artwork.

The core team of leaders meets monthly, and we always build in a half hour of time before we meet just to chat about whatever is going on in life or laugh with one another. This not only brings us closer, it also allows us to stay on task during the business portion of the meeting.[10]

Creating in community. The Elm City Artist Circle meets monthly and is led by Tina Colon Williams, worship leader at the Elm City Vineyard in New

Figure 6.5. A Visual Voice artist works with mosaic glass during a community project. Photo: Jennie Prescott.

Haven, Connecticut. The group is an official ministry of the church but is open to all. The church is small—around one hundred people—but with artistically affirming leadership and a pool of talented artists. It is fertile ground for the development of creativity.

The Artist Circle was formed to meet some of the core needs of artists—community, vulnerability and discipline—and to empower those involved to become better artists in the process. Their meetings are more structured than many arts groups, because they want to actually create something every time they come together. Tina explains how the Artist Circle works. This interview was originally published in CIVA's *SEEN Journal* (winter 2013):

- *Meet regularly.* Our group decided to meet once a month—not too often, nor too seldom.

- *Share art.* Each meeting starts by giving those present a chance to share something they have created. It could be a poem, a photograph or a song—anything that is an original piece of art. Importantly, this time of sharing is not a time of critique or analysis. This keeps the Artist's Circle a safe space for artists with differing levels of ability. For us it is essential to have a space that is free of comparison or judgment.

- *Swap art.* After everyone has shared a piece, each person identifies something that inspires him or her out of what's been shared. For example, a musician can choose someone's sculpture as inspiration, or a graphic designer can choose someone's poem. This transforms the art from something personal to something communal.

- *Create art.* The group then splits up for around sixty to ninety minutes with one task: to create something new using the piece we've chosen as a prompt for inspiration.

- *Share again.* This is the hardest part. Whether or not the new creation feels finished, and whether or not it seems successful, we are expected to share what we've created with one another.

Each time we meet, we are shocked by the kinds of powerful and beautiful art that is created. Not only is excellent art created that would not otherwise exist, but people are genuinely transformed in the process. So many people have come to their first Artist's Circle meeting convinced that they are not artists. In community, in vulnerability, with a little bit of intentionality and discipline, many find themselves making and contributing powerful art. They leave the Circle as artists, less fearful than they were when they entered.[11]

Spirit-led community. Bethel Church in Redding, California, has a vibrant arts ministry and an innovative approach to the arts that enables them to include creative expression in almost everything the church does. In addition to artists based in the area who are involved with the church's arts programs, students from all over the world, many with artistic leanings, attend their School of Supernatural Ministry and are trained to push the boundaries of faith-based art.

Many of these artists get together in a community meeting on Tuesdays at the church. Like most of the creative communities we've talked about, the agenda and flow of Bethel's meetings varies greatly, depending on God's leading. But Theresa Dedmon, Bethel's director of arts, says a few things are constant: "We will always have food, there will always be testimonies, there will always be fellowship, there will always be prayer for people, and there will always be mentorship." They have about forty to fifty people at the Tuesday meetings, and they typically talk about how the artists are doing, how they are processing life. They offer each other prayer support, and there will be times when they break into groups of three or four and pray for one another. Sometimes they work on their art together. There will usually be prophetic words offered to individuals at some point in the gathering.

Testimonies are greatly valued throughout the Bethel Church culture. They expect to see God moving in people's lives on a regular basis, so they love to talk about what is happening as he connects with people through the arts. Not only are testimonies included in the weekly meetings, but once a month they devote most of a meeting to them.[12] Bethel includes the arts in many ministry settings, such as on the stage during services and in their healing rooms, which are open for people to come and receive prayer each Saturday. Artists will paint, dance or practice other forms of art in the waiting area of the healing rooms, and there are always stories to share from those encounters.

Theresa teaches at Bethel's school, so she has an apprenticeship group of students who get training at these meetings before they are released to do art at the church. They are trained in how to operate in the Holy Spirit but also in technique and skill building.

Once a month they have a time during the meeting where community members can bring the art they are working on, and Bethel arts leaders, some of whom teach art professionally, will critique it. They'll also talk about what it seems to be saying.

So the goal is that community members are not only growing their skill set but growing in how to do ministry, how to work together as a team, and how they can grow in their gifting as unique artists, so it's multi-layered. And then sometimes we just have nothing but fun.[13]

Independent arts community. Arts of the Covenant (AOC) is a unique group based in the San Francisco Bay Area that focuses on exploring the intersection of Christian faith and the visual arts. Since 2005 they've gathered monthly for intellectual stimulation, spiritual nourishment, artistic development and the opportunity to use art in ministry and community service. They average about forty to fifty people at their monthly meetings.

AOC is hosted by Menlo Park Presbyterian Church, but they are not funded by the church budget and operate fairly independently. This gives them freedom to pursue a path different from other church-based arts communities. Artists from many different churches within a fifty-mile radius regularly attend their meetings, and the group sees itself as an incubator of sorts, a place where others can come for fellowship and inspiration, and then go back to their own ministries, whether it's making art in a studio or serving in a ministry program at a church.

They stay away from two of the staples of churches and art clubs—Bible studies and art technique workshops—feeling that artists should get in-depth spiritual support from their own church communities and art training from other associations. They'll choose a theme as a sort of umbrella over the year, but it's very loosely associated and designed to nudge people in a new direction of thought or exploration. Founder Marianne Lettieri says:

> One of the reasons for our group's success is that we hardly ever do the same thing from month to month. We don't have a formula. Meetings might feature panels of artists who deal with social justice, producers of children's books, or gallery and museum directors. Sometimes we might have a presentation by an artist of faith who talks about the creative process or a new body of work. We may watch a video about art, such as something from the PBS Art21 series, and then engage in a lively discussion. We often ask pastors to lecture about the theological underpinnings for religious-themed art exhibits prior to our artists creating the work.[14]

Although AOC isn't funded by Menlo Park Presbyterian Church, the church generously provides them with free space, audio/visual equipment, setup and teardown, and a designated pastor to go to for advice and support. AOC gives back to the church by partnering to produce regular art exhibitions, rallying artists to contribute their skills to church outreaches, and assisting groups in the church, such as a Sunday school class, that ask for art-related activities or presentations.

With around 150 artists actively involved in Arts of the Covenant, they feel like their first ministry is to individual members.

When we first started we found that there were many artists within the church who were no longer making art; from a creative standpoint, they had just dried up. We invited them to come and talk about art in the context of their Christian beliefs. They would get excited, and their artistic passion would return. They started to get studios and websites and to make art and enter shows and exhibits. We were just the cheerleaders, but because we provided a format to reengage with art they are now practicing, flourishing artists, and their faith is part of that. A lot of times we just bring artists together and watch them catch on fire.[15]

> "Being in community with like-minded artists has created a bond or family tie where once I felt alone, different and isolated. I feel valued where before I was striving for acceptance. My creativity has become an open line of communication with my heavenly Father."
>
> Sherri Coffield, from a testimony

Empowered leaders. Imago Dei church in Portland, Oregon, has an unusually large percentage of artists, in part because of the creative atmosphere of the city. Around seven hundred people receive their monthly arts newsletter, and a couple hundred attend their quarterly artist forums and twice-a-year artist retreats. Imago worship and arts pastor Paul Ramey has about a dozen lay leaders—mature Christians and accomplished artists who are empowered to lead and mentor other artists in the congregation—whom he meets with quarterly. At Imago this results in support and encouragement being available for artists in the congregation who want it, and a thriving artistic vibe in the church community. Ramey feels that artists should be developed and supported but not separated from the rest of the congregation with too many artist get-togethers.[16]

In addition to a general artist community gathering, there are other forms of community that can work for artists, such as salons and affinity groups.

ART SALONS

Salons are intimate gatherings where specially selected speakers share their work and ideas, and there is lively discussion, food and drink with a group of peers or interested observers. When they originated in the 1700s, French salons consisted of groups of intellectuals brought together by a host in an intimate setting to educate and spark discussion. Writer Gertrude Stein later famously revived the salon model in the early 1900s. Art luminaries like Ernest Hemingway, Pablo Picasso and F. Scott Fitzgerald regularly met on Saturday evenings at her home in Paris.

Figure 6.6. We Make Stuff often has a full house for their Studio Series art salon events.
Photo courtesy of We Make Stuff.

One group of Christian artists that has been working with the salon model is the Vancouver, Canada-based We Make Stuff. Every few months they host an event in an artist studio somewhere in the city and invite a number of artists to present their work. It could be music, drama, visual art, crafts, dance or any other kind of art. The events are open to the public, and there is usually an admission charge of about ten dollars, which goes to support the artists and also covers some food and drinks. Each artist has the floor for ten to fifteen minutes, depending how many are presenting, to just do what they do, and then everybody gets to mingle, have a few drinks and chat together. They generally have a start time but not a definite end time.

The gatherings aren't overtly Christian, although co-organizer Jill Cardwell says, "Many of the artists are not shy about talking about their faith. Predominately they are talking about their creative process, but they are also exploring how their faith works with that." Non-Christians regularly attend, as do artists who may be Christians but have an aversion to the church. The We Make Stuff team has an ongoing conversation about how to be true to what they know they are called to do—following Christ in their lives and art and exploring that—and at the same time finding the right language to welcome everyone to these events. It's an approach that's working well.

People often comment on the wonderful mix of creativity and community they experience on these evenings.

An occasional salon-style evening can add some nice variety to an artist community and could be a good way to showcase artists or invite those outside the community in to see what your artists are up to.[17]

AFFINITY GROUPS

Affinity groups are a branch of creative community that focuses on one creative interest. They usually form organically when a couple of people in an arts community realize they have similar interests or skills and decide to meet in addition to the general meetings. Some affinity groups may be more structured than general creative community groups and often enable the participants to get work done, such as a writers critique group. Affinity groups within a creative community may include painters groups, poetry groups, film or media groups, groups for crafts such as sewing, knitting, scrapbooking, writer's groups and really anything creative that your people are interested in.

Writers groups. The arts ministry of Lutheran Church of Hope in West Des Moines, Iowa, has a number of affinity groups. Their Writing with a Purpose writers group has focused on critiquing each other's work, and they'll have speakers come to it monthly. The writers also get involved in service projects, such as writing all the content for the church's Lenten services and writing greeting cards for the care and missions ministries.

Living Word Community Church art ministry in York, Pennsylvania, has a number of writers that mix in with the other artists at their open studio, but they also do a quarterly writer's retreat on their own. For these retreats, arts ministry director deAnn Roe will gather the writers from 9 to 2 on a Saturday at the church. It's a chance to get out of the busy stream of life and work on their writing. She may give them writing prompts to spark their creativity, but she also keeps the programming light so the writers can focus on whatever writing project they have in mind. The group will meet together to begin the retreat, then break out to other rooms like the church's coffee bar during "writing blocks."

VineArt Boise's writer's group meets once a month as a workshop-based community with plenty of open reading nights.

Scrapbooking and craft groups. Lutheran Church of Hope's strong craft affinity groups include a serious scrapbooking group that meets once a month for two solid days, quilters, and prayer shawl knitters who are dedicated to saturating the shawls in prayer as they make them for those in need.

Arts prison ministry group. Arts of the Covenant doesn't officially have affinity groups, but it certainly encourages people to meet outside of the monthly meetings. This often happens naturally since AOC is focused on their mission and is rather large, so members may feel the need to spend more time with those of similar skills and interests. For example, two women started their own prison ministry group, meeting in the San Mateo County Jail with female inmates and teaching them art. AOC founder Marianne Lettieri says, "That's where we are seeing excitement; our members feel encouraged to go out and make a difference where they are."

Photography group. Visual Voice at Lincoln Berean Church has a thriving photography forum that averages about thirty people at weekly meetings. This affinity group meets on Monday nights in a casual gathering where they might go through a quick lesson or have someone speak. They like to do weekly photography assignments, so they'll look through photos from the past week and give each other feedback.

The team of five or six mature Christians who lead the forum are gifted at making people feel comfortable. It's a tight-knit community, and the leaders model how to love people through the connecting point of a mutual interest. They are sensitive to members' needs and often gather around an attendee that is hurting or needs a little extra attention.

The photography forum also does photo walks and serves together photographing different events for the church and in the community, creating a different type of shared service experience.

Virtual community is also happening regularly through Flickr. The photographers often post images they shoot for the weekly assignments and offer each other feedback.

Actors and filmmakers group. In Boise, VineArts leader heads up an acting and film group and works with actors and filmmakers who are mostly from outside the church.

Mosaic Church in LA had a large improv comedy group called Monkey Butler that hosted free improv classes and developed shows. They currently host a weekly comedy hour at the church and incorporate actors into creative community life and church meetings.

Culinary group. The VineArts culinary arts group meets every two months or so to create amazing hors d'oeuvres and refreshments for special church functions like gallery receptions and prayer training weekends.

Book study groups. VineArts has various book studies and Bible studies for artists that meet weekly or twice a month. Some of these are open-ended, while others have a specific start and end date.

Interchurch artists group. "One of our VineArts leaders founded an inter-church group for artists of faith called Envision, which meets in our church art studio once a month," says VineArts director Jessie Nilo.

> We feature a different speaker each month who shares about their art journey and how their art intersects with their walk with Christ. We tell prospective guests that anyone of any faith is welcome to attend, while acknowledging that the group's leaders are all Christians and the group's vision is to glorify Christ and inspire one another. We do have a couple of professing non-Christians who adore our community and faithfully attend Envision, and often seem visibly moved by the music or speakers.[18]

A LAST WORD ON ARTIST COMMUNITY

Artists' communities can be extremely beneficial—even essential—for your artists. But in order to have a healthy church the artists must be encouraged to join in community with people who are not artists. If you have a small group or home group system at your church, urge your artists—especially the leaders—to participate. Resist the urge to let artist community become your artists' home group. If we want to become mature as the body of Christ, we need to mix it up with other believers who have different giftings and personalities. The home group that has accountants and plumbers and stay-at-home moms needs the creative spark of the artist's personality, and the artist needs the perspective of other believers who are not artists, but creative in their own way. This is one important way to grow a creative spirit in a church: when the artists mix in with the rest of the congregation. We don't want artists or, for that matter, worship leaders or pastors to think of themselves as "very special Christians," isolated from the "average believer." We are all in the body of

Christ together. So while we support each other with the important element of focused arts community, we make sure not to forsake assembling with all types of believing brothers and sisters.

See the online resources and extras for this chapter at JScottMcElroy.com/ CCHandbookextras.

NOTES

[1] J. R. R. Tolkien to Christopher Tolkien, 7–8 November 1944, letter 89 in *The Letters of J. R. R. Tolkien*, ed. Humphrey Carpenter (New York, NY: Mariner Books, 2000).

[2] Tim Chester, "The Good News of the Trinity," *Theology Network* (blog), (n.d.), www.theologynetwork.org/doctrine-of-god/the-good-news-of-the-trinity.htm.

[3] Miroslav Volf, *After Our Likeness: The Church as the Image of the Trinity* (Grand Rapids: Eerdmans, 1997), p. 173.

[4] Insight from Matt Tommey, recorded conversation, January 2014.

[5] German sociologist Ferdinand Tönnies observed "unity of will" in certain communities. Tönnies, *Community and Society* (*Gemeinschaft und Gesellschaft*) (1887; reprint, Piscataway, NJ: Transaction, 1988), p. 22.

[6] Find out more and connect with The Grove Center for the Arts & Media at TheGroveCenter.org.

[7] Written contribution from Jessie Nilo. Connect with VineArts at VineArtsBoise.org.

[8] See the Joyous Moment creative exercise and more in the online resources and extras for this chapter.

[9] Connect with IVAC at http://indyvineyardarts.wix.com/ivac.

[10] From an interview with the author, December 2013. Connect with Visual Voice at http://civa.org/church/visual-voice-lincoln-berean-church.

[11] Visit the Elm City Artist Circle Blog at http://ecvartistcircle.blogspot.com.

[12] See a Bethel testimony form in the online resources and extras for this chapter.

[13] Interview with the author, January 2014. Connect with Bethel Arts at bethelredding.com/content/creative-arts.

[14] Interview with the author, December 2013.

[15] Ibid. Contact Arts of the Covenant at https://Artsofthecovenant.shutterfly.com.

[16] Contact Imago Dei Arts at imagodeicommunity.com/arts.

[17] Connect with We Make Stuff at wemakestuff.ca.

[18] Written contribution from Jessie Nilo.

7

Structure for Arts Ministry

*Do you wish to be great? Then begin by being. Do you desire to
construct a vast and lofty fabric? Think first about the
foundations of humility. The higher your structure
is to be, the deeper must be its foundation.*

Saint Augustine

THERE ARE AS MANY STYLES of administering arts initiatives and ministries in the local church as there are ways of expressing creativity. However, the thing they should have in common is, as St. Augustine says, that the handling of every aspect of the ministry should be done with a spirit of humility. This seems like obvious advice for any ministry, but it is especially important when dealing with the arts.

In modern times the arts have sometimes been associated with pride and arrogance, which has its foundation in the arrogance of Satan, who many believe was the master musician of heaven (Ezek 28:13 NKJV), and his rebellion against God. Pride and elitism crouch at the door, waiting for a chance to sneak in to arts activities. This is because artists are entrusted with the creation of beauty. That can lead people (or angels, apparently) to think pretty highly of themselves.

The need for humility is especially apparent in these areas of administration and structure because this is where we will have to deal with authority, work within a system and then lead others well—the very areas where Satan, once one of the greatest worshipers and artists in heaven, infamously failed.

In this chapter I'll make some suggestions and offer a few practical tips and examples of how budgets, job descriptions, structure and more can be addressed in a spirit of humility. Much of this advice was contributed by Jessie Nilo, director of arts at VineArts Boise.

EMBRACE STRUCTURE

In order to have a successful arts ministry it's important to have a designated church leader that the ministry reports to and a chain of command to get things done. Otherwise there is opportunity for misunderstanding and frustration. The staff may be wary of the arts ministry at first, thinking, *Are they going to ruin the facilities and make a mess? Are they going to make bad art or embarrassing or offensive art? Are they going to do something weird?*

A liaison and overseer on staff can allay fears and advocate for the arts ministry. So it's important that this person have at least an affinity for the arts. They will shepherd projects and ideas through the church's processes and make sure arts activities are in alignment with the church's mission. In some cases this staff member will be—or, over time, become—the director of arts. In other cases this will be a worship pastor or creative director who advocates for the volunteer director of the arts ministry.

The table below provides a quick look at how several arts ministries operate. Each one is unique, but there are commonalities:

- All of these arts ministries do the bulk of their work outside of Sunday services.

- Some contribute art regularly to services, but others rarely contribute, usually because the worship arts department (tech, music, media) handles services.

- With the exception of one (IVAC), all of these arts leaders sit in on staff meetings.

- All have a dedicated budget, which they can spend mostly as they like.

- All can make internal programing and community decisions without consulting pastoral staff.

Many of the specific activities of these ministries are discussed throughout the book, but to see more detail go to the online resources and extras for chapter nine.

Table 7.1. Arts ministries operations.

Arts Ministry/ Church	Department Overseeing Ministry	Director of Arts hrs./wk. (paid)	Volunteer Leaders/ Part-Time Staff	Ministry Presents in Sunday Services?	Church Size
VineArts/ Vineyard Boise	Worship Arts/ Worship pastor	20	18 volunteer leaders	Weekly	3,000
Visual Voice/ Lincoln Berean Church	Worship Arts/ Worship pastor	5	8 volunteer leaders	Rarely	5,000
Infused Arts/Living Word Community Church	Spiritual Formation and Leadership/ Dept. pastor	25	9-12 volunteer leaders	Rarely	1,500
Express Your Faith/ Lutheran Church of Hope	Is its own dept./ Director of arts	25	20 volunteer leaders; 3 p/t staff	Rarely	10,000
Ex Creatis/Saddleback Church	First Impressions/ An executive pastor	Full time	Some volunteer leaders	Rarely	30,000
Indy Vineyard Arts Community/Indy Vineyard	Community Dept./ Dept. pastor	Volunteer	A couple of volunteer leaders	Regularly	450

There are advantages and disadvantages to whatever department an arts ministry is under. Being under the Worship Arts department may allow artists to enjoy more integration of their work and ideas into services, but they may also be forgotten in the hustle to produce the never-ending flow of Sunday services. A ministry under the First Impressions department may have more input into the aesthetic vision for the church and more support for a gallery but may find it difficult to connect with and contribute to Sunday services. If you find your ministry encounters limitations because of departmental structure or the way your church does things, pray that God would open doors in the areas where you would like to have more freedom, but in the meantime, ask him for creative ideas for how you can thrive within your limitations and cultivate humility.

Another element of structure to consider for arts ministry is how the ministry operates from day to day. This can sometimes be a problem area for art leaders who may start out doing everything themselves and have to later learn to delegate. (More about raising up leaders in chapter five.) Leaders will need to designate who handles the art supplies, chairs, microphones, bulletin ads, calendar schedules, web page updates, cleanup, answering emails, coffee and sandwiches. In addition—and especially as the ministry grows—someone has to define gallery entry procedures or schedule monthly workshops and keep the rotating list of workshop instructors. This is the administrative side of arts ministry, and it must be done, if not by the director of arts then by a designated administrator. A good structure will result in more "buy-in" from participants, consistency in programs and schedules, safety for artists, increased creativity, deeper concepts, growing enthusiasm for events and the assurance that the leader will actually be there if people arrive at the advertised time.

Figure 7.1. Designate someone to manage the arts ministry's supplies and materials. Photo: Nina Matthews Photography/Flickr/Creative Commons. License information available at https://creativecommons.org/licenses/by/2.0.

In fact, avoiding structure will kill an arts ministry. If your goals seem tentative, if locations and dates are not set in stone, if procedures are not clearly stated, why would an artist risk the potential embarrassment and waste of time? Even worse, artists will sometimes interpret lack of initiative, interest or communication as arrogance or a rejection of them personally. So invite, set up and show up. Learn as you go, adjusting as necessary.

> "Yet what humanity needs most is for us to set creativity free from this singular category of the extraordinary and release it into the hands of the ordinary. Creativity should be an everyday experience. Creativity should be as common as breathing. We breathe, therefore we create."
> Erwin McManus, *The Artisan Soul*

BUDGETS

Casting a vision for your art ministry (chapter three) will help with setting a budget. Planning what you think your activities will be will give you an idea of what you want to ask for. It's helpful to dialogue with your administrative pastor to get an idea of what is financially possible and to get a good sense of the procedures for budgets. As the arts ministry puts a track record together, your budget should grow.

For their first few years, VineArts didn't have a budget, so they relied on donations of cash and art supplies. When they advertised art workshops, there was always a fee to cover their material costs like copying fees, art supplies and an instructor honorarium. Years later, VineArt's art budget is still small—under $2,000, which covers team training, meals for gatherings, gallery supplies and honorariums for events. This budget does not include the paid director of arts salary of twenty-five hours a week. That comes out of the general church fund. The budget is small partially because Vineyard Boise is situated in the low-income part of town. They intentionally planted themselves there to be close to the poor. But God has always provided. Still, the church values the arts, paying for the VineArts gallery hanging system in 2005, a cable system that cost $2,500.[1] And when they needed gallery lighting ($7,000) the art team raised $4,000 by holding art galas—events where they presented performances and artwork and sold tickets—and the church paid for the other $3,000. This happened because over the years the church has recognized the impact and value of the arts and creativity operating in their congregation.

Arts ministry can be done without a significant budget. We are talking about a ministry of *creativity*, and God will certainly give creative ideas to make it work. VineArts has discovered that there can actually be great freedom in operating on a small budget. The leaders know this ministry would be self-sustaining even if the budget were to disappear. At the same time the church's financial commitment is a great encouragement and is essential for continued growth.

If a significant budget from the church is not a possibility right now, and you know you are called to start arts ministry at your church, ask God to show you how to do it. If you are an arts leader who is called to pioneer this ministry in your church, it will probably cost you something personally, especially at first. That is common. But innovation and faithfulness over time should result in your church wanting to invest in the ministry.

If your church arts ministry is blessed with a good budget, there is some accountability involved. Artists may want to have an additional ministry leader step in to act as the main finance contact if tracking money is not the art leader's strong suit. Of course, this person must be someone who understands and supports the vision of that ministry.

Regardless of who is in charge of your ministry finances, it is important to work graciously with the pastor, leaders and finance board. Humility and persistence are essential. Ensure a respectful and peaceable relationship within your leadership when it comes to your ministry's financial needs, and when told no, forgive them, strive for understanding and don't give up. Know that your Father in heaven sees your needs and he will provide.

Here are a few ideas to supplement your budget:

- *Do fundraisers.* VineArts raises money for trips and outreach through their annual art gala. They'll sell tickets and feature a speaker, music, and booths where their artists can display.

- *Hold art shows and fairs.* This can be a real service to the church, especially before the holidays when people are looking for unique and original gifts. You may also be able to hold performances and charge or take donations.

- *Create work that can be sold.* If a painting or work of art is created for a service and elicits a positive response, your ministry might make prints or recordings of it available for the congregation at a reasonable price. VineArts also has a special salsa recipe that they make and sell when they need to raise money.

Figure 7.2. A church art fair can raise funds for the arts budget, offer a venue for artists and provide a service to the congregation. Photo: mo1229/flickr/Creative Commons. License information available at https://creativecommons.org/licenses/by/2.0.

- *Take a portion of gallery and live painting sales.* Many church art galleries ask for a 10 percent donation (or more) from artists for any work sold. If you choose to do this, add it to your gallery contract so that it's clear. You might also ask for a 10 percent donation from the artist when a platform painter sells a painting. Or you could advise the artist to build it into the price.

- *Ask for small fees or donations for workshops and classes.* This is common in order to cover supplies, expenses and honorariums.

- *Ask for donations.* As the arts begin to touch more members of the congregation you may find that people want to contribute. Give them opportunities to donate with imaginative campaigns and/or direct asks. They may welcome the chance to support the good work your ministry is doing.

- *Ask other ministries in the church that you contribute to if they would cover the cost of your efforts for them.* You may also investigate if the church has a budget for worship services that can reimburse you for materials and supplies when the arts ministry does a project that is used in a service.

WORKING WITH CHURCH LEADERSHIP

Pastors are constantly pursued with personal agendas, which can be exhausting. When approaching your pastor(s) about art ministry, ask him or her first about the vision for the church. Inquire as to how it's going and what you can be praying about. Later, possibly at another meeting, offer your ideas in writing and leave them with him or her to ponder and pray about. You may have to meet a few times before arts ministry comes into existence. Just relax and pray through the process.[2]

As the arts ministry gets going, be intentional about meeting with your pastors at the beginning of each year, if possible, to continue on the path of translating your church's overall vision in artistic, creative ways. Check to see if there is a new focus that you should be aware of, a direction that God seems to be calling the church that the arts ministry can help express.

For those who haven't worked within a church staff structure before, know that you will probably encounter disappointment. The arts are still often misunderstood in the church setting, so there will be times when artists or arts leaders could be offended. You may find yourself thinking or hear your artists saying, "They don't understand how hard I/we worked on this!" "They don't understand the value of (this art/my time)." "They forgot about us again!" "Why would someone put/move our (paintings/art supplies/easels, etc.) here?" "[Fill in the ministry] has as much budget as they want, and we have to beg/get donations for what we need." Again, one of an art leader's most difficult tasks, especially when pioneering art and creativity in the church, can be to keep from becoming bitter by staying humble. And to keep exhorting your artists to do the same.

When you complete a project, leave your church facilities more sparkling than you found them. Be faithful, pleasant and patient yet persistent. Have grace when told no. A large part of what you're doing is educating your leaders—"leading up," as they say. Eventually the staff should relax and be won over by truth and beauty and come to enjoy your ministry. Within a couple of years, they may shudder at the thought of an artless church.

See the online resources and extras for this chapter at JScottMcElroy.com/ CCHandbookextras.

NOTES

[1] Available from www.ashanging.com.

[2] Pastor and artist Dave Blackslee offers a way to approach your pastor in the resources and extras for this chapter.

8

Building a
Creative Congregation

If you can't go to church and at least for a moment be given transcendence,
if you can't pass briefly from this life to the next, then I can't see why
anyone should go. Just a brief moment of transcendence
causes you to come out of church a changed person.

GARRISON KEILLOR,
Interview with *Wittenberg Door*

JESUS TAUGHT US THAT UNLESS we become like a little child—unless we exhibit childlike faith—we won't enter into the kingdom of heaven (Mt 19:14; Mk 10:15; Lk 18:17). What are the attributes of childlikeness? Humility, simplicity, innocence, teachability and creativity. Yes, creativity. What are little children if not creative? They constantly explore and test, come up with new solutions, new stories, new characters. Most little children believe they can create art, drawing and coloring what is on their mind, what they love. Trees can be pink, dogs can sing—anything is possible in their imaginations. Can embracing creativity in our churches enable us to become more childlike in our faith? More humble, simple, innocent and teachable? Absolutely.

It's humbling when we realize that the Creator of the universe designed us to collaborate with him in our creativity. The simple, intuitive nature of art beckons us let go of complex mental analysis and *feel* truth. Innocence is refreshed and cynicism dispelled when, through creativity, our Father touches a soft spot in our heart that we had long forgotten. Art and creativity reminds us that God will speak and teach us in many ways if we will relax and listen. Catherine Kapikian, in *Art in Service of the Sacred*, says,

> What would happen if adults were challenged and/or nurtured persistently by visual stimuli that companioned the Word? What if the religious community began to think seriously about the various aspects of the creative process and to treasure it as a reflection of being in the divine image?
>
> Would a culture of creativity motivate a community to risk courageous action more confidently? Would a culture of creativity stimulate the naturally curious inclinations of our children? Would a culture of creativity give wings to the imagination, enabling leaps of faith?[1]

Yes.

As mentioned earlier, creativity is a family trait; "it's in our blood," as the saying goes. It doesn't have to take the form of art. It can be any form of problem solving and as simple as deciding what to cook for dinner. So our churches, the places we meet with the rest of our family, should be places where the family members' individual creativity is activated and encouraged, a place where we can learn to step into collaboration with our Father, and into our destiny.

For the purposes of this book, I define *creativity* as the ability to arrange or utilize resources in any realm (physical, mental, spiritual, emotional) to address (solve, improve, change, explain, design) any situation (problem, project, void, need). This includes but is not limited to art. Every person is endowed by God with creativity and has regular opportunities to partner and collaborate with him in the use of their creativity. This collaboration will release joy. In addition, creative skill in virtually any area can be enhanced and developed with use. Artists use creativity to arrange materials into works that are often appreciated primarily for their beauty or emotional or spiritual power.

We've looked at many ways to encourage that creativity so far. We've talked about how artists will lead the way in releasing creativity in the church as they embrace their calling and about the necessity of building support systems for them like creative community. And we've explored what it is to envision and grow an arts ministry that's dedicated to fostering creativity. Later, we'll see how displaying art in our churches draws creativity out of people; how artists-in-residence can facilitate creative experiences; and how open studio, arts patronage and arts outreach can enable people in the congregation and community to connect with God and share his messages with others. This chapter highlights more practical ideas that will help build a foundation of expectant creativity in your church.

The number one thing you can do to cultivate creativity is to teach people to hear God's voice. Second, you can help them recognize and become who God made them to be. Third, model what creative collaboration with God looks like. And, finally, lead your congregation in taking risks and putting their God-inspired creativity to work.

> "The fact that we're bastions of boredom rather than bursting with creativity and the release of the arts is such an embarrassment. We should be the place that is known for creativity as we have a direct connection to the Creator."
>
> Leonard Sweet, "Bastions of Boredom"

LISTENING FOR GOD

Learning to hear God's voice is a lifelong pursuit for any Christian. He most often speaks through the Bible, preaching and teaching, circumstances, nature, art, other people and through waiting silently in prayer. Plus any other means that pleases him, such as the occasional donkey. But those seven are the basics. For each of us, God speaks more clearly through some forms than through others. One of the church's most important missions is to help people to recognize how God is speaking and how to respond to it. When a congregation becomes comfortable with this skill it will bring the overall level of creativity up in the church. This is because when we hear God's voice it not only activates creativity and faith in us, but what he leads us to do will often grow our capacity for creative risk.

Your church might consider doing a series on the different ways we can expect God to speak to us, and ask for stories from the congregation about instances when he did that. Waiting in prayer is one of the most consistent ways I hear from God. In chapter five, I highlighted five approaches for waiting silently in prayer. (See that chapter for complete definitions.) They are:

- listening prayer
- prayer journaling
- *lectio divina*
- corporate listening
- personal prophetic art

If an individual is not inclined to journal, meditate or even stand still, encourage them to think about how they most often have heard from God. Maybe it's walking in nature or listening to music. Then urge them to put themselves in those positions and ask God to speak to them there. Encouraging your congregation in these types of activities will set the foundation for creativity in the church.

Help Them Recognize How God Made Them

In chapter five I shared an exercise I use when speaking that can help people come to more of an understanding of who we are in Christ and how beloved we are. This realization is key to being able to unlock the inherent creativity of the individuals in your congregation because it opens the door to freedom. If God made us as we are with a purpose in mind, then we can be empowered to discover what that purpose is and to explore how to creatively collaborate with God to accomplish that purpose. Of course, this realization of who we are in Christ is something that we must be regularly reminded of.

> "The church's central task is an imaginative one. By that I do not mean a fanciful or fictional task, but one in which the human capacity to imagine, to form mental pictures of the self, the neighbor, the world, the future, to envision new realities, is both engaged and transformed."
>
> Barbara Brown Taylor,
> *The Preaching Life*

Tools for discovering how God made us include spiritual gift assessments and personality tests, some of which are available online. The more we can help individuals in our congregations understand about themselves, the more connections they have to see how God is working in and through them.

Chapter five also includes some more thoughts under the "Individual Calling" heading for helping people discern what their calling is.

Model Creative Collaboration

Modeling creative collaboration is easier than you might think. Sharing specific stories of how God has involved us in his work—testimonies—with our congregation is one of the most effective ways to demonstrate creative collaboration with him. Testimonies delivered by members of our congregation also build faith and provide rallying points and community connection. It will cause someone to think, *If Pete can pray for a guy in a cheese shop, then maybe I can reach out to this woman who is crying in the customer lounge.* Make it a practice in your church to regularly collect and tell stories of God's leading, divinely arranged encounters, his provision, healings and more. Sharing stories will help form a culture of creative collaboration and expectant faith.

Collaborative art projects are wonderful showcases for partnering with God as well. It can be thrilling to recognize when God is joining us in the process of creating, making the work more than just the sum of its parts. It might be a congregational activity with artists overseeing the process while individuals contribute, as in the mosaic project described in chapter ten. Or a project where artists collaborate on a work together, and when individual pieces are put together the project has an uncanny flow and resonance of color, styles or meaning. I've often seen this effect when artists take time to seek God's guidance on their projects. Our Father wants to teach us how to collaborate creatively with him, and once you get a taste of that, it's the only way you want to work.

Take Risks and Put Creativity to Work

Of course, the follow-up to modeling creative collaboration is providing opportunities for the flock to step out and put it to work, to take a risk and release what they've learned to the world.

> If the culminating moment of God's creative act was the creation of man, then it is clear that we cannot create without risk. God's ultimate act of creation—creating humanity in his own likeness, with the freedom to choose so that we might become authentic conduits of love—was the greatest risk that God ever undertook.[2]

Seeing creative collaboration modeled should eventually awaken the desire in individuals to try it for themselves. You might encourage them to join prayer ministry teams, outreach teams or personal prayer art teams. Encourage artists to present their art to their creative community. You might organize a congregational prayer and brainstorming meeting, giving people space to share the ideas that God is giving them for ministry or business.

There are many examples of inventors and innovators in history who collaborated with God, asking him for ideas and guidance. George Washington Carver developed over three hundred uses for the peanut, as well as other advances that had a huge impact on the economy of the South. He took a walk with God every morning at 4 a.m., asking for guidance and ideas and said, "Without God to draw aside the curtain, I would be helpless."[3] Samuel F. B.

Morse, with God's guidance, invented the telegraph—the foundation for all modern electronic communication—and sent the famous first message, "What hath God wrought!" He said, "When the Lord wanted to bestow this gift on mankind, he had to use someone. I'm just grateful he chose to reveal it to me."[4] More recently, a ministry to homeless youth in Los Angeles started an inventors club called Technology from Heaven to help them gain skills and confidence.[5] They lead the youth to a relationship with God, then teach them how to ask God for ideas and collaborate with him. The ministry works

Figure 8.1. Inventor George Washington Carver (1864–1943) searched for innovations in collaboration with God. Photo: Frances Benjamin Johnston. Photo is in the Library of Congress and available in the public domain.

with professionals to bring the ideas to life and get them on the market. So far they have nine patents, and their products have sold in places like RadioShack. What ideas might God give us for innovation, invention, business and more if we ask and listen? Encourage your congregation to creatively collaborate with God to bring his kingdom into the world.

MORE IDEAS TO FOSTER CREATIVITY

Let's go back to this idea of being childlike and turn it around a bit. Imagine how someone might develop creativity in a child. What if some similar practices could help promote creativity in our congregations? Of course, you wouldn't do this in a condescending way, treating adults like children, but the ideas might inform our approach to fostering creativity.

Provide a creative atmosphere. Parents play Baby Einstein products for their infants and carefully choose visually and mentally stimulating toys for their toddlers. We want elementary kids to go to bright and creative schools. There is no doubt that atmosphere is important to humans' health and growth.

The same is true in stimulating the spiritual and creative growth of adults.

Pay attention to interior design at your church, and to colors, signage, graphics and stage design (more about this in chapter sixteen). All facilitate an atmosphere of expectancy and creativity. Offer art tables in the sanctuary (chapter ten). Create art galleries on your walls and art fairs in your lobbies and parking lots. Change and rearrange things in lobbies, hallways and sanctuaries. Experiment with drama, dance and live painting in your worship (chapter eleven). Artist Scott Erickson thinks that these things can add a magical sense of wonder to services. Find ways to celebrate innovation and creativity. Have someone who understands new technology and media bring your church up to speed with these tools. Provide the children in your congregation with art materials to play and experiment with. Kids who grow up in a creative church think that creativity and spirituality belong together and they become more creative adults.

Invite questions. It's healthy for children to be curious. It can be a good thing to give them the opportunity to express "divergent thought," to let them disagree with you or to invite them to come up with several solutions to the same problem. Yet many adults just move on to the next thing instead of asking questions about their faith.

> "It's essential for us to develop an imagination that is participatory. Art is the primary way in which this happens. It's the primary way in which we become what we see or hear."
>
> Eugene Peterson, "Cultivating the Imagination," Seattle Pacific University's *Response Magazine,* Autumn 2011

What if our churches encouraged more discussion about faith and theology? We might host regular Q-and-A sessions with pastors or solicit questions from the congregation and post answers on a church blog.

Give them space. In order for children's imaginations to develop, they must have time and space. If their day is filled with non-stop activities, their imagination will suffer, and that can negatively affect their adult life. Nancy H. Blakey shares this brilliant advice about children and imagination:

> Preempt the time spent on television and organized activities and have them spend it instead on claiming their imaginations. For in the end that is all we have. If a thing cannot be imagined first—a cake, a relationship, a cure for AIDS—it cannot be.
>
> I cannot plant imagination into my children. I can, however, provide an

environment where their creativity is not just another mess to clean up but welcome evidence of grappling successfully with boredom. It is possible for boredom to deliver us to our best selves, the ones that long for risk and illumination and unspeakable beauty.

If we sit still long enough, we may hear the call behind boredom. With practice, we may have the imagination to rise up from the emptiness and answer.[6]

There is something here for us and our congregations, as well. Why not occasionally create silent space during services for listening to God? Spaces for meditating on a verse or in prayer? These silent moments might be guided with prompts or simply a free listening time. A short explanation can clarify the concept and set the tone.

Figure 8.2. Congregation members work together to fabricate an art piece under the guidance of professional artist Catherine Kapikian.

Stimulate their imagination. We stimulate our children's imagination

Figure 8.3. The art piece installed in the Garden Chapel at the University of Maryland. Photo: Catherine Kapikian.

by—among other things—encouraging them to think through situations. Jesus was known for engaging his listeners' imaginations with stories that often didn't have a clear meaning and that he didn't explain. We might better engage and stimulate our congregation's imaginations by offering them modern parables through our sermons or through visual art or music. Consider presenting them with a parable that isn't easily understood and requires thought and discussion. What if you offered this through film or drama and then provided a list of discussion questions for home groups to explore? Ask them to express their reaction to the drama and explore why they felt that way. Use the experience as a starting point for a biblical study.

The source material for the entire physical universe is the imagination of God.[7] An active imagination can enable us to envision who God made us to be and how we are designed for a destiny of doing his good works in the world.

Make things together. Many parents know the benefit of making things with their children. It's bonding, mentoring, creative and quality time all rolled into one. (The effect is similar with our heavenly Father when we position ourselves to collaborate with him.)

What if we encouraged our congregations to make things together? In a church that fosters creativity, people who don't consider themselves artists will often be comfortable with trying their hand at making things because they've seen it modeled and it is a natural part of the church culture.

Figure 8.4. Saddleback's arts initiative built giant letters to spell "Zero" and filled them with red balloons for their AIDS eradication Getting to Zero campaign. Photo: Eric Cardella.

Encourage them to be hands-on. Children's museums and interactive exhibits let kids touch and feel things to help them learn and retain ideas and information.

Ex Creatis arts initiative at Saddleback Church often has interactive art available outside of the sanctuary as a way of responding to what has been said during a message. On World AIDS Day weekend, Saddleback church attendees were invited to participate in a response piece symbolizing the global Getting to Zero initiative.[8]

Five thousand red balloons filled a giant installation that spelled "Zero."

Individuals were invited to pop a balloon, symbolizing that they would make an impact in fighting HIV and AIDS. They would then replace the red balloons with new white balloons that were inside the deflated red ones. This represented hope.

Five thousand red balloons were popped and five thousand white balloons were blown up by five thousand different participants. They learned that "getting to zero" is a large task, but by coming together as a single working unit, they can do big things.[9]

Woodman Valley Chapel did one interactive project involving blank art canvases. Cindy West Limbrick says,

> The exhibit was nothing but blank canvas up in frames. We put a notice on the wall that said, "It's January, it's a new start, it's a new blank canvas. What will your canvas look like at the end of this year?" We tied markers with a string onto those canvases and had people write what their goals were for that year.
>
> People drew pictures and wrote many things, so there were different kinds of creativity. We had all kinds of colors of sharpies. This was up the whole month of January.[10]

It was a childlike activity that gave the average churchgoer a chance to interact with the church art gallery and contribute to the community dialogue.

The use of tactile objects in sermons is discussed further in chapter nine.

Encourage to them be themselves. We encourage our children to relax and not give in to peer pressure, and we continue to fight against that as adults. In church environments the impulse to adjust to how we perceive Christians "should be" sometimes causes us to cover up our rough edges in order to appear happy and "Christian-y." We can circumvent that unhealthy behavior by encouraging authenticity in our churches. It's less tidy but promotes creativity because people don't have to put in so much effort keeping up fake appearances, and we can help each other through real failures and issues.

Teach them about art and creativity from the past. Educating children about the art, creativity, innovations and inventions from the past helps them grasp history, how things work, and the times they live in. Similarly, talking about these types of things with our congregations and tying them into faith can help create a culture of creativity in our churches.

Visual Voice at Lincoln Berean Church offers this kind of education and inspiration to their congregation through regular art talks and classes with their theologian-in-residence, where they'll relate the arts to spirituality. They also have studies on the masters of the arts, looking at specific people like Bach or Van Gogh or other accomplished artists. This helps people realize that when you understand an artist, you can better understand their work. Visual Voice also applies this idea to local artists. The ministry hosts artist encounters, where artists from all mediums share about themselves and how they experience God through what they do. These encounters bring more connection and understanding between church members and artists so that they can speak into one another's lives and break barriers of misunderstanding, allowing the body of Christ to be more whole.

Encourage them to observe the world around them. We encourage our children to experience nature and engage their senses as they consider the world around them because we want them to be well-rounded, observant, connected human beings. These principles translate to congregations as well. It is possible to encounter God more deeply by creatively engaging our senses. As

• •

J. Brent Bill and Beth Booram share a prayer in their book that sums up a desire to have our senses awakened to God.

That in the elements of earth, sea, and sky
I may see your beauty.
That in the wild winds, birdsong and silence
I may hear your beauty.
That in the body of another and the intermingling of relationship
I may touch your beauty.
That in the moisture of the earth and its flowering and fruiting
I may smell your beauty.
That in the flowing waters of springs and streams
I may taste your beauty.
These things I look for this day, O God,
These things I look for.

J. Phillip Newell[11]

• •

J. Brent Bill and Beth Booram say in their book, *Awaken Your Senses*, Christianity is a sensuous faith. God can and will speak to us through all of our senses.

> When Jesus spent his last moments with his disciples before his arrest, he did so with a meal. . . . Jesus invited them to receive the cup and the morsel, take them into themselves, and taste forgiveness. He anticipated and commemorated his death on the cross for the forgiveness of sins through the sense of taste.[12]

Teach them that failure is okay.

> Encourage kids to make mistakes and fail. Yes, fail—kids who are afraid of failure and judgment will curb their own creative thought. Share the mistakes you've made recently, so they get the idea that it is okay to flub up. Laughing at yourself when you blow it is a happiness habit.[13]

That's great advice for any church leader, artist or individual.

Failure is one of the most effective ways—if not the most effective way—we learn. Try to make your church a place where taking creative risks is encouraged, and failing is understood to be part of the process. "We have bought into the lie that creative people never fail and hence failure is proof that we are not creative."[14]

Remind people that failure is not an identity, just an event.

More Benefits

Here are a few more ways to encourage and boost creativity in congregations through the arts ministry that haven't been covered yet.

As a resource to other ministries. In addition to its activities in supporting and encouraging artists and providing art and creativity encounters for the congregation, an arts ministry can contribute to the creative life of the church behind the scenes. Arts ministries can help other ministries of the church become more effective by offering ideas for integrating art and creativity into their activities and helping to execute those ideas. This might be a part of an arts director's job description, or artists may contribute on a volunteer or consulting basis. It's wise to specify the amount of time artists will contribute to other ministries and assign a value to their time. They might only take on one or two projects at a time and have a waiting list. But remember that serving other ministries should only be a portion of what the arts ministry does.

Sometimes churches can misunderstand the generosity of artists, asking them to contribute too much of their time and talent for little or no compensation. It's important to develop a sense of value for that so that artists don't get unintentionally taken advantage of. As more of these connections are made, the value of an arts ministry director/leader should go up.

Inviting arts ministry leaders into staff meetings will also have a positive effect on church creativity. This will solidify relationships with other ministry staff and allow the arts leaders to speak creatively into ideas and projects the staff is working on.

Ann Williams says that since she has been included in staff meetings, she's been able to connect with and contribute to ministries like guest services, which had a need for coffee tables for their new coffee shop. Ann was able to mobilize Lincoln Berean's artists to design, construct and paint tables that played on the church's identity and went beyond what the guest services ministry expected.

Express Your Faith, the arts ministry at Lutheran Church of Hope, is in demand to help bring other ministries' programs to life. They work with Celebrate Recovery on the fourth Thursdays of the month, creating art projects with the CR adults and their children. The projects reflect a Biblical message and inspire conversations at home. On the month's first Sunday afternoon, they offer a workshop for families to create art together. And they facilitate art projects three times a month for the Hope en Acción Latino group. With each of these groups the director of arts and her volunteers will study that week's sermon and come up with art activities that tie into it.

To draw artists to your church. Providing a creative and "arts-friendly" atmosphere will also draw more artists to your church, through relationships with church members who invite them and through their own curiosity.

Blackhawk Church in Madison, Wisconsin, makes an effort to welcome artists through hanging lots of art on the walls, mentioning the arts in sermons and hosting the yearly Pulse music and arts festival. Paul Lefeber, associate director of worship arts says "We try and engage visual artists; just kind of do our small part to heal the sometimes broken relationship between the church and the visual artists. [Because of this] we hear artists saying, 'Oh my gosh, I can't believe you guys actually care about this sort of thing. I feel accepted here, like I can belong in some way.'"

As a bridge to build community. In chapter eleven I look at how the arts can help create *bridging events* that draw people into the church who would never come otherwise. But it can be difficult for a new person to connect once they do come to the church, especially at a larger church. Arts ministry can offer a unique connecting point for artists of all levels. And if they can connect there, they'll be more inclined to take that next discipleship class or get involved with a small group.

In addition, as part of serving as a resource to other ministries, the arts ministry can help design creative ways to convey other ministries' messages and help them connect more quickly with people.

In many ways the future of the arts and creativity and the future of the church are intertwined. Both are designed to glorify God, to allow us to know and share his love and to provide ways to collaborate with him in and for his kingdom. And both will benefit when they operate with the other.[15]

See the online resources and extras for this chapter at JScottMcElroy.com/ CCHandbookextras.

NOTES

[1]Catherine Kapikian, *Art in Service of the Sacred* (Nashville: Abingdon, 2006), p. 122.

[2]Erwin McManus, *The Artisan Soul* (San Francisco: HarperOne, 2014), p. 104.

[3]Keith Graham, *Biology: God's Living Creation* (Pensacola, FL: Beka Book, 1986), p. 63.

[4]Tim Hansel, *Eating Problems for Breakfast* (Nashville: Word Publishing, 1988), pp. 33-34.

[5]http://technologyfromheaven.com/.

[6]Nancy Blakey, quoted in "Nurturing Your Child's Creativity," Aha!Parenting.com, www .ahaparenting.com/parenting-tools/raise-great-kids/intellegent-creative-child/child -creativity.

[7]McManus, *Artisan Soul*, p. 94.

[8]See www.worldaidscampaign.org/?attachment_id=106.

[9]See http://excreatis.com/projects/world-aids-day-2013.

[10]Interview with the author, December 2013.

[11]Quoted in J. Brent Bill and Beth Booram, *Awaken Your Senses* (Downers Grove, IL: Inter-Varsity Press, 2011), p. 30.

[12]Ibid., p. 10.

[13]"7 Ways to Foster Creativity in Your Kids," September 16, 2008, http://greatergood .berkeley.edu/raising_happiness/post/7_ways_to_foster_creativity_in_your_kids.

[14]McManus, *Artisan Soul*, p. 7.

[15]For regular updates on building a creative church, go to TheNewR.org.

9

Applications for the Arts and Creativity in Sermons

Understanding is not enough. I do not want to pass on
knowledge from the pulpit; I want to take part in an experience of
God's living word.... It is time to tuck the text into the pocket of my heart and
walk around with it inside of me. It is time to turn its words and images loose on
the events of my everyday life, and see how they mix. It is time to daydream,
whittle, whistle and pray. This is where a sermon becomes art.

BARBARA BROWN TAYLOR,
The Preaching Life

FOR SOME PEOPLE, THE SUNDAY-MORNING MESSAGE will be the most potent piece of spiritual truth they'll hear all week.

There have been numerous books written about making your message "stick," often dealing with use of words, technique, ideas, speaker energy and so on. The spoken word and the Bible are undoubtedly the most important and familiar tools for getting the message across. But many pastors and teachers are looking for approaches that go beyond words, to use additional means to convey the message in creative, artful and moving ways.

In his essay in *It Was Good: Making Art to the Glory of God*, Tim Keller, founding pastor at Redeemer Presbyterian Church in New York City, goes right to the heart of what I want to address in this chapter:

The more various forms in which truth is described, the more we understand and can then communicate truth. We can't understand truth without art. In fact, a preacher can't really express the truth he knows without at least couching it in some artistic form.[1]

If this is true, and it is, what are the artistic forms that can be used to express truth? The more appropriate question is probably what art form *can't* be used to express truth in church? Death metal music? Probably not. Nude pantomime? Definitely not. But there are many more art forms that will work and are just waiting for their shot. This book can only just scratch the surface.

Before we continue, I must offer a little disclaimer: as with any other element of a sermon, the use of the arts and creativity should be subject to prayer and the leading of the Holy Spirit. If adding these things becomes a gimmick to capture people's attention or an attempt to outdo last week's creative extravaganza, then these creative elements can feel more like manipulation than authentic expression. That said, let's take a look at a few creative ways that the arts have been employed to release truth in sermons.

When the Speaker Uses Memorable Material Examples

Jesus often used indelible physical examples in his teaching, things that seared the moment in the heart and minds of his audience and often left them (and us) contemplating what he meant. Everything Jesus did was a direct reflection of what he saw the Father doing. He didn't just come up with a wacky idea to make a point and then throw it out there to shock people. All his actions and teaching were led by the Holy Spirit. He performed a number of dramatic physical healings, including applying mud and spit to someone's eyes. He walked on water to demonstrate faith; he fed five thousand people with a few fish and loaves of bread. He broke bread and poured wine to illustrate the sacrifice of his body and blood, turned water to wine, withered a fig tree, scribbled in the sand, and on and on. Jesus constantly used the physical world to illustrate and drive home what he was saying.

In today's church we do practice a few ways of harnessing the physical world to shed light on the spiritual. Communion is the most common application of the concept. Then there are other practices like the use of ashes on Ash Wednesday or the water of baptism. How else could we follow Jesus' model of illustrating the spiritual with the physical?

My former pastor, Sean Tienhaara, enjoyed gardening. He once brought a large bush on stage and began to prune it, cutting off branches that looked healthy. He appeared to ruin it as he spoke about how God often works with us by removing certain things so that other things can grow. People still talk about that message years later.

Speaker and author Francis Chan used a balance beam in one of his messages, speaking while standing on it, then laying down and hugging it for dear life. He was illustrating the way many people go through life just trying to hang on instead of really living for God.[2]

Christ Church in Montclair, New Jersey, often uses the arts to illustrate sermons. Director of creativity Marco Hernandez says, "One particular message focused on the book of James and talked about how faith without works is dead. So we created gigantic gears. And as the pastor was speaking about the different points of faith, he connected these gears together. Toward the end, when he talked about the connection between works and faith, there was one gear in the center that drove all the other gears. So it was very kinetic. Once he put that last gear in place he spun it, making all the others spin at the same time. Adding gears during his message visually communicated that it is impossible for one gear (faith) to move without other gears (works) moving too."[3]

> "All arts come from God and are to be respected as divine inventions."
>
> John Calvin, *Calvinism: Six Stone Foundation Lectures*

I'm sure you can think of a similarly illustrated message that is lodged in your memory. Really, the sky is the limit in how God may lead in illustrating concepts with physical objects or actions. And these types of Spirit-led examples have great potential to keep speaking to your congregation for years to come.

USING TACTILE OBJECTS

One of the ways that Jesus taught was to use tactile objects to give additional sensory connection to his message. Think of the bread and the wine, the coin in the fish, the widow's mite.

There have been many Good Friday services that have employed some sort of tactile object, such as a nail, to add that sensory touch connection to the reality of the cross. Sometimes services will include allowing the worshiper to actually hammer a nail or other item to a cross.

In chapter ten I share two projects that use tactile objects. The Mosaic Project instructs individuals to bring a piece of something broken that has meaning to them and embed it in a community mosaic during a service. The Sensory Service Experience encourages people to take a piece of cloth and imagine they were touching Jesus' garment like the woman with the issue of blood. Chapter sixteen, on creating sacred space experiences, includes a number of ideas that incorporate tactile things.

Stones can make good objects and take-away mementos from a sermon. One message that I gave included two types of small stones. Volunteers placed rough stones in the pen pockets on the back of the sanctuary chairs before each service. The message was about how, though we may have read the verses that say who we are in Christ, it's possible we don't really *know* it. Is there a lie that we believe about ourselves instead? I asked people to take out the rough stone and hold it as they took a moment of silence to ask God to reveal the lie. It might be, "I'm not good enough," or "Nobody would understand my secret," or a hundred others. I asked them to imagine that the rough stone represents that lie. Then I invited them to bring their rough stones up to the middle of the stage in the front and drop them in a metal bucket, repenting and giving the lie to God. This made wonderful clinking and clattering sounds as the hundreds of stones tumbled in, one by one. Then, before going back to their seats, they went to the side of the stage and selected a smooth stone from a pile there to take with them. This stone was to be an Ebenezer (1 Sam 7:12). They were instructed to ask God for a personal revelation of how he feels about them and loves them unconditionally, and to carry that stone until he spoke to them about that. When he did, they would write the date with a sharpie on the stone. This simple exercise came after praying about how God would like the message illustrated. Some people carried the stones with them years later.

CREATING ACTUAL ART ON THE STAGE

Creating or interacting with art on stage during a message is also an effective tool to widen the impact of the message, help keep the audience's attention and create an indelible moment.

Matt Heard, pastor at Woodman Valley Chapel in Colorado Springs, Colorado, spoke one weekend about stewardship of the earth, of what's around us. One of their artists, Rita Salazar Dickerson, came on stage as Matt spoke and quickly painted a beautiful landscape full of mountains, flowers and fields. When it was completed, Matt picked up a can of black paint and threw it on the painting. All the air went out of the room. His shocking gesture underscored the point that often we are not the good stewards of the earth that God asked us to be.

Chris Dolson, pastor at Blackhawk church in Madison, Wisconsin, did a similar thing with a different topic. He had an artist's painting on stage with him as he spoke, produced a large knife and proceeded to shred the canvas, illustrating how sin destroyed God's beautiful original design for the world and for our lives.

Figure 9.1. Chris Dolson, pastor at Blackhawk church, defaces a painting by spray painting over it. Photo used with permission of Blackhawk Church.

You'll find another effective example of destruction of art, called the Good Friday Live Crosses, in chapter ten.

Lutheran Church of Hope in West Des Moines, Iowa, once introduced a project where members of the congregation were encouraged to add some simple art to a large retaining wall in their parking lot as an act of community and creativity. During a Sunday service the pastor had a facsimile of the wall brought on stage and proceeded to paint a message on it, modeling for the congregation that if he, a non-artist, could do this, they could too.

In chapter eleven you'll read about live painters, such as Bryn Gillette and Scott Erickson, who paint off to the side of the stage as the speaker is delivering the message. They often consult with the speaker

Figure 9.2. Chris Dolson destroys the painting by cutting it with a knife. Photo used with permission of Blackhawk Church.

beforehand about his or her message, then pray and ask God for an image to paint that might complement or illustrate that. This can be very inspiring and invigorating for the congregation and adds a dynamic element to the message.

Dave Blakeslee, a professional potter and former pastor, is an example of someone who actually gives a verbal message while producing a piece of art (pottery) on stage. Chapter eighteen touches on his work and the work of others like him.

> "You cannot tell people what to do, you can only tell them parables; and that is what art really is, particular stories of particular people and experiences."
>
> W. H. Auden, *Prose I*

ART THAT GOES ALONG WITH THE MESSAGE OR SERIES

In this section I'm referring to art that is produced to complement and coincide with a message or series of messages. It will typically hang for a period of days, weeks or months.

Once, during a series of messages about the prodigal son, one of the artists at our church made several large (4' x 8') chalk drawings of scenes from that story, most of them studies of well-known pieces, and hung them around the walls of the sanctuary. I had been searching for a visual to meditate on when imagining myself before the Father God, but when I saw a black and white drawing of the father greeting the son, it repulsed me. The father seemed too close, too intimate as he held his wayward son's head inches away from his and looked into his eyes. Over the following weeks of the series I was continually drawn back to this uncomfortable picture, until at last God broke through to help me understand my position as a son and his intimate love for me. In more than twenty years of being a Christian, no amount of teaching had been able to really bring that home, but that stark chalk drawing did.[4]

Mosaic Church in Hollywood produces a variety of art, ranging from sculptures to dance to films, for their messages and series. Creative director David Arcos will meet with his creative team of mostly volunteer artisans a few weeks to a few months before the start of a sermon series to brainstorm the art and creative elements for it. One series featured the five core elements of the church's mission. Each week they unveiled a new sculpture that artistically embodied a mission point. The sculptures were huge—some twelve feet tall—and located in the lobby, so the congregation would interact with them as they entered the sanctuary each week. One was a giant kneeling man made of driftwood, with a hole in his chest where a child swung on a swing. It illustrated the value of knowing your mission. Arcos says, "The idea was that when you let God invade your plans that there's like a playground inside your chest. . . . You live with an openness where you're free inside because you know you're actually living the way you were designed to live."[5]

Figure 9.3. *Water*, a 12' statue designed and constructed by the artists at Mosaic. It's one of five statues that imaginatively illustrated the core values of the church. *Water* designed by Patrick Diaz. Photo: Josh Anderson.

Imago Dei Church in Portland, Oregon, will change the art in their lobby and/or the images that are projected in the sanctuary for each sermon series. They have five artists-in-residence that rotate in producing the art for the series theme. See more about artist-in-residence programs in chapter eighteen.

Vineyard Boise regularly creates large-scale painted backdrops (50' x 11') that illustrate the theme of the teaching series they are in. On occasion an artist comes on stage during a service and adds something to the backdrop, highlighting the painting's connection to the message series.

Arts of the Covenant, the arts ministry hosted by Menlo Park Presbyterian Church, was recently asked to produce conceptual art pieces for a summer church focus on eliminating extreme global poverty. AOC had a free hand in imagining and designing the pieces, and the church paid for the creation and installation costs. The pieces were installed on all four sides of the MPPC satellite campuses. They weren't just illustrations, but abstract art pieces that were designed to make people wonder, dialogue and try to figure out what the art was saying about extreme global poverty. One piece was a six-foot chandelier made out of empty water bottles that had to be installed with a forklift. It called attention to the 750 million people in our world who do not have enough clean water to ensure their basic needs.[6] The art pieces served to carry the conversation about eliminating poverty beyond the sermon and caused the congregation to think of creative ways that that might be done.

MEDIA IN A MESSAGE

Media—such as movie clips—can be a powerful way to convey or illustrate a message with images or sound and connect with popular culture, as well as tapping into the emotional connection people may have with those songs or films. See the dangers and a discussion on this in chapter thirteen.

CREATING AN EXPERIENCE

Mosaic Church in Hollywood often creates an experience to help the congregation sense the message in unique ways. For one sermon on the church's core values, an artist created a short animated film that complemented the sermon's message about the church's mission. In the film there was a storm, and during the storm scene members of the creative team made live storm sound effects in the sanctuary. Volunteers threw chairs on the ground, broke

Figure 9.4. *Living Water:* This six-foot long chandelier was crafted of hundreds of empty water bottles and suspended from the ceiling of the worship space at Menlo Park Presbyterian Church. It called attention to the 750 million people in our world who do not have enough clean water to ensure their basic needs. Photo used with permission of Arts of the Covenant.

wood and rolled trashcans to give people a sense of experiencing the storm. Of course this can really wake an audience up and get them engaged.

Pastor Matt Heard once gave a sermon in which he talked about the idea of thirst. The ushers handed out a package of two crackers to each person as they walked in, and the worship leader announced, "We know you are wondering about the crackers. They'll be used later in the service, so don't open them now." When Matt got up to teach he asked everyone to take out the crackers and eat one. The sound of hundreds of cracker packages opening filled the sanctuary. He didn't explain anything but instead just kept on going. He talked extensively about hunger and thirst and about three-quarters of the way in he said, "Are you all thirsty?" Former creative director Cindy West Limbrick says,

And of course everyone's mouths were dry and salivating. He had them eat the other cracker. Then he went on speaking. At the end, what they didn't know is that we had tubs of bottled water at the front. So during the last song, which I think was "Hungry," the team invited everyone to come forward to get their own bottle of water. It was crazy and powerful to watch people who could not get to the water fast enough. They would open and gulp them down up front. Or guzzle it back at their seat. But they had a tangible connection to their senses to walk out with. People still remember that.[7]

Creative church stage design, which is discussed in chapter sixteen, can add immensely to the atmosphere of the sanctuary, help reinforce a sermon series theme or elevate the congregation's expectation for the message. It can also be surprisingly inexpensive.

> "Sacred art is theology in line and color, and it speaks to the whole man. . . . The material elements of the image become, as it were, the vehicle of the Holy Spirit, and furnish him with an occasion to reach souls with his hidden, spiritual power."
>
> Thomas Merton,
> Disputed Questions

Another way to immerse the congregation in an experience is by projecting images all around them instead of just on the screens.[8] This is called environmental projection and it's covered in chapter sixteen.

When Ginghamsburg Church in Ohio starts a new sermon series, church designer Kim Miller likes to reimagine what the sanctuary and design elements might look and feel like in order to help people experience the space in a new way.

> Whenever you want to move forward in people transformation, you're probably going to need some kind of physical space transformation too. It's kind of scriptural when you think about that God created the heavens and the earth and then populated that. So when I think about something new that's going to happen, I think, "Well, what's the space that that's going to happen in? How do we design the space so that God can work?" It's like the new wineskin that will hold the new wine.[9]

They might change the stage design, add new design elements or even turn the seating in the sanctuary around so that the front becomes the back.

Working with Artists to Illustrate the Sermon

If there are artists in your congregation that you'd like to work with to illustrate your sermons, take time to get to know them and invest in discipling them. Help them in the process of hearing God's voice if they are not yet skilled in that.

As a general rule, the more time you can give artists or a creative team to incubate ideas or create artwork for your sermon or series, the more creative the end result will be. It also helps to give deadlines for a proposal and the final project so that they can plan their time.

When it comes to presenting the finished work, give them some grace. A lot of artists push right to the deadline, which can cause consternation for some leaders. Dave Blakeslee suggests thinking about it like this: most leaders will tinker with sermons right up until Sunday morning because sometimes the Holy Spirit will drop in little nuggets. That is often what the artist is doing. They might tell you, "I'm working on it, but I want to include every bit, every ounce of inspiration that God can give me for this thing," just like you do. So there is a kind of mutual trust that has to develop in that process.

> "Art has a unique capacity to take one or another facet of the message and translate it into colors, shapes and sounds which nourish the intuition of those who look and listen."
>
> **Pope John Paul II,** *Letter to Artists (1999)*

Creative Exercises for Pastors and Teachers

In my experience, the single most consistent way to get creative ideas is to ask God for them in prayer and then listen to what he brings to mind. Often I don't even ask and ideas come as I'm meditating on him. It's a wonderful benefit of being in relationship with the creative God.

But prayer isn't the only way God inspires ideas. Many times he'll lead us to things that will trigger creativity or cause us to see in a new way. Here are some ideas and exercises that might help spark personal creativity.

- *Listen to others discuss their perspectives on creativity.* TED talks are a treasure trove of creative inspiration and exciting new ideas. You might find a creative shot in the arm, learn something new or be provoked to action. (See TED.com.)

- *Practice* visio divina. This can allow you to see art more deeply and actually hear God's voice through it. *Visio divina* is Latin for "divine seeing." It's similar to *lectio divina* (Latin for "divine reading"), with the difference being that instead of reading Scripture and praying for God to speak through it, you are meditating on artwork and asking God to speak to you through it. *Visio divina*, like *lectio divina*, has four steps:

    1. See. Ask God to lead you to a piece of art. This may be in a gallery or in private. Take it in, at first just noticing the colors, subjects, people, places and objects. Spend one to two minutes with the image. You may want to write down a few thoughts or words that come to mind. Then you may want to leave the art for a moment.

    2. Meditate. Revisit the image and look deeper. Do you see relationships—people or things that relate to other people or things? Is there movement? Avoid analyzing the art; instead observe and enter into it. Does the Holy Spirit convey a deeper meaning to you?

    3. Pray. Dialogue with God about the image in prayer. Pray about what it brought up in you: thankfulness, experiences or issues. If someone came to mind, pray for that person.

    4. Contemplate. Relax and rest in God's love and message for you through this image. Center yourself and breathe deeply. Enjoy God's presence.[10]

- *Take an acting class.* Studying acting can be immensely helpful in public speaking, as well as in empathizing with others and gaining a better awareness of your feelings, senses and body. It can help you loosen up and become more confident.

- *Engage your imagination.* Choose a story from the Bible; then ask the Holy Spirit to lead you, imagining everything about it. Create the scene in your mind and explore it. Follow the Spirit's nudging as you ask yourself questions that require seeing and feeling the scene. Say you are James in the Garden of Gethsemane with the other disciples. What does it look like? What are the smells? Why do you think Jesus has brought you here? What is he doing? What did you pray about when Jesus asked you to watch and pray? Why are you so tired? What were you wearing? Who was the first to fall asleep? How do you feel when the crowd comes? Where did you run to? How did being there at that moment affect the rest of your life?

An exercise like this can lead to any number of creative ideas. Maybe you imagined that James had his favorite cloak on and that he was very comfortable when he sat down to pray, which is one of the reasons he fell asleep. Maybe you bring a cloak with you and show it to the audience, pass it around, and use it as part of a message about getting out of your comfort zone or staying alert. Maybe you make it cold in the sanctuary and describe how comforting the cloak must have been on a chilly night as people touch it and pass it around. You get the idea; let the Holy Spirit awaken and lead your imagination.

> *"Creativity isn't about finding the thirteenth note; it is about arranging twelve notes in a way the world has never experienced before."*
>
> Erwin McManus, *Artisan Soul*

- *Explore other cultures.* Experiments by Northwestern's Adam Galinsky show that

    those who have lived abroad outperform others on creative tasks. . . . The theory is that cross-cultural experiences force people to adapt and be more flexible. Just studying another culture can help. In Galinsky's lab, people were more creative after watching a slide show about China: a forty-five-minute session increased creativity scores for a week.[11]

- *Try free writing.* One form of this is called Morning Pages, one of the foundations of the book *The Artist's Way.* The book is not specifically Christian, but it is full of truth, and it's easy to spot and disregard unbiblical references. The author gives a description of Morning Pages:

    These are three pages of longhand, stream of consciousness writing, done first thing in the morning. *There is no wrong way to do Morning Pages*—they are not high art. They are not even "writing." They are about anything and everything that crosses your mind— and they are for your eyes only. Morning Pages will clear your mind, even if, in fact especially if, what you write is negative, and free you to let go of those thoughts during the day. Do not over-think Morning Pages: just put three pages of anything on the page . . . and then do three more pages tomorrow.[12]

- *Read poetry.* Poetry is believed to offer several benefits for pastors and teachers.

Reading and memorizing poetry trains us to meditate deeply on texts. The compression of language in good poetry forces the reader to pay attention to the details of grammar and punctuation. It thus tends to make us better oral communicators, speaking in memorable sentences, and . . . making our preaching more concise. Lincoln's Gettysburg Address was a little over two minutes long (280 words), while the forgotten oration given right before Lincoln's by famed orator Edward Everett was over two hours long (13,508 words).[13]

The analysis of good poetry should, first of all, be a pure pleasure; but that pleasure can translate into a great benefit for preachers. In the case of sacred poets like Herbert there are personal lessons that may be learned and etched in the memory. This, in turn, can inspire the preacher to pass the most salient lessons on to his congregation.[14]

FINAL THOUGHT

Many pastors would like their sermons to be more creative, artful and memorable. If Jesus were to preach in our church next weekend, it's not hard to imagine that his message would have all three of those qualities. He embodies them. But he claimed that we would do greater works than he did, so the ability he had while in human form—the ability to convey concepts and stories with powerfully simple creativity, using nature, art, beauty and whatever else he brings to our attention—must be available to us as well. Of course this comes from being aware of what the Father is doing and then joining that, like Jesus did.

May we be willing to seek God for the creative means he would use to convey his messages, willing to risk and to empower the artists in our congregations to contribute to what God is speaking to our churches, willing to make room for the arts and creativity to take their fundamental place in communicating the astonishing love story of our creative God.

See the online resources and extras for this chapter at JScottMcElroy.com/ CCHandbookextras.

NOTES

[1]Tim Keller, "Glory," in *It Was Good: Making Art for the Glory of God*, ed. Ned Bustard and Sandra Bowden (Baltimore, MD: Square Halo Books, 2000), p. 122.

[2]See a video excerpt of this message at www.youtube.com/watch?v=LA_uwWPE6lQ).

[3]"Fitting the Arts into Church: Interview with Marco Hernandez," *Leadership Journal*, Spring 2009, www.christianitytoday.com/le/2009/spring/fittingtheartsintochurch .html.

[4]I tell this story in my book *Finding Divine Inspiration* (Shippensburg, PA: Destiny Image, 2008), pp. 38-39.

[5]Interview with the author, January 2014

[6]Email from Marianne Lettieri to the author, February 2014.

[7]Interview with the author, January 2014.

[8]Read more about this at http://visualworshiper.com.

[9]Interview with the author, December 2013.

[10]Inspired by http://episcopalprayer.org/visio-divina.

[11]Po Bronson and Ashley Merryman, "Forget Brainstorming," *Newsweek*, July 12, 2010, www.newsweek.com/forget-brainstorming-74223.

[12]http://juliacameronlive.com/basic-tools/morning-pages/.

[13]Bob Green, "The Forgotten Gettysburg Addresser," *The Wall Street Journal*, June 22-23, 2013, A15.

[14]See Gregory E. Reynolds, "A Model for Preachers," *Ordained Servant* (blog), http://opc .org/os.html?article_id=373.

Five Interactive
Art Projects for Churches

In contemporary society the heart is reached
through participation, and all approaches to worship—
traditional, contemporary, or blended—need to learn how to
achieve services characterized by immersed participation.

ROBERT E. WEBBER,
Planning Blended Worship:
The Creative Mixture of Old and New

WHEN AN ARTS MINISTRY IS JUST beginning to present projects to the congregation, it's good to keep a few things in mind:

1. Leadership needs to be convinced that the arts will work in the context of a service or ministry time.

2. The congregation needs to experience a spiritual and/or emotional connection to the work, which is a phenomenon they may not have felt before.

3. The artists need to present a meaningful, well-executed work.

The five interactive projects in this chapter can accomplish all of these things and will go a long way toward establishing a place for the arts in your church. They also work well in churches where the arts are already established.

1. THE MOSAIC PROJECT

Concept: Create a mosaic art project that can be interactive and that gets part of its beauty from the contributions of average members of the congregation. It could possibly become a permanent piece of art for the church.

Background: A woman at a church in Indianapolis had a dream in which she saw a mosaic picture of a cross with a large heart in the center of it. There were shafts of light shining from the heart, and the heart itself was empty. She saw broken pieces of pottery and other objects placed in the heart later. She sensed that God was inviting her to bring the broken places in her life to the cross and that when she did this, she would understand more of God's heart and purpose for her. He showed her that his light would shine through the cracks created by the broken places. The church's arts group, who had never worked with the mosaic medium before, brought this concept to life for a special service.

How it works: Basic mosaics can be fairly easy to execute and multiple people can contribute, so it's a good beginning project for a newly formed arts group. (Mosaic how-to instructions are easily found on the Internet.) In this group's case, they found the colors of tile and pottery they wanted for the project in random places, like the gardening aisle at Big Lots, Goodwill and their own basements. They sketched out a design, cut a three-quarter-inch piece of plywood for backing, broke the pottery into workable pieces and arranged the colors on the board. Someone had the idea to make the shafts of light out of mirrors, so they smashed several mirrors as well. Others set and polished the tiles and pottery.

A few weeks before the special service, the pastor asked the congregation to be thinking about broken places in their lives that they wanted God to heal. He invited them to bring an object that represented that broken place to the planned special service. The object needed to be about the size of a quarter. The night of the service the mosaic was set up on stage, completed with the exception of an empty heart. As the service began, grout was added to the heart, and soon after that the congregation was invited up to the stage to place their symbolic broken object in the heart. One of the artists stood by to make sure each piece stuck. As the service went on the heart became full of crazy, colorful, meaningful objects.

Result: This project was a success and opened the door for other arts projects at that church. It accomplished the three goals mentioned above:

1. Leaders loved it because it was visual, colorful and interactive. It connected the audience with the message and flowed well with the service.

2. The congregation experienced an emotional and spiritual connection because they (a) contributed something personal to the piece; (b) interacted with it, got close to it, touched it; (c) sensed community as they watched their friends and acquaintances contribute their own pieces while helping make a piece of art together; and (d) sensed redemption because their symbol of brokenness helped create something beautiful. For many this was a new experience in their relationship with and understanding of art's power.

3. The work was meaningful to the artists and congregation, got the artists contributing and working as a team and, though time-consuming, was fairly easy to execute well. It was suitable to show and display. The completed work soon became a meditation point in the sanctuary.

A work like this can become a meaningful part of a congregation's rich history. This piece is mounted in the church's lobby with a placard that explains its history and even an invitation for the viewer to symbolically place their own brokenness in an empty spot on the heart.

Figure 10.1. The completed 33" x 48" congregational mosaic. Photo: JSM.

The mosaic idea is suitable for any service dealing with healing or brokenness. It also works with special services like Good Friday (Jesus takes our brokenness on his broken body and redeems it) or Easter (our past brokenness is absorbed in him and we are given a fresh start).

Details:

- When breaking the tile or glass, make sure to put it into something like an old pillowcase to protect from flying shards. If possible, use tiles of uniform thickness, as this will make the cleaning and polishing part of the grouting process much easier.

- Using tiles of various shapes, sizes and thickness will create an interesting effect, but will require cleaning and polishing each piece individually.

- For backing, use three-quarter-inch plywood or something similar that will not flex. Flexing will cause the grout to crack and tiles to loosen.

Materials needed:

- three-quarter-inch plywood board

- broken pottery, tile, mirrors

- tile adhesive, tile grout

Tools:

- rags, sponges, tile squeegee

- small grout trowel

- hammer, tile clipper

Of course, an interactive, congregational art project can take many forms, but the mosaic project—with church-specific variations—could be a good way to start.

2. GOOD FRIDAY LIVE CROSSES

Concept: Provide a visual assist to the Good Friday story by painting three crosses on four-by-eight-foot sheets of plywood during the service and then immediately defacing them.[1]

Background: The Good Friday story has been told millions of times in many different ways. This concept offers the opportunity to relate the story with the assistance of simple art pieces, painted by members of your congregation as the story is being told.

How it works: First, pray about who your artists should be. Choosing people from your congregation will add to the emotional connection for the audience. They don't have to be excellent artists, because the pieces will be defaced right after they are created.

Set the three sheets of plywood up vertically at the front of your auditorium, spaced out along the stage. The stage-left panel will represent the repentant thief, the center panel will represent Jesus, and the panel on stage right will represent the unrepentant thief. The panels need to be solidly anchored so that they stay still while being painted.

The artists will begin painting their crosses when the service begins, using whatever colors they like, and they paint continuously as the readings progress. The readings could include Scriptures from each of the Gospels, interlaced with appropriate songs. Just before the story reaches the moment of death the artists stop painting and step behind their panels, leaving an unobstructed view for the audience for up to sixty seconds as the story ends. On cue, the artists quickly elevate a bucket attached to the top and back of their panel, and the black paint in it begins to ooze down the front of the painting, defacing the cross they each just painted. This process continues for a few minutes and then the service ends in silence. Sometime during the service, but not right at the end, the audience should be instructed that the service will end in silence. They can then linger in silence, come to the front to pray or leave silently.

Figure 10.2. An artist paints the "bad thief's" cross live during a Good Friday service. Photo: Carol M.

Additional elements might include sound and lighting effects—maybe a thunderclap with a flicker of the stage lights before the black paint is poured, and the sound of rain as it runs down the panel. You might also have the artists remain behind their paintings and turn off their work lights one at a time after the paint has covered the middle of the panel.

Result: This project puts the audience in a meditative state as they watch the artists creating the paintings while the Good Friday story is being read. Some will experience joy as they watch people they know create these

Figure 10.3. The "bad thief's" cross completed. The artist stands behind it. Photo: Carol M.

works. Then the unexpected defacing of the painting really connects the emotions with the moment of death in the story. It's common to hear crying and other emotional expressions throughout the congregation. Many may want to linger in their seats, processing it. And you'll likely hear many stories of how people were deeply affected by the service. This service can become an important link in many people's connection with Good Friday.

Figure 10.4. The artist pours the black paint from behind. Photo: Carol M.

One particularly talkative and outgoing young couple left one of these services in sacred silence, drove the twenty-minute trip home together and didn't speak until nearly an hour later. They then felt compelled to drink a glass of wine as a commemorative sacrament. They still talk about the experience more than ten years later.

Materials needed:

- Three four-by-eight-foot, quarter-inch or half-inch-thick sheets of plywood (per service, if multiple services)
- Three one-quart rigid buckets, with one flat side on each
- Three medium to large door hinges with screws
- Six large plastic tarps (at the very least)
- Three heavy-duty artist easels (preferably not three-legged), or a two-by-four-inch board mounting system that you devise to hold the panels up
- Several medium-sized jars to put paint in. Each artist should have dedicated jars of paint for each color, with a dedicated brush. This is a quick process, and you don't want to have to clean brushes as you work.
- Duct tape
- Paint, brushes and a small table for each artist
- One work light for each artist (attach to top of panel)

Details:

- Use half-inch-thick plywood or very rigid quarter-inch. The board should not flex much or the paint in the bucket on the back may spill. Three-quarter-inch is too heavy and more expensive.

- Prime the panels with white or light-colored paint so that when the black paint is poured it will be easily seen.

- Take the one-quart buckets, with one flat side each (important), and attach one side of the door hinge to the flat side of the bucket. Attach the other side of the hinge to the top back of the panel. You will be lifting it from behind. Place duct tape over the crack between the panel and the bucket, to avoid spilling when the paint-filled bucket is tipped.

- Note that this can be a very messy project. Be very generous with tarps and plastic to cover the ground around and behind each panel, going out several feet in every direction. Tape the tarps securely together to avoid seeping paint. Do everything possible to ensure no paint will get on the stage, sanctuary or surrounding areas. You want to show leadership that a project like this can be done without any permanent impact on the worship space.

- Fill the hinged buckets with black paint shortly before the service. Cover the buckets with an airtight cover to prevent spillage and drying.

- When the artists step behind the panels, they uncover the buckets. When it comes time to tip the buckets, they should tip them quickly to avoid spilling. You'll want tarps behind the panel to catch any spilled paint.

- You might also create a trough with tarps or tape at the base of the panel to catch the paint more effectively.

- I'd recommend that you experiment with the process before the night of the service. You may find ways to improve or simplify your specific application.

3. Pop-Up Drama

Concept: A quick, surprise drama that takes place in the audience and leads into or illustrates the message.

Background: Drama from the stage has been used by a number of churches over the last few decades to bring messages to life. Pop-up drama takes the spontaneous, surprise element of a flash mob (where a group of people suddenly do something, e.g., dance, sing in unison) by placing the actors in the audience. The dramas are sixty seconds or less.

How it works: This project gets its name from the fact that the actors pop up from their seats in the audience when it's time to give their line. Scatter the actors in the audience so that the audience's attention will be drawn from one area to another. Have each one pop up to give his or her line and remain standing.

Result: This will really get the audience's attention because of the shock of seeing someone in the audience stand up and say what they are feeling. In many cases it may be something the listeners have thought but never had the courage to say out loud. When the drama is left open-ended with no nice "Christian" wrap-up, it will lead into the message and create anticipation for what the pastor or teacher has to say when the drama is done.

Materials needed:

- If desirable and available, concealed lapel mics, set at a low volume.

Details:

- This works best when the drama is very short—sixty seconds or less—so that it catches the audience off-guard and keeps them in a heightened state of awareness.

- The drama needs to begin during a point in the service when the audience is seated.

- It's best to have a church leader on stage and have the drama interrupt them. If there's not a leader on stage, someone in the congregation may feel compelled to step in and try to handle the "disturbance," thereby spoiling the moment. The leader might just stand there with a shocked look and let the actors speak without interacting with them.

- When it's possible, use actors who are not well known in your congregation. This will add to the surprise effect.

- In practice, make sure that the actors project their voices, or if you have access to multiple wireless lapel mics, try to conceal them on the actors and run the mics just loud enough to give a little boost to the actors' voices (not at full volume) so the drama doesn't seem planned.

- When the drama is complete, the leader on stage should acknowledge the outburst and maybe repeat the main gist of the material, playing along for a moment. Then he or she may reveal that it was set up, saying something like, "That's what you call a pop-up drama." This is important, as many in the audience will still be confused. You'll hear lots of relief and laughter after this is revealed.

Sample script: The script should be as real as possible and sound like real people actually talk. It should be open ended and pose questions or make observations. Let the sermon provide the answers.

Here is a sample script:

Who Am I?

This script deals with issues of identity and personal value. The drama was performed on a Sunday when it was an "Arts Sunday," with several artistic things going on during worship, like painting and dance. It was also Father's Day.

PASTOR/SPEAKER: (*on stage*) Well, welcome this morning—

PERSON 1: (*pops up from seat and interrupts*) Excuse me. . . . Um . . . I don't want to disrupt, but . . . I just have to say something. I came to church feeling depressed today, and I'm still depressed. I mean . . . this is really cool—people expressing themselves—so much talent! The thing is, I'm not really artistic. And on top of that, I'm not a father either. So I'm feeling a little lost; I don't know how I fit in or where *my* value is. . . . Uh . . . you know what, this is completely inappropriate.

PERSON 2: (*pops up on the other side of the room*) *No* dude! I'm so glad you ·said that! I've been sitting here thinking the same thing. I'm not sure what I'm supposed to do with my life. I'm not creative like they are. . . . This is so embarrassing. But frankly, I'm tired of putting on a good face.

PERSON 3: (*pops up in the middle of the audience*) Um . . . maybe you both should talk to Randy (the pastor)? Make an appointment??

PERSON 4: (*pops up in center of audience near stage and addresses both actors*) No! This is good! We've got to be honest about these things. I've felt the same way. . . . I've actually felt worthless from time to time, but I know that's not right; it can't be right. But I don't know what to do about it.

PASTOR/SPEAKER: (*pause*) Wow. (*pause*) Isn't weird to hear someone saying out loud what we've all thought sometimes: "I feel worthless, but I know that's not right." (*pause*) Well, that is what you call a pop-up drama.

The pastor/speaker then launches into a sermon about who we really are in Christ and how to exchange the lies we believe for God's truth.

4. PERSONAL PRAYER ART

Concept: Use spontaneous art as a form of personal prayer ministry or outreach.

Background: Many churches have ministry teams that pray for people before or after services. Often there will be a word of encouragement given to the person being prayed for; some churches may call it a "prophetic word" or "word of wisdom or knowledge." With this practice you illustrate that word, and it can have a profound, lasting effect on the person who receives it. It can be a part of a special service or become a regular offering at your church. It is also wonderful for outreach, as drawing a picture for someone breaks the ice and opens unique opportunities to speak into people's lives and bless them. This idea was pioneered by Theresa Dedmon at Bethel Church, Redding, California.

How it works: Generally, if you are doing this in a church, it works best if a table is used, which means the prayer art process can operate inside the sanctuary or outside the sanctuary in the lobby. If you are using this as part of an outreach, you can improvise and use whatever is at hand, standing if necessary. It's best to have a few artists at a few stations doing this at the same time, rather than one lone artist. This gives those who receive the prayer art more options and a shorter wait time. There is often a lot of demand for this as people become aware of it and lines can develop. It's also good to have multiple artists and stations so the practitioners don't feel alone or overwhelmed.

(Note: I use the term *artist* here, but this activity doesn't require developed artistic ability, only the ability to hear from God and draw a stick figure. That said, those with artistic abilities will find this very enjoyable because it becomes an experience of collaborating with God.)

1. Artists prepare themselves by taking time to deal with any unforgiveness or anger in their lives, clear their minds, settle their spirits and focus on God. A good practice for clearing the air to hear God's voice is found in my book *Finding Divine Inspiration.*[2]

2. The artists sit at a table with art supplies and, usually after a service is over, invite people (using signage) to have a picture drawn for them.

3. When a person sits down on the other side of the table, the artist doesn't usually ask for any personal details except the person's name. Details may come later.

4. The artist briefly prays for the person, asking if it's okay to put a hand on them, and silently asks God for a picture or word for the person.

5. The artist then waits until a word or image begins to form. This may be just a flash of something, even something seemingly nonsensical. Sometimes it may require a moment more of quiet or meditation for the picture to form. The artist should encourage the person to stay engaged with God and relax while they draw.

    Often the artist will continue to internally ask questions of the Holy Spirit as he or she draws (e.g., "Is the grass brilliant green or more brown?" "Are there three birds or more?" "Is the water rough or calm?" and so on). This may sound scary, but it is astounding how the Spirit will speak when the artist takes a risk to listen and create, prayerfully drawing the images that come to mind.

6. The artist takes a couple of minutes to draw the image, not worrying about perfection or creating a masterpiece, then gives it to the person and asks the question, "Does this mean anything to you?" giving him or her a chance to react to it.

7. The artist then explains what he or she thinks God might be saying or what the picture or word could mean. The artist might write a line of explanation across the top of it.

8. After hearing the person's reaction and taking a moment to process it with him or her, the artist prays with the person about the subject the picture brought up.

9. The artist should make a point to sign and date the picture and encourage the person to write down what he or she thought God might be saying on the back.

The results: This is amazingly effective in conveying God's love to individuals. More often than not, the picture or word has a very relevant meaning for the person, and he or she feels known and seen by the Creator. The person also feels love from the artist, as the artist has taken the time to connect, serve and pray for them. Tears of joy are very common. The artist will often feel an overwhelming sense of joy as well to be able to collaborate with God so clearly. The picture made adds to the impact of the encouraging word and can continue to bless the person for years to come. And God can infuse it with new meaning over time, so that, like many pieces of art, it has a life of its own. Some churches call this "prophetic art," "personal prophetic art," "destiny art" or other variations. Feel free to adjust the name to reflect the culture of your church. This process is simply prayerfully asking God for a picture or word for a person, taking a risk and drawing it out, and then offering it to them as a prayer, always with the qualification to "test it" for accuracy.

Figure 10.5. Artists make personal prayer art as the people they're creating it for watch. Photo: JSM.

Materials needed:

- Tables, art supplies (colored pencils, pens, markers, crayons, quick-drying paint, etc. Stay away from chalk, watercolor or things that can smudge or take a while to dry.)
- Uniform sheets of paper. Five-by-eight-inch sheets work well and can fit in plastic protectors if you want to provide those.

Details:

- Training: Artists who participate in this ministry should go through any training that is provided for other ministry team members. You'll also want to train your artists to hear God's voice and to become comfortable with identifying pictures and impressions they see in their mind's eye that might be from him, then translating them into a drawing. Like most skills, developing this practice requires relaxing and just going with what happens—sort of like floating in water.

- This practice is not limited to pictures but could include words, poetry and so on.

- As a rule of thumb, the images should not be apocalyptic or threatening, but uplifting and affirming, just as prayer ministry will usually be.

- If the image or word does not resonate with the person, suggest that he or she keeps the drawing and tuck it away somewhere. It's not unusual for God to reveal meanings to the recipient some time later. Also, always leave room for the possibility that the artist got it wrong. They take a risk, and sometimes it is not completely accurate. This is okay. The artist will usually want to qualify the presentation of the drawing with, "I think this may be what God is saying, but I could be wrong. Test it and see what you think."

5. Sensory Worship Service

Concept: Create a worship experience—as a special service—where the congregation's senses are engaged.

Background: A sensory worship service can awaken additional ways of grasping spiritual truths and create wonderful opportunities to incorporate the arts. Sensory practices are uncommon in most evangelical churches, but other traditions have been successfully incorporating sensory worship for centuries.

How it works: Here is one model that a medium-sized church recently put together. The setting was a mid-week service that was focused on prayer, specifically kicking off the opening of a season of 24/7 prayer. In planning the service, the leader felt God's encouragement to base the message of the evening on an invitation the pastor had given at a recent Sunday service. The invitation was the question Jesus asked the blind men: "What do you want me to do for you?" Another point of inspiration for the evening was the thought that the woman with the "issue of blood" had: "If I can only touch the hem of his garment, I will be well." These were two very simple yet profound ideas. The sanctuary was set up with stations so that the attendees could contemplate these thoughts and make them into a prayer. There were five stations: a group of art tables in the center of the room, two posting walls on either side of the room made up of four-by-twenty-foot sheets of white paper, and two prayer stations on either side of the room that included candles and an incense bowl.

After brief acoustic worship, the leader gave a short message that focused on the two stories from the Bible. When the woman's story was recounted, the audience was invited to take a small cloth from a basket that was passed around and imagine that they too could touch Jesus' garment. They were invited to grasp it and feel it as they prayed. The speaker then gave instructions on how to interact with the stations, and the people were encouraged to move around the room as they felt led. Two musicians led simple and beautiful worship while the people visited the stations.

Figure 10.6. Members of the congregation express their prayers as drawings. Photo: JSM.

The art tables were stocked with colored pencils, markers, watercolors, paper and scissors and engaged the senses of touch and sight. People were encouraged to illustrate their prayers, or just freely express themselves to God. They could affix what they made to the posting walls or draw directly on the posting walls. The prayer stations were to the sides of the stage and engaged the sense of smell, with many different sizes of candles burning toward the back of the table and an incense bowl toward the front. This bowl was full of one-inch square cloths that were soaked in a pleasant scent. People were encouraged to come up, pray and inhale, imagining that their prayers were like sweet-smelling incense to God (Ps 141:2; Rev 8:4). People were also invited to walk up on the stage and view and contemplate the art altarpieces closely. The audience could visit the stations in any order and as many times as they liked. In addition, three artists painted images that inspired them on easels set up at the edges of the stage.

The result: Many people found this service to be a unique and freeing experience for several reasons. It's not often that worshipers—especially Protestants—are invited to engage multiple senses in church or to move around freely. This was a new experience for many; there were comments that it was "fun," felt "joyous," "sacred," "moving" and "Spirit-led." The leader described that at one point about midway through, it seemed like a dream that was being choreographed by the Holy Spirit. The music and the movement of the people around the room, everyone in a posture of prayer and art-making, seemed like a unified prayer in collaboration with God himself. According to the leader, it felt like a piece of heaven. Several people were deeply affected when they connected their prayer with the pleasant incense smell of the bowls, imagining what God might be sensing as they prayed.

This event also provided a wonderful opportunity for the church's artists to experiment and stretch. Since it was a midweek service and very freeform, one artist who is working to overcome perfectionism felt comfortable to paint from the stage, a breakthrough for him. He even left his image up for the Sunday service and had offers to buy it. Two other artists painted a piece together and were transformed by the joy they felt in collaborating. These two had so much fun with what God was doing that when they sat down they couldn't stop giggling, something that both of them needed.

Materials needed:

During the service:

• Fabric to represent Jesus' garment, cut into small one- or two-inch squares

Art tables:

• Folding tables

• Plastic tarps for under the tables. Always cover more than you think is necessary.

• Art supplies for the tables

• Large paper or tarps to cover the tables

Prayer stations:

- An assortment of candles. You can make them various sizes with random holders, or uniform.

- Bowls

- A couple dozen small, one-inch square pieces of cloth

- A bottle of pleasant scent, preferably subtle, nothing too strong or specific. You might try a prayer oil like myrrh or frankincense or a scent from a place like Yankee Candle.

Posting walls:

- A roll of craft paper, three or four feet wide

- A couple tables with a couple of baskets with art supplies in them (see "Details" for more specifics)

Details:

During the service:

- You might consider having acoustic worship music for the service to encourage the attitude of simplicity and intimacy.

- When you pick the fabric to represent Jesus' garment, look for linen with a rougher twill. Imagine what someone would wear two thousand years ago.

Art tables:

- If you provide paints at your art tables, make sure to tape your tarps— under the tables and on top of them—together.

- Children will be attracted to the art tables, so make sure there is adult supervision.

Posting walls:

- Tape the white craft paper for the walls with painter's tape or a tape that will be gentle on your walls. Don't use packing tape.

- Supply pens, pencils, markers and things that won't create a mess at the posting wall. It's best to not have paints or chalk available at the posting walls. Congregants can instead paint at an arts table, let their work dry, and then affix it to the walls.

- If you'd like to cover the floors next to the posting walls, you can find carpet-protection film at the local hardware or carpet store, or online. It provides a clean, organized look because it's clear and the adhesive backing means you don't need tape to keep it down. If your floors are not carpet, look for film that works on hard surfaces. Carpet-protection film will be difficult to get off your hard floor and may pull the shine off.

You'll find more project ideas, categorized by type, season and difficulty level in the resources and extras for this chapter.

See the online resources and extras for this chapter at JScottMcElroy.com/ CCHandbookextras.

Notes

[1]Based on an idea from Jim Mathias, pastor at Common Ground, Indianapolis.
[2]J. Scott McElroy, *Finding Divine Inspiration* (Shippensburg, PA: Destiny Image, 2008).

Live Art in the Church

*Art is a human activity consisting in this, that one man
(or woman) consciously by means of certain external signs hands
on to others feelings he (she) has lived through, and that others
are infected by these feelings and also experience them.*

LEO TOLSTOY,
What Is Art?

INVITING ARTISTS TO PRODUCE THEIR WORK LIVE in the church is a key to unlocking the creativity of a congregation. It is invigorating to witness the creative process unfold in front of us, in the flesh. Sparks can start to kick up in hearts as they watch—sparks of desire to connect with God creatively, to feel the freedom of collaboration with the Creator that the artist models. It's a desire that can ignite faith to believe for God's creative touch in the daily details of life.

If you want to cultivate a creative church, consider incorporating live art. This chapter gives some detailed examples of live art being produced in churches. I'll start with the developing area of live painting.

LIVE PAINTING

Watching an artist paint live can be magical: the anticipation of the blank canvas, the dance of brush strokes and color choices, the vision that materializes through the artist's intense attention. Pair that process with inspiring worship music, and an even stronger emotional connection with the audience is created. Have the painter illustrate or react to what a speaker is expounding on, and you engage more of the viewers' senses as they listen. When the painter is in tune with the Holy Spirit and asking God to give images that speak to the congregation, you may see reactions like tears, repentance, joy, affirmation and more from viewers. These are some of the reasons live painting is gaining popularity in churches around the world.

The phenomenon started getting attention with a few live painters who travel to churches and put on a sort of performance, usually to a track of music. They generally create a specific pre-planned image that is chosen from their collection of religious images, such as the face of Jesus, the cross or a scene from the Bible. Maybe you've seen some of these talented people on the Internet, speed painting Jesus' face upside down to an inspirational song. These performances are guaranteed crowd pleasers, professionally done with a predicted outcome: a recognizable, quality image and an appreciative audience. They're neat experiences, a special event that can be a way to introduce an appreciation of art to a church.

More recently, another stream of live painting has come to the forefront of churches, literally. It's often done by someone from the congregation and takes place on the stage or to the side of it. These painters may be professionals or hobbyists but they paint whatever they feel led to, usually during the worship part of the service and sometimes continuing while the speaker is bringing the message. They generally are not the featured part of the service—not a performance—but one of the elements. It's another creative expression of worship more than a novelty or special event. Depending on the church culture, they may be called prophetic painters, platform artists or just live painters. It's common for them to ask God for an idea or an image of what he would like to say and then, when they get an impression, they'll paint or draw it. This may be more mystical than some non-artist Christians are comfortable with, but it makes complete sense that artists would identify God speaking to them in images, since they are fluent in that language.

> "Art is sensory. It is physical. When it's working well we should have a physical, visceral, vocal experience with and response to it."
> Luann Jennings, *Church and Art Network* blog

For any church desiring to encourage creativity in their services and congregation, live painting can provide plenty of rewards. For this chapter I talked with several talented and experienced live painters and came up with some important tips and advice. Just to clarify, I won't be focusing on the professional performance style of painting (that's dealt with in chapter twenty) but rather the style that often empowers artistic members of the congregation to paint for their fellow worshipers.

First, let's define "live painting" more precisely. There can be live painting on the stage, in front of the whole congregation, which I'll call platform painting, and live painting done by individuals in the congregation as a personal expression, off to the sides of the church, in the back or in the pew. It's

Figure 11.1. Artists from the congregation paint live during a special service. Photo: Nathan Siner/The Siners Photography.

similar to the arrangement of worship leaders singing on stage in front of the whole congregation and individuals singing at their seats in the sanctuary.

The following questions are answered with the platform painter in mind, but most of the principles also apply to those who are painting off of the platform for personal expression.

Who should do the live platform painting? Well, who do you look for to lead worship? People who have talent, character enough to handle being on stage, a solid relationship with God, and can sense the Holy Spirit's leading in the moment. You'll want to look for the same things in a live platform painter. A person who is lacking in one of those areas may do in a pinch, but you want them to grow if they are going to continue to lead from the stage.

Where should the platform painter set up? Generally the platform painter will be on the stage but off to the side (not center stage) or off the stage but still in the front. It's not uncommon to have two painters on stage, one on either side, during a service. This way people on both sides of the auditorium have the option of watching and benefiting from the painting process.

Figure 11.2. Three artists paint live on stage as a dancer moves nearby during worship at Bethel Church, Redding, CA. Photo: JSM.

Bethel Church in Redding, California, occasionally has up to eight people painting on stage during worship, four on each side. Director of arts Theresa Dedmon says their reasoning for this is that one type of painting may touch a certain type of person in the audience, and with more painters you have the opportunity to affect more people. "So number one, you're welcoming diversity in the body of Christ," Theresa says. "Number two, you are acknowledging the fact that God can speak to each one of us differently. And number three, you're creating a lens where the audience can start to see what God is saying from different perspectives, different art genres or different expressions. Also, painting by yourself can kind of be lonely, so as a painter there is camaraderie, just like you'd get with a band."[1]

If you are considering multiple painters, it would be more natural to have this during worship but not during the message. Pray and experiment, and see what God seems to be saying.

How long should the artist paint? Some professional performance painters (like those you see on the Internet) are able to produce a painting during a single song because their images are usually simple, often on a spare background, and they have painted the same image many times. On the other hand, most platform painters are painting an original image that matches the moment and may be more complex or something they've never tackled before. Still, some platform painters can do an original painting in twenty or twenty-five minutes during worship, while others need longer. While Scott Erickson, a platform painter based in Portland, was the artist-in-residence at Ecclesia Church in Houston and painting weekly there, he would generally take forty-five minutes to do a painting, working through the worship and continuing while the pastor spoke. (See more about Scott in chapter nineteen.)

Bryn Gillette, from Walnut Hills Church in Connecticut, varies in the time he takes: "A lot of times it's a one-shot deal and I start and finish in one service. [Bryn also paints through the entire service.] Sometimes it depends on size. The biggest one I've ever done in one service was 10' x 15' feet. I used rollers and latex paint. There are days when my task is to catch what the Spirit is doing in a particular service. On a morning like that I'll do two separate paintings during separate services. I might go back later and putter on them or tighten something up, but often at least the heartbeat of what the Lord seems to be saying comes through in the painting itself."[2]

When should the artist paint? When to have the artist paint depends on the church, the speaker, the painters available and the topic. Painting during worship is certainly a good way to start out. Many live platform painters only paint during worship because it often flows with and complements the worship. It takes courage to do any form of platform painting, and being up there with the band generally makes it a more natural and enjoyable experience. It also gives the congregation a chance to become accustomed to the presence of this exciting new element. In addition, some audience members or speakers will find it distracting if the painter continues during the message.

It takes even more courage and a level of technical mastery for a painter to feel comfortable to continue painting during a sermon. The focus that was distributed over the whole worship team now becomes narrowed to the speaker and the painter. But it can be a wonderful experience if the painter's work interprets or complements the message.

Scott Erickson feels that in our current culture, where multiple activities and multiple focuses are common, having a painter creating on stage while someone is speaking is not an issue, especially in congregations who have grown up in a multimedia culture. But this doesn't need to be something that happens every time. In some circumstances, a singular focus on the speaker is going to be the best avenue for learning.

Obviously, some speakers will never be comfortable sharing the stage with someone who is doing something potentially distracting. Others may find it energizing to have someone else partnering with them to convey the message.

Figure 11.3. Scott Erickson paints live while a speaker delivers his message. Photo used with permission of the artist.

What should the artist paint? The main ways a platform painter knows what to paint is by asking God to give him or her a relevant image and by connecting with the speaker about their topic. Then there is the consideration of what might be appropriate in a particular church setting. If a church is new to live art, then it might be better to paint an image that's more easily understood. Consider how people in the back rows will perceive it. At the same time, more artists are finding it's not necessary to paint literal paintings of biblical events or traditional religious symbols for a painting to be "Christian" or used by God. Look at God's imagination in creating the world and its sometimes fantastical plants and animals. He can speak through images that can be interpreted many different ways, creating a personal impact on many different viewers.

Scott Erickson says, "For me, live painting is proclamation . . . just like preaching and music. I see it as the visual word, . . . and it's to be partnered with the verbal word and the musical word. It's our jobs as leaders and curators of those proclamation roles to be listening to the Spirit, . . . and if we do, he will give us direction and tie all those elements together for revelation."[3]

Should the painting be explained? Given that live art is new in most churches, and Christians' general lack of understanding of the arts, I think it's important to take a moment early on in a service to explain why there is a painter on stage and then to explain the meaning of a painting at the end of a service. We want people to feel welcome in our services. If they see something like this and are confused, it can make them feel uncomfortable. If God has given the artist a special word or interpretation, this can be extremely helpful to the congregation in the moment. And it can cause the painting to speak to someone at another level. It's best to limit explanations to two minutes. Any longer and it's possible for an artist to overexplain the painting, the process or the symbolism and actually become irritating. In churches with an active and established arts ministry, explanation may not always be necessary.

What mediums work best? Many platform painters prefer using acrylic paints because they are water-based, dry quickly and have no fumes. Painters who work with large canvases will often use latex paint from the hardware store. Some will use charcoal or chalk, and occasionally I'll see someone use watercolor. A few use oils and have found ways around its challenges.[4]

Most platform artists paint on canvases because that's the standard process, plus a painting on canvas looks nice when it's hung. The drawback is that it can be expensive. One alternative is to buy canvas, build frames, stretch them yourself, then gesso them to take paint, but it's a process. Scott Erickson has found a cheaper and faster way to make his paintings. He paints on wood composite board. "It's super cheap, especially when you're making work big enough for people to see from the back at multiple weekend services. You can put paint down faster and it dries faster too, which is good when you're trying to put layers down. Canvas keeps the paint wet."[5] Scott gets tempered hardboard or masonite from Home Depot or Lowe's in four-by-eight-foot sheets and cuts them down to three feet by four feet. "Three feet by four feet fits in anybody's car, so it's a good size if people are going to take it with them."

Figure 11.4. The Sower. Oil on canvas. Painted live on stage by Bryn Gillette during a service at Walnut Hills Church, CT.

What do we do with the paintings? Generally the artists are considered the owner of the painting unless they have agreed to give it to the church, which may be the case if they have been paid an honorarium or a fee to paint. Imago Dei Church in Portland will sometimes give the painter a choice of receiving an honorarium or selling the painting. Most churches allow the artists to sell their paintings after they create them. Some may even announce beforehand that the painting will be available.

A painting may also be hung somewhere in the church as decoration or a remembrance. For Scott, his paintings often feel to him like modern Eb-enezers. Bryn Gillette sometimes feels like he is making a visual record of what God is doing in the congregation. Or sometimes the word is just for that day and it gets painted over. "Sometimes I'll blog on a particular painting I did during a service and then let the church know the image and story associated with that particular sermon is online so they can link it," Bryn says.[6]

On the other hand, when Tom Clark, a California artist with a penchant for painting barefoot, paints at a church that's not his home church, even though the church keeps the original, Tom retains the image rights. So if they want to make prints and sell them, they go through him.

When Scott Erickson was the artist-in-residence at Ecclesia Church in Houston he would paint during five services a weekend, often five different paintings. Many times people wanted to buy the paintings he created, and he would sell them, often for whatever the person could afford, and put the money in the church's arts fund. This wasn't a requirement of his position, but his preference. He didn't feel he should keep it for himself because he was a paid (part-time) staff member. Since he painted with quick-drying acrylics people could take their painting home with them that day.

When Bryn Gillette paints at Walnut Hill Church he often sells them, but might also give them away: "A lot of times it's clear that the painting was for someone specific and blesses them. Whether they can or can't afford it, a lot of times the painting ends up being a gift for them."[7]

If someone is interested in a painting I have done on stage, I will take time to talk with them while listening for anything the Holy Spirit might say to me. We may discuss what it means to them or what I felt God was saying through it. I may pray for them as God leads. I have a typical amount I ask for paintings of a certain size, so I have that in mind, but if I feel God is telling me to sell it for what they can afford or give it to them, then I'll do that. I may not do it at that moment, but wait until later, making it a special gift and giving me time to photograph and document it or add a few more touches.

I'd recommend that even if an artist likes to give his or her paintings away, they still a set value for them. It's human nature to value something more highly if people know it has a significant worth. A free painting may eventually end up in the trash because the artist didn't assign a monetary value to it.[8]

WHAT THE CHURCH PROVIDES

The platform artist invests significant time and effort into making a painting for a service. Artist materials can be expensive, so the least a church can do is pay for those. This includes canvas, paints and possibly the artist transportation costs. Any church that intends to make live painting a regular part of services should invest in at least one quality easel, preferably two. Make sure you have a clip-on work light and extension cord to go with them. This will save the artist from having to haul too much equipment back and forth. The church should also provide protection for the environment around the painter. One very professional-looking way to do this is to use adhesive-backed film that comes in rolls and covers carpets and hard floor, available at hardware stores. Make sure you use the correct kind for your floor. It's preferable if the facilities staff can talk with the artist beforehand to determine the areas that need to be covered. If you can't find the adhesive-backed plastic film, then use canvas on the floors (plastic sheets without adhesive backing can be slippery) and plastic on walls and tables. Then take care to tape the material down before the painter arrives. (Use painter's tape on walls, testing it first to make sure it doesn't take the finish off.) This puts the burden of protecting the church's investment in carpet, flooring and wall paint on the church and not the artist. And it shows the artist that the church supports them. If the church can't provide the environmental protection, then staff should give the artist access to the sanctuary ahead of time to set up the protection, easel and canvas.

Figure 11.5. An artist paints live during worship at a Midwestern church. Photo: JSM.

The church should also provide a clear line of communication so that the artist knows who to report to, who can share the service themes and timing with them, and how to get access to needed materials.

The Artist's Responsibilities

Generally the artist is responsible for seeking God for an image, preparing spiritually, communicating with staff, making sure adequate protection is in place in the area that they are painting in (whether they or the church provide it), being on time, being available to interact with people about the painting and possibly talk about it from the stage, and cleaning up so that everything they touch is spotless.

A LOOK AT THE PROCESS OF LIVE PLATFORM PAINTING

Preparation. The artist should start with talking to the pastor or speaker about the message of the service—themes and Scriptures—to get a feel for how God is leading. Then artists should have a personal time of prayer to ask God for an image to paint. The artist might picture him or herself as a priest with the privilege of translating God's mes-

> "The mastery of our craft should be paramount, for without it we will never have the language to tell the full story of our lives. To leave our gifts and talents unmastered and undeveloped is to leave unwrapped precious treasures entrusted to us."
>
> Erwin McManus,
> *The Artisan Soul*

sages to the congregation and pray as David did that God would search his or her heart and cleanse it.[9] Scott Erickson asks God the question, "What do you want us to see?" and then waits to see what pictures come.

Next, artists may want to do some research on the image they are getting: print out pictures of similar images for reference, sketch it out and maybe even do some studies with models. Many artists take their research with them for a reference while they paint live. Sometimes I'll even take my smartphone to pull up reference images while I'm painting.

The painter may not fully understand what the image is about, and that's okay. Scott Erickson says, "Sometimes it's an exact translation of the sermon. Sometimes it's complementary. It's not for me, it's for the community gathered . . . although I do get the joy of seeing all the connections."[10]

Preparation will provide a great foundation. But I still hear success stories of people who jump into platform painting with both feet, experience or not. I've seen God impart some ability to a person who has never painted before. In fact, I've asked God to help me paint beyond my ability and had him grant me that. But this should be the exception, not the rule. We wouldn't expect people who have never played an instrument or led worship to get on stage and take a shot at it, believing that God will suddenly make their work good. Art doesn't magically happen, at least not consistently. I tell artists that if God does call you to step into live painting, quickly follow up your experience with practice, study and prayer. He calls us to steward and develop the talents and abilities he entrusts to us. And when we do that he multiplies them.

Execution. Live painting is different from studio painting in that there is a limited time frame to do the work. There will often be a freedom to the painting and less attention to detail. This can be liberating for painters; the work is what it is, and it may be easier than usual to trust God to add his touch to it.

It can be a powerful experience to paint live during a service. If the painter is on the stage, the band may be worshiping in front of her, the congregation worshiping behind her, the music all around her and a strong sense of God's presence bubbling in her chest. "It's incredible worship for me many times," Tom Clark says. "I might be weeping. You feel God working and go, 'Oh wow, this is just too much.'"[11]

The painter's practice, research and knowledge of technique will actually allow him or her to have a more worshipful experience while painting, and to relax and enjoy the process.

Afterward. It is not uncommon to feel drained after painting live. Tom Clark uses his whole body in the painting process, and Scott Erickson would often (understandably) feel like a zombie after painting at five services. Artists are sensitive and can feel things strongly—which is one of our best attributes—but we can also be susceptible to spiritual attack after serving like this. It's important to have people praying for you. Also be intentional about being filled with the Word, getting plenty of meaningful fellowship, eating well and getting plenty of rest.

TIPS AND A PATHWAY FOR BEGINNING PLATFORM PAINTING

If your church is thinking of starting a platform-painting ministry, the rule of thumb is to start small. Invite painters to create live off of the stage in safe environments like an evening prayer session or worship night with a casual atmosphere before having them paint on a Sunday. The painters are not as restricted and can practice in these settings, and the leadership can see them functioning in that gift. This also gives you the opportunity to identify who is ready to move to the next level. Ask those you think have the right mix of skill, character and courage to pray about creating on stage.

If you are an artist with a desire to step into platform painting, again, start small. Start drawing or painting in a notebook at your seat, then ask to paint off stage during a worship night. Begin doing it as personal worship to God, without thinking about an audience. If you haven't done a lot of painting in the past, give yourself time to develop. I know several painters who were invited on stage by their pastors when they were ready. If you know any accomplished platform painters, see if you can meet with them and get some tips or even paint by their side as you start out. Take some painting classes and pick the instructor's brain for techniques on how to paint quickly. Watch some Bob Ross videos.[12] Consider doing plenty of prep work before you paint to smooth out the experience.

Tell your director of arts or worship pastor of your desire to paint on the platform. Ask them what you need to do in order to step into that. If they are not open to this, do not be offended. Ask if you could paint off stage at other casual church events or kids' events.

LIVE ART NOT ON THE PLATFORM

There may be artists in your church who will not ever feel comfortable or skilled enough to paint on the platform but who enjoy worshiping while making art. Art tables (see more on these below) may fulfill their desires, but you could also try making a designated, protected (floor and wall coverings) area where they can set up an easel and paint. This might be out of the line of sight of the congregation, in the back by the art tables or somewhere similar.

TESTIMONIES

Wonderful testimonies are common from congregations that experience live painting. You'll find many on my website,[13] but here's a quick one.

Pastor Bill Johnson tells the story of how they were having a pastors' advance (like a retreat) at Bethel Church in Redding, California, and as is Bethel's custom, artists were painting on the stage during worship. One morning during the service Bill got a call from one of their missions teams in Thailand telling him there had been a magnitude 8.1 earthquake, and a tsunami had formed and was expected to hit their shores in fifteen to twenty minutes, causing catastrophic damage. As the pastors prayed, someone pointed out a painting an artist on stage had done the night before of a large white wall blocking a giant wave. This image immediately sparked faith in the pastors and gave them a specific way to pray, and they did so with power and authority. Shortly, they got a call from the ministry team saying the tsumani had been downgraded and only small waves hit the coast with no significant damage.[14]

ART TABLES

Art tables are different from personal prayer art (see chapter ten) in many ways. They do not focus on person-to-person prayer, ministry or making art for other people. Art tables are simply areas in the sanctuary that are available for personal expression during services.

Concept: Create a space in your sanctuary for visual processors to journal and create small, simple artwork as a personal response to God during the Sunday message. In addition to the standard rows of pews or chairs, a few tables are provided on the side with simple art supplies for anyone to use in the art table area. It's a quiet area to hear and respond to God through color, line and writing.

Background: Art tables began as an experiment when the pastor asked VineArts Boise to create a place in the sanctuary where people could meditate and draw or paint whatever God seemed to be speaking to them during a special New Year's Eve service. The tables were well received by the congregation and soon became a regular addition to Sunday services.

How it works: Occasionally the pastors explain from the pulpit what the art tables are for. Just before every service, a volunteer turns on the table lamps, pours clean water into containers and puts a small stack of watercolor paper on each table. Then the volunteer sits at one of the tables during the service. When the worship music starts, people of different ages, abilities and genders start coming over, and they stay seated at the tables through the whole service. A large church may average a dozen people each service, usually a random cross-section of the congregation: a mix of creatives and regular folks. Most will be adults, with a child or two mixed in. Some artists bring their own pens, pastels, professional markers or watercolors to worship God or illustrate the sermon in their journals. Jessie Nilo often draws or paints her sermon notes using her own watercolor kit. Visual processing helps her grasp God's Word in a deeper way than listening alone.

Details: Consider positioning the tables on the side of the sanctuary that's closest to a water supply. You don't want the art tables to feel relegated to the back of the sanctuary, nor do you want them to feel too scary or prominent to approach in front. You may want to start by putting drop cloths under the tables and then determine if you really need them later.

People working with art supplies during a service can cause unexpected and distracting noises. Here are some ways around that:

- Cover tables with padded outdoor tablecloths. This will eliminate sounds of things being dropped on tables, which happens a lot.

- Dampen the sounds of brushes tapping water containers by lining the tops of the containers with foam strips.

- Cheap, thin paper can make a surprising amount of noise. Stop paper rustling and crinkling sounds by providing nice, thick card stock instead, with a watercolor paper-type texture. If you cut the paper into smaller sheets, there is less tendency to fold it (more noise) because it's so small to begin with.

- Use cushioned sanctuary chairs around the table to avoid noises made by plastic or metal chairs.

Table lamps are necessary if the overhead lights ever dim, but keep water containers a bit separated from the lamps because of electricity. Twisting the lamp's cord around a table leg a few times will ensure nobody trips over it. Also, tape loose cords onto the floor with acid-free gaffer's tape for safety.

Art tables are not a place to discuss things—not even great things like art or ministry. All of these can wait until after the service. Of course, prayer is the one exception; don't stop someone from quietly praying with another person when they feel led.

VineArts has signs on their tables that say, "Art Tables: Please HONOR THE SILENCE as you make things in worship and contemplation." There is also a small sign on their paper basket saying, "Please only use two sheets of paper per person."

Age requirements are necessary for people to process deeply spiritual content. If there are not clear age requirements and the purpose of the art tables is not communicated, it quickly dissolves into a never-ending babysitting job. VineArts now keeps a stack of fliers on each art table that says: "Parents: Please come over and sit with your child at the art tables." They give that slip of paper to any children they find sitting by themselves.[15]

Materials (for 3 art tables):

- three tables with chairs
- three or more padded tablecloths (lined with soft fleece on the underside)
- three table linens that can get marked up, to go over the padding
- three table lamps, extension cords and gaffer's tape
- nice, new Crayola crayons (soft and oil pastels are too messy)
- sharp colored pencils
- one or two watercolor sets per table
- four to five watercolor brushes per table

Figure 11.6. Art table supplies. Photo: VineArts Boise.

- one water container per table, top lined with a silicone or insulation strip (to mute brush tapping)
- three cups lined with cloth to store colored pencils
- three small boxes lined with cloth to store crayons
- three skinny boxes lined with cloth to store watercolor brushes
- one ream of white card stock watercolor-textured paper, pre-cut into halves or fourths (office supply stores charge under two dollars to chop a whole ream of paper at once)
- place the paper, along with erasers and a small pencil sharpener in small baskets (you might attach a small sign to the baskets with, "Please only use two sheets of paper per person.")

The result: An arts leader who regularly hosts art tables says, "Adults sometimes approach me in tears, saying they never knew God cared about their creativity until they discovered our art tables."[16]

At Vineyard Boise some people have come to Christ through connecting with God at the art tables. For many others, expressing themselves creatively during the service has opened up a whole new way to relate to and worship God and has brought new life and excitement to their church experience.

ART IN THE PRAYER ROOM

It really is astounding how much art will be created in a prayer room if people are given permission to express themselves in that way. It can become a beautiful, colorful space where everyone gets to play with art as a mode of prayer.

If you were to visit one of these prayer rooms you'd see all levels of ability in the art, from unencumbered preschool scribblers to adult experimenters to talented professional artists. These prayer room artists have found that "making art as a prayer, rather than trying to make 'good' art, can free us from self-judgments and inhibitions that stop us not only from expressing our own creativity but from entering that loving expansiveness where our hearts can be aware of Holy Presence."[17] (More about prayer rooms in chapter sixteen.)

During my home church's annual Lenten 24/7 fifty days of prayer, it doesn't take long for the art to spill out of the prayer room onto the walls of the sanctuary. The presence of the prayer room encourages a general culture of creativity in the church and creative expressions in prayer.

One artist who had difficulty finding words during a one-hour prayer slot brought some paper-modeling tools into the prayer room and discovered that his time connecting with God was transformed as he made his creativity a prayer. He created a beautiful shadowbox that was later displayed in the church gallery.

Art from the prayer room can make a wonderful gallery exhibit. Gather some of the best or most visceral art at the end of a prayer room season and frame it or

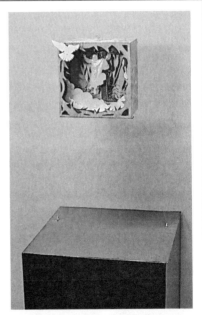

Figure 11.7. Prayer room art by Ian Smith. The box was later displayed suspended in midair using fishing line in order to give it a floating effect. Photo: JSM.

prepare it to be hung in the gallery for a time. You could make the show anonymous, as many of the art pieces will be. Or contact the artists who have signed their work and ask for permission to hang it and if there is a story to go with it. Hanging the work can be very encouraging for the people who made it and can build a sense of community and reverence in the congregation.

If you have scrapbookers in your congregation, you might also talk with them about cataloging all the art that is created in each prayer room season.[18]

LIVE PERFORMANCE

Drama. God is obviously a fan of drama and story, having used it to deliver his messages for thousands of years. He often had his prophets act out what he wanted to convey with performance art. The Jewish festivals and feasts often reenacted significant historical events. Jesus was a master storyteller, and the Gospels are full of drama. It would make sense that God would still use drama to speak to us today. Alison Siewert, in *Drama Team Handbook*, says,

> We need drama. Drama is the compression of human experience into a story we can view on stage. It's a way of communicating what is and has been important, of describing our condition, of making symbols and stories in which people can find meaning, release and hope.
>
> Dramatizing our experience helps us understand the world, see ourselves more clearly and see God as he is. Theater can ask hard questions by pointing to them on the stage, and we can say things in the context of theatrical dialogue that we would struggle to speak in any other context.[19]

Short-form drama has been used extensively in the church in recent years. Churches like Willow Creek, outside of Chicago, pioneered the modern church drama in the eighties. It's become an innovative way to convey truth, set up or illustrate a message or ask a question in many churches. (The pop-up drama in chapter ten is an example of a fairly simple project churches can do.)

Here are a few tips for doing drama in your church:

- Make it short.
- Make it real (authentic).
- Don't offer easy answers.
- Don't be preachy or produce Christian propaganda.

- Grow your drama ministry organically. It is better for it to naturally arise from the passion of people who want to do it than for you to decide to do drama and have to search for the people to pull it off.

For a complete understanding of how to perform short-form drama ministry in your church, I direct you to Alison Siewert's book *Drama Team Handbook*.

Long-form drama has been a part of church worship for centuries. Cantatas, mystery plays, passion plays, and others continue to bring meaning to times and seasons of the Christian calendar. This book does not deal specifically with those expressions, though they can play an important role in a church's creative and spiritual life. Due to space constraints, this book focuses on newer and less developed expressions of the arts in the church, although I will share one interesting example of a contemporary church that has embraced long-form drama.

Many years ago when Grace Community Church in Westfield, Indiana, thought about encouraging the arts in their church, they asked themselves some questions. Jeff Unruh, creative director, says, "We asked who God had given us, what do they do, what dreams do they have?"[20] They discovered they had a number of people in the church who were passionate about drama, so they invited them to create.

> We started by doing a kind of variety show at Christmas, and that evolved into our first show, which was a musical version of *It's a Wonderful Life*. That actually birthed our drama team because of the great experience those people had in the show; we didn't want to lose that. That was back in 2000. Now there are about fifty people involved who meet weekly for relationship building, skill building and show development.[21]

They focus on redemptive stories that people are familiar with, such as *To Kill a Mockingbird* and *Godspell*. Over 6,600 people came to their staging of *The Sound of Music* one weekend. People in the local community know they put on good productions, so they come out to see them. This is a great example of a church bridging event (see chapter seventeen).

Grace's casting calls are often open to the community, so they'll invite actors who aren't believers. "Our desire would be that . . . being in our environment—the conversations we have as a cast, the emphasis and prayer time—they'd say, 'What is this? I've never experienced anything like this before.' We want to draw them into following Jesus."[22]

The leaders also have to deal with issues like language in the plays they put on. They'll pray through what do in these circumstances. In the case of *To Kill a Mockingbird* they created a hybrid word to replace the *N*-word in the play.

> There is a cost to this type of program, financially but also in deciding "does anything go?" Are we compromising something? It's complicated. But it's a risk we feel is worth taking. I feel like it's easy for a church to play it safe.[23]

These plays are bridging events, inviting people who might not be believers into the church building. Unruh says,

> I think this is a way that we can break out of the mold of existing for this time of the week and this group of people. Otherwise it becomes an extremely closed community. In that case you really only attract people who are already like-minded.[24]

Dance. Dance is a powerful, up-and-coming art form in the church, so it is covered in its own chapter, chapter twelve.

Poetry. The Bible is full of poetry. The books of Job and the Song of Solomon are dramatic poetry, the book of Psalms is lyrical, and Ecclesiastes is didactic poetry.[25]

Figure 11.8. Nick Benoit delivers a spoken word performance at Rock Harbor Church, Costa Mesa, CA. Photo used with permission of the artist.

The prophets were also known to use poetry. As far as scholars can tell, Hebrew poetry did not rhyme but had mutually corresponding sentences or clauses. Our modern poetry often rhymes but can also be in the form of non-rhyming free verse or blank verse. But any way you construct it, poetry can convey truths quite effectively. "[Poets] can give you an unusual turn of phrase or image that focuses your attention on something in a completely new way. Commonplace objects and events take on a new meaning when tackled by poets."[26]

A landmark study commissioned by the Poetry Foundation found that the number one benefit of poetry that users cited was "understanding."[27] Poetry helps us understand not only by revealing things in a new light but also by connecting with our feelings. The way the poet captures a feeling in a phrase can add a layer of delicate beauty to a service and evoke a subtle sense of wonder. And we all want more beauty and wonder in our churches.

At one time we had a resident poet at our church who had freedom to share his poems during services. If he felt God leading him, he might write a poem there in the service and, after alerting a leader that he had a poem, share it during worship over instrumental music or as the service concluded. His poems were often free verse and reflected what God was doing in him or in the congregation. They often captured or created a moment and fit with the flow of the Spirit in that service. There is something special that happens in the hearts of a church community when artists step up and do what God is calling them to. Not only does the work offered benefit the community, but watching our brother or sister take a risk encourages us and builds our faith. It becomes a transcendent act.

Maybe there is someone in your congregation who is capable of making this kind of contribution. It could be that they just need encouragement from a leader in order to step out.

Even if a poem isn't original and freshly written it can still have a powerful effect on a congregation. Poems from the ages, especially if read over music during worship, will at the very least add another element of creativity to the service. God can move in surprising ways to touch the congregation, especially if the Holy Spirit is consulted in their selection.

When experimenting with adding poetry into services it is always good to go slowly. Don't expect your poets to go on stage and be instantly brilliant. Help them hone their skills by encouraging them to write and then bring their work to leadership without expectation of presenting it on stage for a time. Have them share their poetry in smaller venues instead of Sunday-morning services at first.

Spoken word. Spoken word is a mixture of poetry and performance, often presented dramatically with emphasis on certain words. Spoken word usually rhymes and has a definite rhythm. It is usually written by the person performing it, who will almost always have it memorized.

As spoken word has gained popularity, some younger congregations and African American churches have begun including it in their services. Done well, it can stir emotions and convey ideas in a visceral manner. Spoken word artist Blair Linne says,

> People are drawn in by the good storytelling as well as rhythm, rhyme, and the performance element so common in the genre. One of the wonderful aspects about using spoken word . . . is that you have the ability to communicate an important message in a catchy rhythmic format, which allows for many words to be expressed in a short amount of time. Also there is what is called the "Slam" element of using powerful punch lines to grab the listener's attention, compelling them to consider the thesis of your poem.[28]

Spoken word can be done in a hip-hop style or more straightforward manner, but it's not uncommon for it to be forceful and lively. It may not fit in some more traditional church cultures, or it could be the thing to shake up a typically more staid church. Of course, make sure all leadership is on board before you try to pull it off! In a more contemporary church setting a well-done performance can connect with tweens to fifty-year-olds and be a catalyst for a church to take more risks with creativity.

Again, go slowly. Let your spoken word poets develop their skills in smaller venues and services before featuring them on a Sunday morning. This is a form of performance, and they need to be prepared for it. Letting them loose before they are ready would be like expecting someone to sing a solo without making sure they are qualified to do it. The result can be embarrassing and awkward. With preparation and God's grace, however, it can be brilliant.

SPECIAL LIVE ART EVENTS

There seem to be primarily two kinds of special art events: those that feature artists that are not a part of your church and those that feature talent from your church.

We'll look at the first kind in chapter nineteen and give a few examples of homegrown events here.

Open mic/variety show. Most arts communities include a variety of artists working in different mediums, some of whom rarely have an opportunity to share their talents at church. Why not give them a chance to express themselves in a special event at the church or even off site?

Think about having an open mic/variety show. It might be a relaxed event where anyone can bring anything to share in five minutes or less, or it might be as organized and polished as having entrants audition and an emcee present. You might come up with a way to build a show around a narrative and incorporate all your artists' talents. It might be a fantastical narrative or a parody or something like a soap opera. Ask God for ideas, use your imagination and have fun. Make it more about the people involved and less about the end product, and it will grow and enrich your arts community and your church.

One note: these types of events generally work better for church community building and community fun than for outreach. For outreach purposes you might consider taking a polished version of your event out to places pre-Christians frequent.

Night of worship and art. Some churches have regular or occasional nights of worship where the focus is on music and song, with little or no spoken message. These evenings can provide the perfect casual atmosphere for artists to experiment with platform painting, spoken word, art tables or many other forms of expression. If your worship leader is willing and you have artists available, why not set an expectation that each event will include art?

A WORD ABOUT HOW TO TREAT ARTISTS

With each of these examples of live art, there is a caution: don't put the product or the program ahead of the people involved. It's important to have someone in place, such as an arts ministry director or staff leader, who can advocate for, lead and minister to the artists. As we've discussed throughout the book, artists can contribute profoundly to the creativity and growth of your church, but they also need community and leadership. With so much to give, they can get burned out or be wounded by a leader who doesn't understand how they work.

Yes, part of artists' learning to step into their role in the church requires them to pursue an increased maturity and a thicker skin. But this is a process, and it takes time, care and understanding.

FINAL WORD

Live art in the church, including live music, can be a vibrant part of any church's creative life. It will create a sense of excitement and immediacy in your congregation and be a catalyst for skill and relationship growth in your arts community. Try to approach live art as more than a novelty, more than something to hook people in. Like any other form of creativity in the church, let the role of live art grow naturally. Don't try to program it or force it, but let it grow out of the passions of your artists and the needs of your church. Live art should be compelling and purposeful, adding something to the spirit and message of the service and the church.

See the online resources and extras for this chapter at JScottMcElroy.com/ CCHandbookextras.

NOTES

[1] Interview with the author, December 2013.

[2] Interview with the author, January 2014.

[3] Interview with the author, November 2013.

[4] See Bryn Gillette's process of painting live with oils and eliminating turpentine fumes in the resources and extras for this chapter.

[5] Interview with the author, November 2013.

[6] Interview with the author, January 2014.

[7] Ibid.

[8] See thoughts on pricing paintings in the resources and extras for this chapter.

[9] See my book *Finding Divine Inspiration* (Shippensburg, PA: Destiny Image, 2008) for more on how to hear God's voice in your creative process.

[10] Interview with the author, November 2013.

[11] Interview with the author, December 2013.

[12] Bob Ross was an American painting instructor who hosted the TV show "The Joy of Painting" on PBS for many years. He painted quickly and with unique flair, using the "wet-on-wet" technique with oil paint. This technique can also be applied to acrylics using a medium additive or water. Purchase Bob Ross videos online or search the Internet for episodes.

[13] See more testimonies in the resources and extras for this chapter.

[14] "We Stilled the Storm," GodSpeak.net, May 3, 2006, www.godspeak.net/mytest/my_9 .html.

[15] For more helpful details on Art Tables see the extras for this chapter at http://JScott McElroy/CCHandbookextras.

[16] Lisa Marten and the VineArts team provided most of the material for the art tables project.

[17] See http://day1.org/1791-art__prayer_workshops.

[18]Some thoughts here were gleaned from www.charlotte24-7.com/prayer/prayer-room/prayer-room-photos.

[19]Alison Siewert and others, *Drama Team Handbook* (Downers Grove, IL: InterVarsity Press, 2003), p. 15.

[20]Interview with the author, October 2013.

[21]Ibid.

[22]Ibid.

[23]Ibid.

[24]Ibid. For more information, contact Allison Cook at alisonc@gracechurchin.org.

[25]M. G. Easton, *Easton's 1897 Bible Dictionary* (Edinburgh: Thomas Nelson, 1897), http://www.ccel.org/e/easton/ebd/ebd/T0002900.html#T0002976.

[26]Ali Luke, "Six Reasons You Should Consider Reading Poetry," DumbLittleMan.com, February 14, 2009, www.dumblittleman.com/2008/02/six-reasons-why-you-should-read-poetry.html.

[27]John Coleman, "The Benefits of Poetry for Professionals," *Harvard Business Review* blog, November 27, 2012, http://blogs.hbr.org/2012/11/the-benefits-of-poetry-for-pro.

[28]Quoted in Matt Smethurst, "The Viral Power of Spoken Word Poetry," thegospelcoalition.org, January 24, 2012, http://thegospelcoalition.org/blogs/tgc/2012/01/24/spoken-word-poetry-slam-and-the-power-of-language.

······ 12 ······

Dance in the Church

*Church was designed by God to be the dance studio. A gathering becomes
a church when a group of Christians together hear the music of heaven's
party and the laughter of God enjoying Himself and begin awkwardly
dancing with the Trinity into the relationships and circumstances
of life in order to bring heaven's way of doing things to earth.*

Larry Crabb Jr.,
Real Church

FOR MANY CHRISTIANS, ESPECIALLY THOSE over thirty, it's much
easier to embrace the poetic metaphor of dance than it is the actual act of
dancing in church. In fact, most church leaders will tell you that dance is the
most difficult of the arts to integrate into the church. It's mentioned many
times as part of worship in the Bible, so it is hard to debate its biblical va-
lidity, but sometimes it's difficult for Christians to get past its essential
fleshly connections. Many of us are just not comfortable with the human
body, largely because our culture is so obsessed with it, but also because of
the faulty belief that only the spirit is good and the body is bad. Some have
the general feeling that dancing is inherently a sinful or impure activity, because that is how our culture tends to use it. Christian men, trying their best
to navigate around lust and pornography, will often feel uncomfortable with
dance and avoid it, at least initially, in the church. If a church can educate its
congregation and get past these things, then there are the problems of
finding people who can dance well and do it with the right amount of
modesty, in the appropriate context. It can all seem like so much work.

Churches might feel it's better to sidestep dance and embrace less problematic areas of the arts.

But what if we are missing out on something wonderful by not exploring dance in our churches? What if there are times when the expression of dance might be the *perfect* thing, the God-ordained thing to take us to another level of worship, truth or understanding? To break through spiritual barriers and proclaim here on the earth what God is doing in the heavens?

Maybe dance is low on your list because you've seen cheesy Christian dance presentations. I've seen my share too. In fact, my inclination was to include a small section on dance in this book. But as I prayed about it, I felt God saying that there is something important here and that we need to look into what he might do in our churches through dance. We may not be comfortable with this expression in the beginning; David's dance made a few people uneasy, but it was right and God loved it (2 Sam 6:20-22). I imagine there's nothing cheesy about the angels' dancing and rejoicing when someone gets saved (Lk 15:10); it's got to be incredibly beautiful and thrilling to see. Couldn't we ask God to give us the creativity to bring that kind of dance into our churches? It doesn't need to be included in every service to be effective. Just finding ways to bring it into special presentations could release a new level of creativity and worship.

If God is nudging your church or someone in it to embrace dance, he can put it together in his perfect timing.

> "Art is born when the temporary touches the eternal."
>
> G. K. Chesterton,
> *Fancies Versus Fads*

Like any other area of arts ministry in the church, significant prayer should go into bringing dance into services. This is especially true because of the difficulties with dance as well as the incredible spiritual potential it has. God can and will use it to break though spiritual barriers and proclaim his truth and glory, but a premature start can set you back and cause consternation in the congregation. Plus, it's a form of spiritual warfare, and Satan would love to find ways to stop it from coming to fruition. So pray thorough what God would like to do with dance in your church, and ask him for wisdom in how you might go about it. Then, look at the artists you have in the church. Is there someone with a passion for dance? If not, then maybe the timing isn't right, or maybe dance really isn't for your congregation. You don't want to force any area of the arts, but to let it grow organically. On the other hand, sometimes you have to follow God's leading and step out in faith.

BENEFITS FOR THE CONGREGATION

Done well and appropriately, dance can have a profound effect on a congregation. Dance and movement stir the air and break up the atmosphere not only in the physical realm but also in the spiritual. Executed with prayer and the guidance of the Holy Spirit, dance will announce God's victory in the spiritual battle going on around us (Eph 6:12). He can also use it to get past our personal barriers. Dance can bypass the intellect so that the beauty and symbolism of the movement touches our hearts in unexpected ways. It can proclaim to the eyes and the spirit God's thoughts and intentions. He will sometimes use it in healing the mind-heart disconnect so many of us suffer from. Dance gets the viewer's blood pumping and engages them more fully in worship. God can reveal the glory of creativity and creation through it. And dance can bring a prayer or the meaning of a song to life.

Saara Taina, dance leader at Bethel Church in Redding, California, and author of *Encountering God Through Dance*, says, "I heard someone say, if you want to make people hungry, eat in front of them! I think the same is true about worship and worship dance."[1] Through our worship, we can stir up hunger in other people's hearts for God and for intimacy with him. Jesus himself said, "And I, when I am lifted up from the earth, will draw all people to myself" (Jn 12:32).[2]

Finding a way to incorporate dance into special events will help welcome God's presence and sustain peace in your congregation. It may very well be the perfect missing element you're looking for in worship.

BENEFITS FOR THE DANCERS

St. Irenaeus is quoted as saying, "The glory of God is man fully alive." It's hard to imagine a person more fully alive than a dancer as their body, mind, heart and spirit all engage in ardently worshiping God and revealing his glory. "Dance . . . is a wonderful gift from God because we can use it to express deep feelings we might not even have words for."[3] There is something that happens when we dance—something that is far more than just the movement of our body or what we can see.

> When someone fully surrenders and allows the Spirit to move them to step out in faith, 1) God takes pleasure in this obedience, 2) dancing and praising the Lord brings freedom to that person, and 3) it causes victory over the enemy's footholds.[4]

After Saul was anointed by Samuel to become king, the prophet told him he would meet a company of prophets on the road who would be dancing, playing music and prophesying. "The Spirit of the LORD will come powerfully upon you, and you will prophesy with them; and you will be changed into a different person" (1 Sam 10:6). Joining with God's Spirit and his prophets in the arts profoundly and immediately changed him.

Nick Benoit, former director of arts at Rock Harbor Church in Costa Mesa, California, loved to see dancers step into their calling when the church did dance presentations, and he recognized the effect it had on them.

> "In as much as Christ's mission was to bring all things into submission to God, and to restore not only humanity, but also the whole creation to its proper purposes, to make straight what is crooked, and to redeem both humanity and the creation from the curse of sin, then herein can be found the possibility for a full and wholesome realization of human artistic activity."
> **John Walford**

> It's not until really the second service that the (new) dancers understand what they're really a part of. Because, in the first service, they got to do this thing that they rehearsed a million times. But when they see the way that God uses it, and see the audience respond to it, they see people raising their hands to commit their lives to Jesus, they see them getting baptized on Easter morning, then they realize that they were a part of the work of God in a more powerful way than they ever understood. Then they recognize the potential (of what they do) as an artist in Christ that absolutely defies their expectations.[5]

CATEGORIES OF DANCE IN THE CHURCH

Among those who practice dance in the church, there are varying opinions about what is appropriate and what the types of dance are called. For our purposes I'll boil the categories down to three main ones—presentational, liturgical and personal—*all* of which involve worship. Obviously a single chapter in this book can't provide an exhaustive study on dance in the church, but I'll try to give you a practical overview.

Presentational. Presentational dance is done in front of the congregation, either as a focal point or as part of a program. It's usually meant to lead others into God's presence with worship.

These dance presentations may include only one dancer or many. The dance may be choreographed to the music, spontaneous and improvised, or

Figure 12.1. Presentational dance during a service at Bethel Church, Redding, CA. Photo: JSM.

a mixture of the two. If it is part of a program, is shouldn't be distracting but instead be complementary to the worship.

Saara Taina also considers a dancer's skill level in dance technique when choosing them for a worship dance team.

We don't just randomly take people without any experience or training to sing or play instruments on a musical worship team. The same common sense should be used when choosing dancers. I don't mean that all dancers should be professional prima ballerinas. They should, however, know how to use their bodies in a way that's not distracting but rather turns everyone's focus to God.[6]

Having said this, I want to add that we should never put God in a box. Lack of training does not hinder God from using anyone. He wants us to release freedom through movement in worship. I have seen God powerfully use little kids who danced spontaneously. That is why it's so important that we constantly stay sensitive to the Holy Spirit and do everything in love.[7]

Saara suggests that the presentational dance team communicate clearly with the worship leader and musicians before the service on practical things like the space used and timing, and that there be a designated dance leader who can direct the group and handle changes. If it's possible to practice with the worship team, that is optimal. Saara also advises that the dance team spend plenty of time dancing together in worship while not in a public service.

> The more the dancers dance together, the better they learn each other's "movement language." This makes improvising in worship as a team much easier because the dancers don't need to pay so much attention to each other anymore. . . .
>
> When our dance team danced in worship services, we used both choreographed and improvised dance. Sometimes we chose one of the dancers to lead the improvised parts and we followed the leader, either mimicking the leader's moves all at the same time or doing the movements in cannon or just picking up similar shapes and rhythms. For all of this to work, it requires both practice and the anointing of the Holy Spirit.[8]

Liturgical. Liturgical dance is often done in front of the congregation but isn't seen as presentational because it does not stand outside of the liturgy. Rather, it is "liturgical" because it expresses what is happening during worship.[9] It is generally choreographed and often literal in its interpretation of the messages in the songs.

Jane Wellford, professor of dance at Elon University, says,

> Liturgical dance is dance or gesture used within worship for the glory of God. It is intended to add depth and dimension to the spoken or sung text and/or music within the worship service by use of visual display, as enhancement for the words as they come to life through movement and drama. Liturgical dance may also be performed in silence without the use of words or music. Many of the movements choreographed are literal and easily understood.[10]

Liturgical dance is not currently officially sanctioned by the Catholic

Church, so you'll rarely see it there. It is, however, practiced by a number of mainline Protestant denominations.

Personal. Personal dance is practiced as personal worship or expression, not in front of the congregation, although it may drift into the view of the congregation. It's generally done to the side or in the back of the sanctuary in a church. Certainly personal worship is going on in presentational or liturgical dancing, but it's still presentational if it's performed in front of the congregation and not part of the liturgy.

Personal dance is a good place to start in bringing dance into a church. You might invite people to practice personal dance one Sunday a month in the back of the room or to the side and see how it goes. You'll want to communicate guidelines somewhere in writing, such as designated areas where dancing is welcomed and what conduct should be—things like, "Be aware of others as you dance; be free but don't disrupt the service; children should be supervised"—all communicated in a loving and welcoming tone.

If your church wants to start a dance ministry or incorporate dance into services but there is no dance leader emerging, making room for personal dance could enable an untapped person to find their passion and step into their calling. If you feel God nudging you to create a designated area for personal dance, watch and see who embraces it over time, then pray about approaching them to see if they may be inclined to be discipled as a dance leader.

Seven Types of Dance

All of these types of dance can be practiced in each of the categories of presentational, liturgical and personal dance.

- *Praise.* A dance of thanksgiving or giving glory to God by using your movements to testify to others of his goodness (Ps 149:3-4).

- *Worship.* An intimate dance between you and the Lord. Movements are personal, reverent and yielding (Rom 12:1).

- *Celebration.* This might be an exciting victory dance that celebrates anything from God's grace to answered prayers to financial blessing—whatever God has placed on your heart to celebrate (see Zeph 3:17 Jerusalem Bible).

- *Warfare.* A forceful dance full of confidence and boldness that speaks to your circumstance or to Satan with directness (see Ps 149; Rom 16:20).

Many of us know that dance can bring a lot of destruction when misused by the enemy, but we don't always seem to realize how much havoc Holy Spirit-filled dance can cause in the camps of the enemy.[11]

- *Travail.* A dance of encouragement, either to yourself or to others, in times of discouragement or trouble. It can also express sorrow or injustice. It reaches to God for help, guidance, direction and relief (see Ezek 6:11).

- *Prophetic.* A God-given dance that ministers to a person's heart for a specific word of encouragement, direction or confirmation (Ex 15:19-21; 1 Sam 10:5-7; 18:7).

- *Intercessory.* A dance of prayer and intercession for others.

  There is no formula for how to dance prayers. The main thing is to be led by the Holy Spirit. We often started by putting the person who was receiving prayer in the middle of the room. We prayed for a while . . . then started dancing in front of or around that person who was receiving ministry. Sometimes all the dancers danced at the same time or sometimes we took turns, depending on how the Holy Spirit was leading in each situation. Sometimes we used music in the background and sometimes we danced in silence. Often God also gave us dancers scripture verses and words of encouragement and we got to share the prophetic words after we had danced.[12]

> "The Lord wants double edged artistry, praising God's name and setting things straight."
> Calvin Seerveld, *Bearing Fresh Olive Leaves*

STYLES OF DANCE USED IN THE CHURCH

Typical worship dance may incorporate many styles of dance, mixing them together. Here are a few of the styles that might be included.

Contemporary dance. Contemporary dance is the most common form of dance in the church. Although originally informed by and borrowing from classical, modern and jazz styles, it has since come to incorporate elements from many styles of dance.

Ballet. Ballet has been globally influential and has defined the foundational techniques used in many other dance genres. It requires years of training to learn and master, and much practice to retain proficiency. Due to the skill required, churches may not have members who can do pure ballet. Traveling Christian dance companies will often offer ballet as a part of their repertoire.[13]

Figure 12.2. AnnaRose Girvin presents contemporary dance worship during a service at Indy Vineyard Church. Photo: Hailee McElroy.

Hip-hop dance. Hip-hop dance refers to street dance styles primarily performed to hip-hop music or that have evolved as part of that culture. It includes a wide range of styles, primarily breaking, locking and popping, which were created in the 1970s and made popular by dance crews in the United States.[14]

> "Art tends to show rather than tell. It allows people the opportunity to experience another way of seeing the world. But if we are not there, people are denied the opportunity of encountering our perspective."
>
> Steve Turner, *Imagine: A Vision for the Arts*

EXAMPLES OF CHURCHES WITH DANCE MINISTRIES

Rock Harbor. Because of its location in LA, where dancers tend to migrate, and its proximity to Disneyland, where many dancers are employed, Rock Harbor Church finds that dance is actually their most common art form. This ten-thousand-member church often includes large groups of contemporary dancers (as many as one hundred) in its Christmas and Easter services. Their dancers range from professional to beginner. The dancers are also regularly requested to perform during Sunday services and have the freedom to suggest dance presentations and ideas for upcoming services if they get inspired. Their focus is currently on presentational dance, though they would like to encourage more personal praise dance.[15]

Bethel. Bethel Church in Redding, California, also embraces dance during services, occasionally with presentational dance on the platform but regularly

Figure 12.3. Dancers perform at Rock Harbor Church, Fullerton, CA. Photo: rockharbor.org.

with personal expressions off the stage. Bethel operates with an atmosphere of freedom during worship, so many people will often be worshiping with dance together. The music is loud and the atmosphere ecstatic, so the expression fits. Even though this is often done toward the front of the auditorium next to the stage, it's still considered personal dance because the dancers are not presenting to the congregation.

Practical Tips

How often to do dance in services. Saara Taina thinks that less can be more with presentational dance. For instance, if a large number of dancers are pre-

senting, she suggests there should be less movement and more synchroni-
zation so that the dance doesn't look haphazard or too busy. In fact, she suggests having periods of time during worship when there is no movement or
dance going on.

> Of course, the key for breakthrough is not the amount of dance but being
> sensitive to the Holy Spirit.
>
> When a new dance group is just starting, it is easy to get so excited about
> this new ministry that the dancers want to dance all the time. However, in
> corporate worship settings, dance tends to work in a similar way to a solo
> instrument. It's lovely to hear the oboe or flute being played once in a while,
> but if it's being played nonstop though the whole worship time, it can get a
> bit annoying.[16]

Randall Flinn, founder of the professional dance troupe Ad Deum Dance
Company, goes a bit further in saying that he believes that dance shouldn't be
used in every service.

> Since dance is a physically viewed expression, it becomes a focal point
> when it's on the platform. Even though, quite clearly, you can offer worship
> and communicate spiritual truth, it . . . has the potential to actually become
> a distraction if not treated with great sensitivity.[17]

Starting slow. What goals do you want to reach with dance in your church?
Set guidelines so that people who are doing any type of dance in your church
know what the expectations are and what the boundaries are.

Start by incorporating dance during a special service like Christmas Eve or
Easter and working it into a musical presentation or dramatic presentation.

Explain what you are doing. It's helpful, especially when you first start
presenting dance in services, to assist the audience in understanding what
they are seeing by offering some explanation. When Colin Harbinson was
traveling and leading Christian drama and dance programs, he would have the
choreographer say:

> "In this dance production you are going to see tonight, things will be re-
> peated in different places. We call them dance motifs. And we want to show
> you a few of these, so that when you see them, you'll understand what's
> happening." They would take a few moments and bring a dancer out and

say, "Here is what we are trying to express when you see the dancer doing this type of movement or this sequence." So then when the show starts you can see people smiling and saying, "Yeah, I'm actually beginning to understand this now." I think we have to do that in all sorts of different ways, because people need to be educated about how to understand art.[18]

Dress. God has given us freedom, but we shouldn't let our freedom become a stumbling block to others. We're called to serve one another in love (Gal 5:13-14). Randall Flinn says,

Cover yourself up completely even though you may believe you have a lot more liberty than that. Let go of your rights and your entitlement and go and serve. If that means you have a turtleneck and a long skirt on, and under that skirt you have another skirt and you're going to burn up when you're dancing, then that's what you do.[19]

Figure 12.4. Dancers dress modestly during worship at The Well Christian Community, Livermore, CA. Photo: The photography ministry of The Well Christian Community.

A helpful dance document available on Docstoc.com offers a few additional guidelines:

- Don't let anything you wear (or don't wear) draw the attention of the audience away from the message of the song. Jewelry should not be flashy.

- Be modest! Ministry is not your time to be cute or handsome and noticed.

- Keep all of your "bouncy elements" wrapped up, tied down, and/or pulled in.[20]

Dancers' preparation. Prayer and fasting prepares the heart for worship and ministry by focusing our attention on God. Internalize the message of the music if you are dancing to a particular piece; listen to it over and over. Spend plenty of time practicing—alone, with the dance group and with the worship band, if possible. Record a video of yourself and your team so you can study it and improve.

> "Our story begins with a kiss, mouth to mouth resuscitation (Gen 2:7), God pressing against us. We begin when God exhales and we inhale. This is the level of intimacy and synchronicity for which we were always intended. While all creation declares the glory of God, we humans bear the image of God. The more clearly we reflect the divine, the more we reflect that which is good and beautiful and true."
> Erwin McManus, *The Artisan Soul*

FINAL THOUGHTS

Although it may not fully happen here on this earth, I look forward to a time when, as Christians, we are mature and healthy enough to see the whole person and not be overwhelmed with the fear of objectifying other people's bodies, so that we can appreciate the expressions that they want to offer God through them.

I'll end this chapter with a very insightful thought from Heidi Leyshon, a dance leader from the United Kingdom:

> It has been amazing watching my daughter learn to move. It is programmed in her to dance when she's excited, to jump when she's happy, and to clap her hands when she's pleased. Somewhere along the way we lose this, we start to worry about what others think. God calls us back to child-like faith, when his face is all we see (Mark 10:15).[21]

See the online resources and extras for this chapter at JScottMcElroy.com/ CCHandbookextras.

NOTES

[1]Saara Taina, *Encountering God Through Dance* (Shippensburg, PA: Destiny Image, 2008), p. 74.
[2]Ibid., p. 75.
[3]Ibid., pp. 68-69.

[4]"The History of Dance in the Church," www.refinedundignified.com/the-history-of
-dance-in-the-church.html#_ftn49.

[5]Interview with the author, January 2014.

[6]Taina, *Encountering God Through Dance*, p. 130.

[7]Ibid., pp. 131-32.

[8]Ibid., pp. 135-36.

[9]Thomas Kane, "Types of Liturgical Dance" in *Introducing Dance in Christian Worship*, rev.
ed., ed. Ronald Gagne, Thomas Kane, Robert VerEecke, Donna La Rue and Gloria
Weyman, (Portland, OR: Pastoral Press, 1999), pp. 99-110.

[10]"What Is Liturgical Dance?" March 9, 2011, available at www.docstoc.com/docs/73274517/
What-is-liturgical-dance.

[11]Taina, *Encountering God Through Dance*, p. 55.

[12]Ibid., pp. 99-100.

[13]See "Ballet," *Wikipedia*, http://en.wikipedia.org/wiki/Ballet.

[14]"Hip-Hop Dance," *Wikipedia*, http://en.wikipedia.org/wiki/Hip-hop_dance.

[15]See Rock Harbor's wonderful Easter dance and spoken word presentation, "Cataclysm,"
which included over one hundred dancers, at www.rockharbor.org/media/rh-films/
cataclysm-easter-2012.

[16]Taina, *Encountering God Through Dance*, pp. 137-38.

[17]Randall Flinn, interview with the author, January 2014.

[18]Colin Harbinson, interview with the author, January 2014.

[19]Flinn interview.

[20]"What Is Liturgical Dance?"

[21]Heidi Leyshon, quoted in John Shorb, "Worshipping God Through Dance: A Q&A with
Heidi Leyshon," Church Health Reader, http://chreader.org/contentpage.aspx?resource_
id=699.

13

Media, Film and Video

He told stories of fish to fishermen, stories of farming to
farmers, stories relating to business and finance to businessmen,
and stories of weddings, family relationships and other general tales
to the crowds. He did this so everyone could connect truth to something
concrete in their daily experience. And God does the same thing
for you and me today. He uses words to paint pictures of
what he desires on the screen of our imagination.

JOHN BEVERE,
Extraordinary

IN THE TWENTY-FIRST CENTURY, visual media, like music, has become a common element of many church experiences. Whether projecting song lyrics over a pleasant background, an announcement video, movie clips, a closer view of the speaker on the stage or PowerPoint, visual technology has been a boon to creative communication in churches. It's enabled us to bring ideas to life on the screen and speak the language of our visual culture.

Since the use of visual media is already fairly common in churches, I'll simply offer a few tips and advice from professionals in this chapter. By now you've surmised that this book is not a technical manual, so I'll leave the considerable technical discussions to the experts, who are easily found in the online resources and extras for this chapter. In fact, this area of creativity in the church is always evolving, and the online resources and extras will link you to online communities and sites where the discussion of media, film and video can be continued.

Jason Moore of Midnight Oil Productions cautions that churches should not use media, film and video "just because we can," because we have the technology.[1] Using too many of these things can seem inauthentic and showy. Use them purposefully, remembering that less is often more.

PROJECTED SONG LYRICS AND GRAPHICS

When choosing text fonts for song lyrics, announcements and PowerPoint text, generally go with clean and simple over fancy or funny. No Comic Sans. In these applications you need the words and message to be clearly communicated.

With series or sermon title graphics, experiment more with fonts and create a design that conveys the attitude of the message; then use the same graphics throughout all your material and promotion. Create a cohesive look to tie all mentions and information on the series or sermon together. Some churches have been able to develop design teams that take every element of a series, service and message into account and develop a plan to make it all work together to achieve the maximum effect of cohesively communicating a truth.[2]

BACKGROUNDS

Backgrounds for text and graphics can vary from static and simple to moving and highly stylized. They provide an opportunity to add creativity to the service, but they shouldn't be so creative that they overwhelm the message of the text and graphics. A general rule of thumb is to stay away from cheesy, overly sentimental or overused images. Generally only a minimal amount of movement or motion is needed. Jason Moore believes that backgrounds can sometimes include a metaphor or image that will be used in the series or message. Reaffirming and redeeming that metaphor or image in the series and message can cause it to take on a new meaning for viewers and continually point them to the gospel when they see it in the culture.[3]

ENVIRONMENTAL PROJECTION

Environmental projection consists of using two or more projectors to create large images on the walls of the church, expanding far beyond what typical screen projection does. This can generate a feeling of being in another time or place, helping viewers enter into a story or message. It can be a very effective way to make creative use of the large blank walls of many churches. Note, however, that environmental projection is intended to be background support for the series, service or message, and overuse of it, as with any of the creative elements in this book, can dull its effect or become a distraction.

See more about this innovative use of technology in the online resources and extras for this chapter.

Figure 13.1. An example of the effect of environmental projection. EP system design and photo from VisualWorshiper.com.

FILM AND VIDEO

It's been said that cinema is the most powerful of all the modern art forms because it encompasses so many of them. Story, performance, sound, symbol, color and lighting all come together to make an impact on the viewer. In the case of a movie theater showing, you get something that is rare with art; a viewer sitting in a dark room, completely focused on the art form in front of them.

With advances in digital photography, the line between film and video has become blurred. Where once film was the only choice for a professional cinematic look, now digital video can not only mimic but, some say, surpass the clarity and depth of film. For the purposes of this book, we will put film and video together and instead differentiate between short-form and long-form film and video.

We'll start with short form, since that is most commonly used in churches.

Short-form film and video. The use of this medium has exploded across the world since the arrival of YouTube in 2005. At the time of this writing, YouTube reaches more US adults ages eighteen to thirty-four than any cable network. Over six billion hours of video are watched each month on YouTube—that's almost an hour for every person on earth. And one hundred hours of video are uploaded to YouTube every minute.[4] This really is astounding. But YouTube isn't the only video site. There are hundreds of others, including Christian sites like GodTube and GodVine.

With so many of us watching and enjoying short-form film and video, it makes sense for the church to be able to speak this language as well. In fact, many churches have been incorporating video in announcements and services since well before YouTube was born. The main areas short-form film and video have been used in the church are

- during announcements
- as a sermon illustration or enhancement
- to record services or events

Twenty years ago, you needed hundreds of thousands of dollars of equipment to produce a video. Today, the same video can be made at a fraction of the cost. Some churches are blessed to have their own video team that's able to produce pieces that spice up the announcements. This can be fun for the congregation, especially if the video features recognized members of the staff or congregation or talented actors and is produced well. And some churches have the staff, talent and equipment to create more complicated pieces that speak specifically to a sermon's message.

If you don't have a team for these types of production but want to expand into this area, there are a number of things you can do.

- Consider having a professional volunteer produce videos for the announcements or for sermon illustrations. This is a lot of work for a volunteer, so take that into account and let them set what they can do.
- Look for students in your church who are taking classes in film and video or who have some experience with it. Make sure they work closely with the staff member in charge of services. Frame it as an experiment that may or may not work.
- The simplest solution to having regular access to high-quality sermon illustrations is to utilize online content sites that are searchable by topic and price. See the links in the online resources and extras for this chapter for

more. The material on these sites is original, so the licensing is covered by the provider. You shouldn't need a special license to show it.

Movie clips. As mentioned in chapter nine, movie clips can be a powerful way to convey or illustrate a message and connect with popular culture, as well as tap into the emotional connection people may have with those films. Note, however, that there are some dangers to using clips from movies in a service. You have to be careful not to use these elements for shock value. They can elicit strong emotions, disturb people, or distract them and make them think about the rest of the movie instead of listening to the message. So if you are using a strong movie clip, make sure your follow-up and message are equally strong. And, of course, don't just plug something in because it seems to fit. Again, ask the Holy Spirit for his guidance in what clips to use or whether to include these things in a particular message at all.

> "Art is mainly about wrestling with material reality, not striving after a spiritual ideal."
>
> Jeremy Begbie, *Voicing Creation's Praise,* paraphrasing Calvin Seerveld

There are a number of websites where you can download short scenes from movies; the choices are plentiful and the topics are searchable.[5] Wingclips .com, in particular, edits the movies to hone in on the desired point, adjusts the picture for church screens and, most importantly, obtains the licensing required to show movie clips in your church.

The importance of licensing. It used to be that if you wanted to use a movie clip for a sermon, you'd just play it from the DVD or video. Did you know that is actually illegal? According to the Copyright Act of 1976, pre-recorded videocassettes and DVDs are for home use only, unless you have permission to show them in public. Without permission, you may be in violation of the copyright act and subject to substantial penalties. Viewing outside the home requires a license granting specific authorization. This is the case for each organization that uses videos—even for nonprofit groups, even if admission is not being charged and even though the video has been purchased. This is what that warning we never read at the beginning of every movie states.[6]

Sites like WingClips handle the licensing for you. But you can also purchase a low-cost, yearly, renewable license from Christian Video Licensing International (CVLI). This license is similar to the Christian Copyright Licensing International (CCLI) license many churches purchase to cover the use of music and song lyrics. The CVLI license is a partnership between the Motion Picture Licensing Corporation and the local church that allows the church to show rented or purchased videos publicly during worship. (Nurseries, day cares, youth meetings, retreats and so on may be added as a rider to the license for a small additional charge.) As with the CCLI music license, it is always the responsibility of the church to be certain the video is from one of the many motion picture studios or producers represented by CVLI. You can check this on the list provided with the license when it is issued. The cost of the license is based on church attendance and on which license you purchase.[7]

If you want to show a YouTube video, you would need to contact the producer of it to get permission. If that video contains any copyrighted material that the producer does not own, like music, you would need to obtain permission for that as well.

Producing short-form film and video. If you are considering producing your own original short-form film or video, there are a few things you can do to make it look more professional. Emmy Award–winning producer Eric Poland

> "What is Christian in art does not lie in the theme but in the spirit of it, in its wisdom and the understanding of reality it reflects."
>
> Hans Rookmaaker, Modern Art and the Death of Culture

of Poland Productions offers tips that are available in the online resources and extras for this chapter.

Long-form film and video. Through much of the one-hundred-year history of moving pictures—and certainly the last fifty years—the Christian perspective has often been lacking. One church decided to do something about it.

After reading an article by George Barna indicating the influence of the church in the culture had fallen behind the influence of sports, education, movies, media and music, Sherwood Baptist Church in Albany, Georgia decided they would try to change that. A 2001 staff retreat to Disney World challenged them to think about being as committed to excellence in the church as Disney is with its theme parks and creativity. They developed a sports park, Sherwood Christian Academy and Sherwood Pictures.

Since 2003 Sherwood has produced a number of feature films through the efforts of filmmakers, former Sherwood staffers Alex and Steven Kendrick, and hundreds of volunteer cast and crew members from the church. Their accomplishments have been somewhat miraculous. The films—

including *Flywheel, Facing the Giants, Fireproof* and *Courageous*—have reached millions of people with a Christian message and grossed millions of dollars over their budgets, in spite of mixed reviews. *Facing the Giants* was made for $100,000 and grossed $10 million, and *Fireproof* was made for $500,000 and grossed $33 million in theaters and $25 million on DVD. They accomplished all this as a ministry of the church, with mostly volunteer cast and crew, and support of church members, although they did, wisely, hire professional cinematographers.

This is an example of a church looking at who they had in the congregation—in this case two staff members, the Kendrick brothers, in whom God had developed the desire to make films since they were kids—and how the church could get behind them to meet a need in the culture. At the same time, the church was able to carry out one of their missions: to influence the culture.

This required risk on the part of the leadership of the church. Making films calls for lots of investment and lots of courage. It is a long process that can cost thousands or millions of dollars, depending on your vision. The key to Sherwood's success, though, was prayer. The staff and filmmakers prayed through every step of the process. And then prayed some more.

Darren Wilson of Wanderlust Productions is a filmmaker who makes movies not as an outreach of a church but as a ministry *to* churches and Christians. His documentaries, including *Finger of God, Furious Love, Father of Lights* and *Holy Ghost,* have inspired millions of Christians in their faith. Darren's film *Father of Lights* recorded a number of divine appointments and miraculous healings as they happened, and *Holy Ghost* was shot entirely through prayer, with the locations set by the leading of the Holy Spirit. Darren and his team are working on new distribution models to bring more movies to churches, enabling them to become partners and hubs for presenting quality, God-honoring films in communities.

Certainly there are more Christians producing long-form film and video today than there were twenty or even ten years ago. There is ongoing concern about the quality of Christian filmmaking, with laments about poor scripts and wooden acting. It will get better, but I appreciate the effort of anyone willing to take the risk to make a movie that honors God. He wants to speak through this powerful medium, in the cinema, in our homes and in our churches.

There seems to be no end to the hunger for stories brought to life on film and video, as evidenced by the growing number of ways to access them—DVD, online, on tablets or phones, in the theater—and box office records continually being broken. How can churches and congregations speak into this? Most churches don't have the means or opportunity to produce movies, but they can support Christian brothers and sisters who do. Filmmakers who follow Christ often walk a very difficult road. And you can get involved with organizations like the Hollywood Prayer Network, support filmmakers' crowd-funding campaigns, and invest your time and effort promoting worthwhile films. And pray. Pray that the God who gave us the capacity for imagination would find more willing collaborators to divinely inspire.

See the online resources and extras for this chapter at JScottMcElroy.com/ CCHandbookextras.

NOTES

[1] Interview with the author, February 2014. See also http://MidnightOilProductions.com.

[2] For links to free and custom church graphics and more information on design teams, see the online resources and extras for this chapter.

[3] See other resources for backgrounds available in the online resources and extras for this chapter.

[4] See www.youtube.com/yt/press/statistics.html.

[5] See the online resources and extras for this chapter for these.

[6] Josh Reeves, "Why Should I Use WingClips™ Instead of Playing a DVD That I Rented or Purchased?" http://help.wingclips.com/entries/102663-Why-should-I-use-WingClips -instead-of-playing-a-DVD-that-I-rented-or-purchased.

[7] The information in this paragraph comes from Dean MacIntyre, "Using Movies, Videos, and Film Clips in Worship," UMC.org, www.gbod.org/lead-your-church/contem porary/resource/using-movies-videos-and-film-clips-in-worship.

14

Creating an Art Studio and Workshops to Foster Creativity

There is not a square inch in the whole domain of
our human existence over which Christ, who is
sovereign over all, does not cry, "Mine!"

ABRAHAM KUYPER,
"Sphere Sovereignty," in
Abraham Kuyper: A Centennial Reader

ONE OF THE BEST WAYS TO NURTURE CREATIVITY in the church and your creative community is to provide opportunities for hands-on art making. Open studio time and arts workshops are excellent venues for this to happen. And, as you'll see, your church doesn't need a permanent, dedicated art studio to make these things work.

Most of the arts ministries featured in this chapter find that their ministry activities change often. As they seek God for what he desires to do in and through the ministry, every year looks a little different. Still, some form of the activities in this section remains a part of what these ministries do, because artists need to create. And there is joy when they can do it together.

ART STUDIO TIME

Most churches don't have a dedicated art studio space, but that doesn't need to stop you from offering regular studio time. You can easily set up a temporary studio in any available, well-lit space. The caveat would be that, as I've mentioned before, your cleanup of the space is impeccable. In many cases the arts ministry will need to earn trust with leadership and facilities management at this most basic level of cleanup before it can move on to bigger and better things.

Infused Arts. Infused Arts at Living Word Community Church in York, Pennsylvania, sets up and takes down their studio space every week. They do this in a multipurpose area that also houses a coffee bar and an art gallery. Director of arts deAnn Roe keeps all the studio supplies—tablecloths, paintbrushes, paints, paper and other things they need—in a big, heavy rolling cabinet. On studio night they'll roll out the cabinet and get the supplies ready. The facilities staff will set up the tables in the area of the room with linoleum floors and put them away later. When the studio time is over volunteers help clean everything up and put the room in order.

Figure 14.1. Artists experiment with watercolor during the Infused Arts open studio. Photo: deAnn Roe.

The Infused studio takes place the first four Thursdays of every other month. Each month has a different theme or topic. "We recently explored the life of artist Jackson Pollack, then we invited people to experience painting like Pollock," deAnn Roe says. "I got these 30" by 30" canvases for ten dollars, which workshop attendees paid for. Everyone donated old house paint that was sitting in their basement. Of course we had plastic all over the floor for protection. It was a lot of fun! We later hung those canvases in the gallery."[1] Infused workshops are often about learning a new technique or studying an artist and creating work in that style. This is a good time for people who haven't come to the studio before to join in, try something new and get a chance to play with art.

Every fifth Thursday of a month Infused will host an open studio where anyone can do anything they want with any medium they want. They do charge five dollars on open studio night, which includes the use of the art supplies and an 11-by-14-inch canvas panel. deAnn provides creative prompts for those who are interested, but most people come in having an idea of what they want to create or what medium they want to try.

deAnn says, "I cannot tell you how many times people walk into the studio and say something like, 'I don't know why I'm here. I'm not an artist.' My heart is to encourage them, to help them embrace their creativity, no matter their current level, and then discover how God will speak to them and through them while in the creating."

Express Your Faith. Express Your Faith arts ministry has a similar situation in that space is at such a premium in their church that they have to share their studio space with many other ministries. The arts ministry does have a desk in this room, as well as storage cabinets filled with art supplies, a workbench, several tables, a sink and a potter's wheel. They schedule room use through the church computer system to keep things straight.

Express Your Faith hosts open studio in this space on the first and third Thursdays of every month. Adults and high school students can come in and bring their own supplies or use provided supplies for a freewill offering. They also have a service component where sometimes they'll make things in the studio that will be taken to places like nursing homes or given to missions partners in the United States and abroad.

Ex Creatis. Ex Creatis, the arts initiative at Saddleback Church, currently has open studio, which they call Open Create, on Fridays and Saturdays from 1 p.m. to 6 p.m. They can accommodate the typical studio arts, plus woodworking, graphic design, photography and more.

They also hold their weekly Arts Collective on Thursday nights. This includes discussion, a group art project or workshop and two hours of Open Create, ending at midnight. The collective is a rich time for artists to personally connect with each other, ask questions and discuss integrating their faith with their art. Basic tools are provided by the arts ministry, and they cultivate a supportive atmosphere where artists can be in community but work on their own projects.

Ex Creatis initially started with an open creative space and then shifted to a weekly program in order to be more intentional about fostering creative and spiritual growth. Altogether they have eighteen hours every week during which artists can use the studio space. See their website at ExCreatis.com.

VineArts. The VineArts studio is always humming with activity. They've occupied a 40' by 40' space since 2009, filling it with everything an art studio and arts ministry home base would need. In addition to weekly arts affinity group meetings, workshops, book studies and more, they offer weekly open studio time to anyone in the church and community who would like to come. "We've seen numerous lives transformed through our open studio," Jessie Nilo says. "Many have found a church home after coming through the art studio door."

Figure 14.2. Artists enjoying the VineArts studio. Photo: Sherri Coffield.

VineArts open studio operates the first Wednesday of the month from 3:00 to 8:30 p.m. and Saturdays from 1:00 to 6:00 p.m. They average twenty-five to thirty guests at those times, many of whom are from outside the church. They suggest a small donation for materials and supplies from those who use the studio.

With this volume of people coming through, and the frequency of open studio times, VineArts decided to put a volunteer studio host/monitor system in place. Several people take turns hosting open studio once a month. These "monitor ministers" help people feel comfortable in the studio, answer questions and serve their needs.

WORKSHOPS AND CLASSES

Visual Voice. Visual Voice arts ministry is known for their arts classes and workshops. You may find one operating any night of the week. "Some of the classes are specifically skill-based, like drawing or painting or sculpture, etc.," says director of arts Ann Williams.

> Then we also have two classes that are designed to just get artists together. One is a discovery class, a sort of "how does this art-and-God-thing work" where we use Janice Elsheimer's *The Creative Call* book. The other class is called Creative Connections. It has five major components: Bible study, arts history, arts skill building, a professional practices component and a conceptual component, where we'll take an entire class period and go through Scripture and conceptually come up with a piece of art and sketch it out. This process helps people think through the journey of creating a piece of artwork.
>
> Classes are usually held on a weeknight, often on Wednesdays because that's when the youth clubs go on, enabling parents to attend and have childcare covered. We also have a photography group that meets every Monday.[2]

(For more on the photography group, see "Affinity Groups" in chapter six.)

Express Your Faith. Express Your Faith arts ministry is quite busy most weeks, hosting workshops and planning sessions. They have an art workshop the second Saturday morning of each month that usually runs two hours long and is based on themes. There are three different activities, all with a biblical meaning.

A volunteer leadership team plans "Rekindle Your Creative Spirit" events, which serve to create arts community and bring more awareness to volunteer opportunities in the arts ministry. Featured artists will share about their process and how their faith influences their art. Then everyone will go to the art studio and spend time working with whatever art form was talked about. They'll have refreshments and sign-up opportunities. The following Monday will be a full evening of "how-to" with that art form, whether it's pottery, collage, painting, sculpture or whatever. Then the artists who presented and instructed will have the opportunity to display their own artwork in the church gallery.

VineArts. Jessie Nilo, VineArts director, says, "Over the past several years, long before we had a studio, we hosted low-cost art workshops in the gym or the lobby or chapel, wherever we could. We hosted workshops on drawing and communication, Chinese brush painting, copyright basics, acrylics, clay, plein air, photography, Adobe Photoshop, printmaking, and many more."

VineArts provides their workshops at a low cost but asks attendees to pay beforehand so that they can cover supplies and the instructor's honorarium.

Many of the topics covered in this book could be turned into workshops. You might page back through the chapters and see if anything seems to stand out as a workshop idea you'd like to try. For more workshop ideas, see the resources and extras for this chapter.

Figure 14.3. A painting workshop led by Dean Estes at VineArts Boise. Photo: Jessie Nilo.

Through hands-on studio time, workshops and classes on the arts, artists in your church can contribute and develop their talents, the level of creativity in the church can be raised, and individuals and ministries in the church will benefit from the sharing of creative gifts. And people who would never have entered a church will be drawn in by the power of arts.

See the online resources and extras for this chapter at JScottMcElroy.com/ CCHandbookextras.

Notes

[1] From an interview with the author, December 2013.
[2] From an interview with the author, November 2013.

15

Displaying Art in Your Church

In the Gallery and the Sanctuary

Yes, would to God that I could persuade the rich and the mighty
that they would permit the whole Bible to be painted on houses, on the inside
and the outside, so that all can see it. That would be a Christian work. . . .
If it is not a sin but good to have the image of Christ in my heart,
why should it be a sin to have it in my eyes?

MARTIN LUTHER,
Luther's Works, vol. 40, Church and Ministry II

Art enables us to find ourselves and lose ourselves at the same time.

THOMAS MERTON,
No Man Is an Island

IN 1719, A YOUNG COUNT NAMED Nikolaus von Zinzendorf visited an art gallery in Denmark where he viewed a painting—Domenico Feti's *Ecce Homo*—that showed Christ dying on the cross, with this inscription: "All this I did for you. What are you doing for me?"[1] Zinzendorf had been a Christian for nearly a decade but had been groomed to live the life of a nobleman. When he saw this painting, the Holy Spirit spoke to him, and his life's call became instantly clear. He would give everything to live solely for Christ. Zinzendorf went on to become the founder of two major moves of God that continue to this day: the Moravian missionary movement—the forerunner to the modern missions initiatives—and a 24/7 prayer meeting that ran continuously for one hundred years and sparked the modern 24/7 prayer movement.[2]

What if God used art displayed in your church to inspire the next Zinzendorf?

In addition to providing a unique way for God to speak to individuals in your congregation, adding works of art can be one of the most effective ways to beautify a church building and foster an attitude of creativity in a space quickly, even inexpensively. Art can open spiritual eyes and enrich the church experience for everyone, even those who don't realize it is having that effect. If artists from the congregation contribute to it, gallery art or sanctuary art can help further a sense of community in the church. To see the work of our brothers and sisters on display adds meaning to the artwork, their gifts edify the community, and we sense that the body is working as it should. Art displayed in a gallery or the sanctuary beckons to the artists on the fringes. Some will begin to desire that their work might too be shown one day. A gallery asks viewers to slow down and observe how God might be speaking (a reminder we all need), and it educates us in how to view art for edification. Spiritual experiences are also broadened for children who grow up with works of art in their church. They'll come to understand that God speaks to them not only through his Word but also through art, and in fact, if they learn to listen, he can speak through anything.

So the reasons to make room for works of art in your church building are numerous. The next question is how to go about it. First, we'll look at how to start and maintain a gallery.

> "Unless a kingdom perspective of the lordship of Christ over every area of life permeates our understanding of mission, we will continue to express a reduced story that communicates a reduced vision of the overarching work of God to restore all of creation (the cosmos) back to his original intention."
> **Redeeming the Arts**

LAUNCHING AN ART GALLERY IN YOUR CHURCH

The first thing you'll want to do in establishing an art gallery is decide what the overall purpose of the gallery space will be. Everything else will flow out of that. If you have an established arts ministry, this will be a good discussion for your arts team. This question applies to whether your gallery is on church property or off-site.

Possible reasons for having a gallery are listed below. You might discover that your gallery eventually fulfills most of this list, but it's good to focus your

Figure 15.1. The VineArts gallery. Photo: Jessie Nilo.

vision and then keep it focused, because plenty of distractions will come along.

(Note: You'll also find the following questions in a printable form in the online resources and extras for this chapter.) Rank these purposes 1 through 4 in order of importance to you, with 1 being the most important purpose, 2 being a secondary purpose, and 3 and 4 being side effects that you'd like to see. You might also place an X next to any goals you would *not* want to see fulfilled in this gallery.

____ Showcasing artistic excellence

____ Facilitating art sales

____ Communicating truth/biblical principles

____ Leading the congregation in worship and adoration of God through visual art

____ Communicating prophecy through visual art

____ Educating the congregation on the value and purpose of art

____ Equipping artists in the church to become a voice in today's culture

____ Being a voice for social critique/commentary/awareness of issues

____ Giving new artists a chance to display their artwork

____ Giving established artists a place to connect at our church

____ Other: _____

Thinking through this list will also be helpful if there is not yet an arts ministry in your church and you'd like to make the gallery a first step.

It's important to consider these questions because a gallery is a public forum that touches many areas of the church. Pastoral staff may have to explain or defend it from time to time, facilities staff will have to work with and around it, and design/aesthetics staff will want to have a say in its planning. You want to make sure these folks understand what you hope to do from the start. The more you think through the process, the better you'll be able to communicate the vision and execution.

To that end, here are a number of other questions to consider.[3] You'll find advice about many of them later in the chapter.

Who will be exhibited in this gallery? (Check all that will apply)
____ By invitation only (Who will do the inviting? _____
_____)
____ Professional artists
____ Emerging artists
____ Amateur artists/non-artists

Will there be an entry fee?
____ Entry fee: $_____
____ No entry fee

Affiliation of artists
____ Members of our church
____ Members of other churches
____ People who don't attend any church
____ Christians
____ Non-Christians

Age
____ Ages allowed to exhibit: _____ and up
____ No age requirement

What criteria will you use to determine whether something is accepted into your gallery?
____ Artistic excellence (Is the technical skill and overall effect of the work important?)
____ Theological accuracy (Are the theological statements or ideas portrayed in the work important?)
____ Presentation (Will you have set standards of professionalism in framing, presentation and so on to ensure a uniformly excellent display? Or

would more casual display formats be acceptable in your church culture?)

____ Thematic content (Are you concerned with a cohesive, unified presentation in the gallery visually, content-wise or both?)

____ Other_____

Will your gallery have a jury? If so, who will be on it? (See more about jurying below.)

Will you award "Best of Show" or other titles that recognize select artists?

How strict will you need to be about art entry deadlines?

Will you offer a preparation gathering for artists to create or prepare their entries for the gallery?

If the art is available for sale, how will you handle that?

What percentage of your viewers will likely be members of your church?

_____

What percentage of your viewers will likely be unchurched people? _____

Will the public have direct access to the gallery? If so, what will the hours be?

Is the gallery in a high-traffic area or relatively secluded? Will people go out of their way to see the art? If so, you might be able to exhibit edgier themes.

Will children be exposed to your exhibits during a typical week?

Will your gallery announce themed exhibits? If so, how often?

If so, what kind of themes do you imagine you'll have?

If so, who will determine the upcoming gallery themes? How will they decide?

Will you provide those who are rejected with future opportunities to grow artistically?

Who is interested in helping install and administer? You don't want the work to fall to a single person.

What kinds of lighting and hanging systems will you have?

How will you handle insurance and/or releases?

When you have a good idea of what a gallery in your church might look like, write everything out in the form of a vision/mission statement. You might refer to the arts ministry vision worksheet in the online resources and extras for this chapter. (You can also see an example of a VineArts gallery invitation

Figure 15.2. Sojourn Community Church Gallery, Louisville, KY. Artwork by Gene Schmidt.

and release form there.) Then take that vision to the pastoral leaders who oversee the arts ministry to determine the next steps.

PRACTICAL ADVICE

VineArts Boise has maintained a gallery in their church since 2004. It hangs in the main hallway outside of the sanctuary and gets a lot of traffic. The church has invested in gallery lighting and a professional hanging system to give the space a professional appearance and make the art easy to install and view.

The following practical observations were contributed by Jessie Nilo, director of VineArts, except where noted.

Operation.

The VineArts Gallery Team consists of a gallery coordinator and a gallery installation team of volunteers (about 8-10 people), who our coordinator recruits, trains and oversees. This team installs our exhibits in the gallery four times per year, always on a Saturday. The gallery coordinator also solidifies ideas for themes that our team has prayed about corporately, and she helps to make the final timeframes alongside the VineArts director. She also schedules the dates for receptions, and she takes down the artwork when exhibits are over.

Our gallery is housed inside our church, so it remains open during church office hours (Tuesday through Friday 9-5), Sunday mornings and any time the church is open for evening events. Our facilities staff turn on our track lighting as part of their routine for opening and closing the church.

Themes.

Our exhibits run quarterly and have a theme that's announced ahead of time, allowing the artists to dig deep into a concept. We find that the more specific the theme, the more original their ideas.

Location. Chris Brewer, in his excellent article "How to Start an Art Gallery in Your Church," advises:

> Work together with the folks [on the pastoral, facilities, and design teams] to select a gallery space that suits your purpose. If you're showing work tied to the preaching schedule or liturgical calendar you might consider selecting a space in the main foyer or sanctuary. If you're looking to show work as a sort of community engagement/outreach you'll want to be sure that the space is accessible and provides room for proper viewing and reflection.[4]

Some questions you'll want to ask in regard to where to put the gallery include:

How many pieces will you be showing? What type of works will you be showing (e.g., paintings, sculpture, etc.)? Will the work be concentrated in one area or scattered throughout the church? Do you want the work in high or low traffic areas? Do the works need to be in a secure area or protected with a security hanger?[5]

"The idea that art is a luxury that we can well live without is refuted by the enormous amount of art made in WW II concentration camps and by the poorest peoples of the world as well as by the irresistible need of believers of all kinds in all parts of the world to create art. . . . Art is a necessity for our humanity and an expression that human beings are made in the image of God, who is Creator and Ultimate Artist."

Laurel Gasque, ArtWay.eu

JURYING

Someone at some point has to make a decision about what works will be shown in a church gallery. This may be a single person who is capable of curating a show and who can take into consideration all the possible scenarios for how the art might be perceived and received. Or the decision about what is accepted in the gallery may be up to a jury of staff members or artists.

There are some differences between an art gallery in a church building and a gallery anywhere else. Possibly the biggest difference is in the audience. A gallery in a church has a specific audience to be faithful to—an audience that sometimes has strong opinions about what is appropriate and what is not. For many viewers, the specific works shown in the church gallery can be a direct reflection on the church. A non-church gallery doesn't have as many concerns or people to answer to and can often take more risks in what they show.

Similarly, the function of a jury in a church setting and a jury in association with any other gallery can be a bit different. Typically a jury in a non-church gallery setting serves the purpose of making sure the artworks accepted meet certain criteria, often with excellence being the greatest concern. A church gallery, on the other hand, often must balance excellence with accessible content and presentation. And the church gallery jury must be concerned about how the audience will perceive the art. Will the art be suitable for families and children to view? Will the pastor get complaints? Will it introduce confusion or unorthodox views of God?

THE JURYING PROCESS

Jessie talks about jurying the gallery:

> Have your pastors/staff or other leaders in your community be part of the jury for your art exhibits. Having them on the jury will allow your pastor(s) and leaders early access to the artwork, giving them the opportunity to learn about the art, ask questions and get behind your artists before the exhibit is displayed to the public.
>
> You might also invite art professionals from the community to be on the jury, though I suggest keeping your arts ministry leaders off of it. This will allow your art leaders to enter their own artwork into exhibits without a conflict of interest.
>
> We usually invite several church staff members to be on the jury and ask each juror to look at about five art submissions closely. They carefully read the artist statements as well. If the jurors have any questions, concerns or red flags,

they mark the artwork or statement with a Post-it explaining their concern.

Then our worship and senior pastor will come in and review all the pieces marked with Post-its. The gallery coordinator and I have a great time answering conceptual questions and explaining artistic approaches to our pastors. In most cases the flagged work is allowed into the show. Our pastors make the final decision on anything questionable.

If the artwork is rejected, our gallery coordinator calls the artist and encourages him or her while gently explaining the reason for the decision. We reserve the right to edit artist statements for "length, content, or clarity," so we may remove distracting rabbit-trails or theological inconsistencies.

POSSIBLE REASONS FOR REJECTING ARTWORK

You can (and should) set standards for what is and isn't selected in your gallery. Every gallery needs to determine what is visually acceptable for their location and culture. Generally this should be decided on a case-by-case basis, so if you make guidelines, keep them flexible. A few issues you should have basic philosophies about are:

- nudity and partial nudity
- violence
- profanity
- depiction of sin/darkness
- unconventional depiction of holy relics, God or people

OBJECTIONABLE/CONTROVERSIAL ARTWORK

If you notice a submission that is potentially controversial or inflammatory in any conceivable way, you should pursue your senior pastor's total support for the particular artwork before launching it into public scrutiny. Tell them they must be able to "go to bat" for the artwork, no matter who complains about it. If your pastors can't guarantee their full support for the piece, it shouldn't be accepted into that particular venue. You will get complaints about it, and after the third or fourth complaint, your pastors may decide to remove the art early, which would be absolutely devastating to any artist.

Figure 15.3. The lobby gallery at Imago Dei, Portland, showing the work of artist-in-residence Justin Hall. Photo: Erik Railton.

Here are a few of the more potentially controversial submissions we've received:

- A twelve-year-old boy's drawing of an angel smoking a cigarette while guarding the artist's teenage brother (The boy's older brother had died in an accident that summer and he was processing his death.)
- A blood-soaked rag in a frame
- A self-portrait of a nude dancer, which was largely abstracted and integrated with the background
- A drawing of a nude pregnant woman in a bathtub, the water obscuring most but not all of her body
- A collage that included a small, realistic nude angel
- A color photograph showing a sixteen-year-old girl with her back to the camera. She was wearing no shirt and had large handprints covering her exposed back to convey the atrocities of human trafficking.

Keep in mind that our gallery is in a main hallway inside our church.

After deliberation, all but the last two pieces were accepted and backed up by our elders and pastors.

- The collage that included a tiny nude angel was rejected for too much exposure, because everything on the figure was exposed.

- The photograph of the sixteen-year-old girl was rejected at the advice of our youth pastor, who was concerned for her protection as she's a minor. We contacted the girl and commended her concept and artistic excellence, and she shared with us that her mother had taken the picture. The girl was very understanding about the decision and seemed encouraged by our genuine appreciation of her work.

Each work of art is unique and so is the culture of your church. Additionally, seasons change. What might have offended your congregation a year ago may not offend them after further education, discussion and exposure to art. Conversely, if your church is recovering from a recent artistic disaster, they may be overly touchy or suspicious for a while.[6]

GALLERY EXAMPLES

Below are four more examples of galleries operating in churches. Some exist in the best location in their building that you could ask for, or have state-of-the-art lighting or hanging systems, or feature only professional-quality art. Others use natural or ambient light, hang art from a nail on the wall or will accept art from any skill level. Whether you want to showcase excellent art that glorifies God or to provide a place for artists in the community to reveal their talents, whether you can find the money to provide an infrastructure for a first-class gallery or are working with nails, baling wire and worksite lights, a gallery is worth doing.

Visual Voice galleries. Visual Voice (the arts ministry at Lincoln Berean Church in Lincoln, Nebraska) operates five gallery spaces throughout the multiple levels of their building. The auditorium is on the first level where people come in, so they have designated that to be a photography gallery since this art form is very visually accessible and easily understood. The work in this gallery centers around a theme that the church is currently focusing on. The gallery on the next level up is also theme-based but populated with paintings. The artists process what they are learning and what God is speaking to them through that theme. Both of those galleries are semi-permanent, which means the work will be up for one to three years depending on what the theme is and how the church is working through it.

The other three are considered rotating galleries. They might show anything from solo artists to a themed show to art from a local gallery or university to work from a retirement community.

Figure 15.4. A display in one of five galleries at Lincoln Berean Church. Photo: Carolyn Miller.

Visual Voice arts ministry director Ann Williams oversees the galleries, but the hands-on work is handled by a dedicated team of eight or nine artists who install and administer the galleries. In addition, the photography forum administers the photography gallery.

Westminster Gallery and Archive. Westminster Presbyterian Church in Minneapolis really has an optimal gallery situation. With over one hundred thirty feet of wall space for hanging art and a museum-quality lighting system (with motion sensors that dim automatically), all situated in a commons area that is a center for many activities, the art is professionally presented to a large audience. A custom-designed archive with workroom, office, library and storage rooms supports the church's growing art collection. Full-time curator and archivist Dr. Rodney Allen Schwartz runs it all.

How did all this come about? Dr. Schwartz says, "It happened in a place like Westminster because we're a downtown, mainline Presbyterian church that has always been an engaged, well-educated and very curious congregation that tends to make things happen. So it was a magical set of circumstances happening in the right place."[7]

It also helps to have leadership who appreciate and see the value of the arts. Their minister's wife is an artist, and both of them were raised in families that valued the arts.

The gallery is in a common area furnished with comfortable chairs and lower tables. It's one of the places coffee is served on Sundays and a gathering area for a lot of church events. There might typically be about thirty art pieces hanging and also display cases containing three-dimensional work.

The gallery is run like a museum, following standard museum practices. They use a particular framer who works with acid-free archival materials and UV-filtered glass. While they are not a sales gallery, they do purchase art and have over 200 works in their permanent collection. They'll have about six exhibitions a year and generally work two years ahead. Dr. Schwartz will often go to local artists and borrow a couple of pieces that get woven into a theme with a lot of other artists, although they have presented solo shows by major artists like John August Swanson and He Qi.

Schwartz believes that encountering the building's aesthetics helps people

Figure 15.5. The Westminster gallery. Photo: Rodney Schwartz.

prepare for worship experiences. The exhibitions are supplemental to worship, for example, during Lent when the gallery is filled with Lenten and Easter art. It becomes a place for meditation and contemplation. Dr. Schwartz says, "It's very typical during those times that I will come in and find people in the gallery in tears."

Dr. Schwartz didn't start out full-time when the gallery first opened. He was the architect of the gallery from the beginning, working as a volunteer, and as his responsibilities increased, his position transitioned to full-time. His salary and benefits come from the church's general operating budget, just like any other employee. There is a modest budget for supplies and materials to support the expenses of the gallery and archive. Some major expenses like the addition of the lighting system and the ongoing acquisition of art are often supported by individual donors. "It's all supported by gift money. We don't ever take money out of the offering plate to buy art," Schwartz says.

Ex Creatis Gallery. The gallery at Saddleback Church is a beautiful space with reclaimed barn wood walls laid horizontally, professional lighting and hanging systems, and easy accessibility at one of the church's entrances. They present a new show every two to three months, sometimes tied in with a sermon series. The art is of the highest quality, setting a tone of excellence and creativity as you enter the church.

The gallery is run by the Ex Creatis arts ministry team, led by Jason Leith, and the arts ministry falls under the leadership of Saddleback's First Impressions team, who are responsible for the aesthetics of the church. Accordingly, the gallery is designed to fulfill the

Figure 15.6. The Saddleback Church gallery.
Photo: Eric Cardella.

goals of creating a general environment of creativity and the arts on campus, and also to build community. When visitors encounter the gallery as they enter the church, the hope is that the space feels creative, artistic and inviting in a fresh, new way. And the gallery can be an entry point for people who have been looking for a place to express their creativity in community. See more about the Ex Creatis arts community in chapter three.

Fireside Gallery. Woodman Valley Chapel's Fireside Gallery began showing artwork in 2000. They installed track lighting for the art fairly early on, but it wasn't until recently that they got a professional track hanging system. This saves the work of patching and repainting the walls after every show.

The gallery can accommodate eighty to one hundred pieces of art and ex-

GALLERY OPENINGS

If your church has any kind of an art gallery, a gallery opening or reception can be a fun community-building event. There can be lots of opportunity for creativity at such an event; you could make it black tie and glitzy, build it around an unusual theme, have a costume party, do a benefit for a local charity or just invite people to come by after Sunday services. An opening will build camaraderie in your creative community (especially if you plan and execute it together), pique interest in the arts among your congregation, draw fringe artists in to an easy-access event and could generate funds for your artists through sales or your ministry through donations or tickets.

It makes sense to present an opening when you hang paintings for a new show, but if your gallery is permanent, you might construct a reception around one of the paintings or invite one of the artists to make an appearance.

You might consider tying your openings or receptions into things that are happening in the community, such as First Friday if your church is in an area around other galleries. Or tie in with church events like an evening service or worship night. Another option is to hold a casual reception immediately following morning services if you want to expose people who wouldn't normally make a special trip out to experience art.

Try to have snack food or hors d'oeuvres and live music. Maybe have poetry or book-excerpt readings. If you make them fun and classy, these events will become an anticipated special event for your growing creative church.

tends all along a large outer hallway that surrounds the auditorium, so you pass through it to get to the service. That means families encounter it weekly, so the art must be accessible for all ages.

Shows in the gallery typically run for eight weeks. Curator Cindy West Limbrick says, "Sometimes we invite artists personally to exhibit, and other times I'll do an open call for entries and have one day where any artist can bring three or four art pieces in. We jury it, and if they are accepted we schedule them for a year to a year and a half out, so they know, say from May to June next year they'll be exhibiting at Woodman."[8]

They also host the annual show of the Colorado Art Guild, a mainstream organization, providing a unique opportunity to invite non-Christian artists into the church. I talk more about that in chapter seventeen.

INCLUSIVENESS

Here is another thought from Jessie Nilo on how VineArts invites the community to participate in their gallery.

> Our church is situated in the poorest area of Boise; we have a heart for the poor and less fortunate, the "less skilled." Our gallery reflects that heart, and we like to offer everyone the chance to express themselves in our exhibits. To me it represents both the non-exclusive love that our church wants to offer and the leveling effect of grace.
>
> So we accept art from amateurs and professionals, all within the chosen theme of the exhibit.
>
> Our choice to display amateur and professional works side by side has had an interesting effect on the quality of the shows, sort of in the same way the more talented singers in the congregation during worship create a better singing experience for everyone around them. And this practice of acceptance has also had the unexpected effect of providing a humility check for the professionals. I've seen artists' initial defensiveness give way to an excitement for inclusiveness, a mysterious change I never anticipated.
>
> And I've seen the overall quality our exhibits skyrocket over the years. Often amateurs come into our community, show in our gallery and become more serious about their art, and at the same time become closer to the One who is infinitely creative and artistic.
>
> We believe that art shouldn't just be practiced by the talented and edu-

cated, but that artistic expression is an area where everyone should get to play. And we want to celebrate that.

Of course, I'm not advocating our gallery approach for everyone. Each church's culture and purpose within the body of Christ is different. Many churches are called to a higher level of professionalism in their galleries. But I encourage you to spend some time praying about the issue of inclusiveness in your art ministries and see if God might give you some creative ways to address it.[9]

DISPLAYING ART IN THE SANCTUARY

Throughout the history of the church, the way that art has been displayed in sanctuaries has ranged widely: from the staggering beauty of marble sculptures and enormous stained glass windows in one-thousand-year-old cathedrals, to small Protestant churches that display a single cross; from Orthodox basilicas filled with icons and gold-leaf splendor, to bare-walled evangelical megachurches that project images on screens during worship.

With the growing interest in embracing creativity in churches, there is renewed focus on what it looks like to bring visual art into the sanctuary. Art displayed in the church sanctuary can have an ongoing, profound effect on the congregation. It can help a church remember who they are as a people or envision who they might become. It can set the tone for worship. It can turn the eye and the heart toward higher truths. It can completely change the atmosphere, or it can gently and consistently whisper revelation. Art in the sanctuary can help define the personality of a church for decades. There are a number of things to consider when thinking about introducing visual art into the sanctuary.

Art that works in the gallery may not be appropriate in the sanctuary. A gallery is generally a place where the congregation passes through and occasionally meditates, so the work shown there may have a wider subject matter and a different purpose (such as to express the artists' thoughts, or challenge the viewer) than what you'd see in the sanctuary. Art in the sanctuary will usually have some meaning for the whole congregation, and will serve to assist or lead them into worship and/or reaffirm the mission and vision of the church. Gallery art may be displayed for months, while sanctuary art may be part of the worship experience for years. Whereas a jury may choose the art for the gallery, ensuring that it doesn't conflict with the standards and culture of the church, it's advisable to have a dedicated committee decide on the art for the sanctuary. This committee might work with the artist on the design and meaning of the sanctuary art and represent the concerns of the congregation and staff. A gallery jurying process could take an hour or two, whereas a sanctuary art committee's process could take months.

What should the art look like? Any style of art that your congregation and staff are comfortable with could work. Something to consider is the scale of the work: Is it large enough to be seen by

> "For an artisan, the completed work becomes a prayer to which the community can say 'Amen.'"
>
> Mary Lou Weaver, "Artisans and Worship," *Liturgy* 5:4 (Spring 1986)

people in the back rows? Does it look too large or small for the space? You can address these questions before the art is made by modeling it on a computer or in 3D.

It's advisable to stay away from designing works of art are that are too instructive or didactic, because visual art is often stronger and more authentic when it retains an element of mystery.

Where does the art fit? Some liturgical churches have specific places where art should go, while evangelical churches may not. As a rule of thumb, the art shouldn't overwhelm or distract from worship wherever it is positioned,

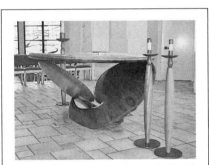

Figure 15.7. The altar at Holy Trinity Parish in El Dorado Hills, CA, designed by Roger Hogan Studios. Photo: JSM.

but instead add to the experience. Some questions to ask include: Is the style, color scheme and execution complementary to the overall aesthetic of the church? How will it be displayed? Will it be lit?[10]

Will the art be permanent or temporary? Art that is permanent or at least semi-permanent will help define the personality and identity of the church. Temporary art that is displayed for a season or a short time can refresh or put an exclamation point on that identity. For specific examples and pictures, see the online resources and extras for this chapter.

Examples of permanent art include:

- Pulpit
- Baptismal
- Altar
- Visual art altarpieces or stations
- Windows
- Architecture and embellishments
- Floor designs
- Vestments and paraments (although they rotate for the seasons)[11]
- Sculpture and 3D artwork
- Banners
- Symbols
- Furnishings

Temporary art could integrate with or illustrate the seasons of the Christian calendar, a sermon series, a season of growth or learning the congregation is going through, an event, or anything else in the life of the congregation that could benefit from artistic elucidation. Examples of temporary art:

- Seasonal or series-specific banners
- Seasonal or series-specific artwork and art pieces
- Seasonal or series-specific textile decorations
- Seasonal or series-specific 3D installations[12]
- Sacred space experiences[13]
- Curated worship experiences[14]
- Special exhibits
- Environmental projection[15]
- Screen-projected images
- Prayer room art[16]
- Art that was produced live during a service[17]

Who should make the art? Generally, art that is displayed in the sanctuary should be of highest quality and not amateurish or technically undeveloped, so permanent art especially should be made by skilled artisans. This artwork will become part of the worship experience for your community for quite a while, so it needs to be well thought out and well-executed to stand the test of time. The artists will need to be able to work with the arts committee to present a vision, budget, timelines, material choices and logistics for display.

The art may be made by artists from within your congregation, which can add an extra element of connection for the church, or by commissioned outside artists. If the latter is the case, see the thoughts in chapter eighteen on working with outside artists.

The exceptions to the rule of having skilled artisans create the work would be in the case of a display that features the work of children or amateurs, or the creation of participatory artwork that involves the congregation making the art piece under the guidance of a professional artist. This kind of collaborative art made by members of the congregation can be especially powerful in that it really is "the work of the people," made by and for the community. An-

Figure 15.8. Artist Richard Cummings created this cross from discarded objects, transforming them as an act of redemption. During Holy Week a tattered torso is placed upon the cross as a wonderfully disconcerting reminder of Christ's incarnation and sacrifice. The torso is removed before Easter Sunday and the cross remains bare for the rest of the year. (RichardWCummings.com)

other notable exception is in visual art that is painted or made live during a service by someone with skill, then temporarily displayed in the sanctuary afterward. In this case, the design wouldn't usually go through an arts committee, but would be fairly spontaneous and simple.

Should the art be explained? I do believe that art in the sanctuary should be explained. Having the artist talk about their process and the meaning of the work when it is initially installed will help in the congregation's connection to it. Posting an explanation somewhere in the sanctuary or in the bulletin will be helpful and welcoming to new visitors who want to know more about it.

Some questions to ask about potential sanctuary art:

- What does the visual art say about your church community? Does it welcome people? Does it confuse them?

- Is it theologically accurate?

- Is it high quality?

- Does it work aesthetically and fit with the overall design of the church sanctuary?

- Is it communal in nature rather than personal or esoteric?

- Does it evoke rather than instruct? (You want it to evoke, involve, refresh or engage the worshiper.)

- Does it have courage and integrity?

- Is it imaginative?[18]

Done with care, displaying art can be a very effective and efficient way to encourage a creative atmosphere in your church. Through including the visual arts in a church gallery or in the sanctuary, the congregation will be inspired, challenged and led into worship. The church building will be beautified and refreshed, and the artists in the congregation will have opportunities to share their talents and insights for the benefit of their brothers and sisters in Christ. Art displayed in your church can contribute uniquely to building up the body of Christ.

See the online resources and extras for this chapter at JScottMcElroy.com/ CCHandbookextras.

NOTES

[1]See http://usrenewal.squarespace.com/home/having-a-child-like-heart-for-jesus-this -christmas-part-2.html.

[2]Claude Hickman, "Count Zinzendorf," *HistoryMakers*, www.historymakers.info /inspirational-christians/count-zinzendorf.html.

[3]Most of these questions were provided by Jessie Nilo of VineArts.

[4]Chris Brewer, "How to Start an Art Gallery in Your Church," http://gospelthroughshared experience.blogspot.com/2012/03/how-to-start-arts-ministry-at-your.html.

[5]Ibid.

[6]Written contribution from Jessie Nilo.

[7]From an interview with the author, November 2013.

[8]From an interview with the author, January 2014.

[9]For additional information and ideas on church art galleries, I recommend these resources: the VineArts gallery brochure and release form in the resources and extras section for this chapter; the book *Seeing the Unseen: Launching and Managing a Church Gallery,* published by CIVA and available at CIVA.org; the article "How to Start an Art Gallery in Your Church" at TheNewR.org.

[10]For a discussion on hanging and installing art in the sanctuary, see the online resources and extras for this chapter.

[11]Vestments are the liturgical garments worn by clergy, servers and choir. Paraments are liturgical hangings that add depth and beauty to sanctuary appointments: pulpit falls and Bible markers, burse and veil sets, frontals and super-frontals, etc. Vestments and paraments are generally designed to be used over and over again, but are changed according to the season.

[12]Any sort of three-dimensional or interactive artwork that is not permanent. These could include sculptures in wood, metal, stone, clay or any other medium.

[13]See chapter sixteen.

[14]See chapter sixteen.

[15]See chapter thirteen.

[16]See chapter eleven.

[17]See chapter eleven.

[18]Several of these questions are adapted from Nancy Chinn's thoughts in "Evaluating Visual Art for Worship" in *Music and the Arts in Christian Worship, Complete Library of Christian Worship IV,* ed. Robert Webber (Nashville, TN: Star Song, 1994), pp. 646-48.

Creating Sacred
Space Experiences

As I listen to the silence, I learn that my feelings about art and my feelings
about the Creator of the Universe are inseparable. To try to talk about
art and about Christianity is for me one and the same thing,
and it means attempting to share the meaning of my life,
what gives it, for me, its tragedy and its glory.

MADELEINE L'ENGLE,
Walking on Water

And I heard a loud voice from the throne saying, "Look!
God's dwelling place is now among the people, and he will dwell
with them. They will be his people, and God himself
will be with them and be their God."

REVELATION 21:3

WE KNOW THAT EVERY BELIEVER is a sacred space, since God's Spirit
lives in each of us (1 Cor 6:19-20). And, in fact, all space could be called sacred
space, since God is omnipresent. Both of these thoughts provide rich material
on which to meditate.

But God in his wisdom also provided us less ethereal models of sacred
space, places where people could encounter his presence and escape distractions. He designed the tabernacle and temples of the Old Testament for these

purposes, and allowed a manifestation of his presence to be contained in their small, enclosed spaces.

It is so merciful that he did that—the multiple-omni God making himself fit in a small room in order to be more accessible to his people. It was a clear foreshadowing of the incarnation and of the unfathomable privilege we now have through that to be his personal temple.

But before the incarnation, the sacred space of the tabernacle and temple provided a place of focus for the community, so that the people could reach out to God *together,* thus strengthening their bonds and their faith. The visuals and rituals they encountered there stayed with them so that when they were not together, they could recall what they had experienced and feel connected and encouraged. Because they were prone to forget, as we are. We often need to be reminded who we are in relation to God—beloved, accepted children, temples of God. So God created tangible, material sacred spaces, not for his benefit but for ours.

In the past several decades some streams of Christianity have focused only on the sacred space inside us, often with an emphasis on the space above the shoulders. The spaces of the world around us and the churches we meet in

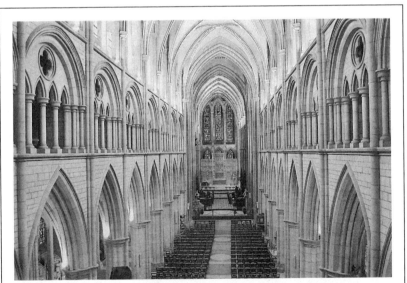

Figure 16.1. The interior of the magnificent Truro Cathedral, Cornwall, England, designed by John Loughborough Pearson in the Gothic Revival Style. Photo and caption: Jack Pease/Flickr/ Creative Commons. License information available at https://creativecommons.org/licenses/by/2.0/

have sometimes been downplayed or neglected because of their temporal status. However, more congregations are now realizing that intentionally designed sacred spaces can help us engage with God in meaningful and intuitive ways. This chapter looks at a number of ways to create sacred space experiences that can enrich the lives of believers and communities.

To be clear, this chapter is not specifically about designing church sanctuaries. That would get into things like sanctuary architecture, acoustics, denominational traditions and so on that we don't have space to cover here, although I touched on related areas like displaying art in the sanctuary in chapter fifteen. Instead, I am talking about additional ideas for sacred space, some that can become a part of a church sanctuary. Most of these examples and ideas will work within the current architecture and design of any church. If you are interested in church sanctuary design, see the online resources and extras for this chapter.

But first let's touch on two other areas typically thought of when sacred space is discussed: exterior church architecture and interior design.

ARCHITECTURE

Church architecture is perhaps the most recognizable yet controversial representation of sacred space. Tremendous resources have been and can be spent on architectural design. With the advent of the new evangelicalism in the 1950s, many believers began to think that beauty in the church—specifically in the form of elaborate architecture—was a waste of resources, especially when those resources could be used to win souls. The thought of building new cathedrals like in those of the past seemed downright offensive. As time went on, new churches began to build out spaces in warehouses and office buildings. New freestanding churches often resembled those structures as well. For many evangelical churches, their spaces were simply a utilitarian meeting place.

Today, church leadership in many denominations is recognizing that beauty and creativity—which God undeniably affirms (Ps 19:1-2)—can go hand in hand with the fundamentals of the faith, such as soul winning. And, in fact, if any stream of Christianity extols the essentials without engaging the imagination, we risk being both boring and unbiblical.

Still, each congregation must decide where their priorities lie and what they are called to in their community when thinking about architectural design. A relevant question to consider is "What do we want to say to our community with our architecture?" Because your building *is* saying something. A well-designed church can have a positive impact on its community 24/7: lifting spirits, providing inspiration and hope, exhibiting a recognition of and care for the community, and affirming the value of those who live there. Architect Duncan Stroik says,

> Religious buildings are symbols of the faith, and our churches have the possibility of being evangelistic in the sense that many people walk by them, drive by them, who might not ever step foot in them. So, what do our churches say about [Christianity] on the outside: In a sense, it's the cover of the book, and does it have anything on the outside that makes you want to read it? What does it tell you?[1]

At the same time, the question of wise stewardship of church funds must persist. Wouldn't finances used to create attractive architecture be better spent on the poor or on missions? Perhaps so. Each congregation must wrestle through that in prayer. Still, there are many ways to accomplish attractive design and environmental friendliness without spending excessively. I would suggest that we owe it to our community, congregation and the God of beauty to investigate the possibilities.

> "There is the lively awareness that beauty imitates the divine nature; that to create beauty is to imitate the divine activity; and that to be a lover of beauty is to be a lover of God."
>
> Jane Merriam de Vyver,
> *The Artistic Unity of the Russian Orthodox Church*

Finally, consider that Jesus taught us, particularly in the story of Mary of Bethany in Matthew 26:6-13, that sometimes the extravagant act of seemingly wasteful beauty can be the exact thing that love calls for.

So if your congregation has the opportunity to create or change the architecture of your church, you probably don't need to build a cathedral, but consider how you can communicate God's love and personality to those who interact with your building.

INTERIOR DESIGN

Good interior design is one of the greatest tools for crafting sacred space. The art and science of creating a comfortable and welcoming experience through design is sometimes overlooked in churches, but our spaces do significantly color our feelings and receptivity to God's spirit.[2]

We have the opportunity to help prepare people to enter into a sacred experience even starting in the parking lot. Good design choices in the lobby or common area and sanctuary can help hearts feel welcomed and relaxed. Attention to the elements of line, shape, form, color, texture, space and lighting will all contribute to the overall experience and help prepare worshipers to receive from God.

Andy Stanley, pastor of North Point church in Atlanta, says in his book *Deep and Wide*, "Every ministry environment communicates something. There are no neutral environments. Environments are the messages before the *message*. The messages your environments communicate have the potential to trump your primary message."[3] He observes that some people won't return if they don't feel comfortable in your church's environment.

Kim Miller, campus designer at Ginghamsburg Church in Ohio, writes:

I'm happy that the Church was expanded by its use of gymnasiums in the 80s and 90s, but we lost something profound, we lost the sensuality of spirituality and replaced it with song after song in the key of C, metaphorically speaking. I love music, but we've underestimated the power of physical

Figure 16.2. Interior design at Holy Trinity Parish, Eldorado Hills, CA. Photo: JSM.

design. Environment is how we exist on earth! Not my idea, but God's. You may not feel that you are "into Design," but because we are humans created in God's image, design is wired into us.[4]

In *Redesigning Churches* Kim shares a helpful list of church design basics:

- Always use fresh flowers and plant life, nothing artificial, plastic or silk. (The exception would be in a temporary sacred space like the Well, discussed below.)

- Keep fabric window treatments to a minimum. Shades, shutters, blinds or bare windows all present a clean, more professional look.

- Replace bulletin boards with mission statement walls or enlarged framed photographs of your church's mission, servant activity or other inspiring images.

- In public hallways and spaces, remove anything that does not pertain to the majority of your people and new guests.

- Soft, ambient lighting is always preferable to harsh, overhead florescent lighting.

- Clean carpets, windows and restrooms speak volumes.

- Empower one trusted person (who possesses a sense of style) to oversee public areas to ensure a clutter-free, guest friendly and aesthetically pleasing environment.[5]

You may want to do a physical design audit with an interior design professional to see if you have spots that are hindering the experience for your congregation and guests. And pray for eyes to see how God can use interior design and decoration in your church to help creatively facilitate the message that he wants to share with your congregation. See the New Renaissance Arts Movement site, theNewR.org, for more tips and help.

Now, let's branch out into some less traditional ideas about sacred space.

WORSHIP CURATION

Worship curation is a relativity new concept, having been developed in the late 1990s by Mark Pierson and others. It uses many of the elements of interior design but focuses them on the sanctuary and experience. The idea is that a person or team would create or curate a worship experience for a congregation or a group of people by designing a sacred space with certain worshipful elements to it, seeing this process as more of an art form than an organizational task.[6] The curator finds the best ways of encouraging people to engage with God.[7]

> The curator of an art installation is responsible for the selection and design of that installation.[8] . . . In a similar way, the worship curator is responsible not just for the singing part of a church service (as the misnamed worship leader normally is), but for the whole event—from the moment people enter the door until they leave and everything in between. A good worship curator unpacks the elements of the service in a particular space she has thought about and deliberately arranged. She is aware of lighting levels, temperature, seating, projections, sound and every element that contributes to the worship experience.[9] . . . It is also possible to be the curator of a single element of the event—say, the prayers of confession. The curator might be the pastor, but is just as likely to be a layperson.[10]

The idea is to provide an intentionally designed worship experience, with every element geared toward facilitating an encounter with God. This lines it up with author Leonard Sweet's idea of worship being E.P.I.C., the acronym for Experiential, Participatory, Image-Driven and Communal.[11]

For more on the fascinating field of worship curation, see the book *The Art of Curating Worship* by Mark Pierson.

DESIGNING SPECIAL SACRED SPACE EXPERIENCES

The purpose of creating a special sacred space experience is to allow people to step out of their busyness and step into a space where they can recognize God's presence, expecting he will meet with them. Sacred spaces can evoke a feeling of holiness of place and time where heaven seems to touch earth and we find ourselves aware of and filled with the Spirit.[12] Often these spaces will be temporary, or adjust to the seasons.

Living Word Community Church has a thriving arts ministry in Infused Arts that operates almost exclusively outside of Sunday services. Creative expression during services is usually limited to music and media, but director of arts deAnn Roe has found another way to share the arts with the congregation. The arts ministry designs and operates a quarterly sacred space experience in an area of the church that allows people to connect with God on a deeper level. There are several stations in the project that are designed by artists at the church, and writers in the arts ministry put a booklet together to guide worshipers through the experience. This project, The Well, is explained in detail at the online resources and extras page for this chapter. Their sacred space experience is an artful place for members of the congregation to encounter God, and many say they have been profoundly touched by going through it.

Figure 16.3. A station in The Well sacred space experience. Photo: deAnn Roe.

SACRED SPACE POP-UP INSTALLATIONS

What if we could occasionally bring sacred space to people, instead of expecting them to come to us?

If you've read *Blue Like Jazz* you may remember the scene where Donald Miller and his friends create a confessional booth, set it up in the middle of a hedonistic festival at their college and invite people in.[13] The kicker was that they turned the confessions around; instead of the guest confessing his or her sins, the Christian host confessed to the guest the sinful things that had been done in the name of Christ over the centuries and asked forgiveness. Miller recounts how God used this whimsical sacred space to witness to dozens of people, how it was the beginning of a fruitful time of outreach on their liberal campus and how, when Miller manned the confession booth, God did major spiritual work in him.

Mark Pierson suggests that Christians set up "pop-up" sacred spaces during times of tragedy, such as a national or world crisis. We might reach out to our community by setting up a spot "on a riverbank, a public park, a parking lot, a front yard, or anywhere else people will gather as they deal with the crisis at hand."[14] Just some seating, a tray of candles, devotional material and peaceful music could be a wonderful, loving gesture. Similarly, you could also create a pop-up sacred space somewhere in your church building at such a time and make it accessible to the surrounding community.

> "Looking at art is one way of listening to God."
> Sister Wendy Beckett,
> A Child's Book of Prayer in Art

You might spend some time praying and thinking about how you and your church could model God's love to your community though your own unique pop-up sacred space ideas.

Prayer Rooms

Prayer rooms have been common fixtures of world religions for millennia, but their place in modern Christian churches has increased over the last few decades due to the 24/7 prayer movement. There are prayer rooms or houses of prayer in most large cities in the United States and around the world that function either continually or on a more occasional schedule. Many are hosted in a church but operate independently of their host. Increasingly, churches have designated prayer rooms of their own that may be open 24/7 during certain seasons, over dedicated weeks or weekends, or on occasional evenings of prayer and worship. People will usually sign up for hour-long increments of prayer time. A prayer room may be a special space in a sanctuary or separate room or chapel. It may be set up in an unused classroom or office. It may be permanent or taken down at the end of a season.

Prayer rooms are not only a great example of sacred space but also provide a wonderful place for individual creativity to be expressed in worshiping God. They are often bursting with signs of joyous creativity from all age groups and skill levels. Chapter eleven talks more about art in the prayer room.

Some elements of a prayer room might include:

- Comfortable chairs and sofas: you want the room to be relaxing and cozy.

- Music: an MP3 player or computer that is available to play a variety of supplied worship music.

- Soft lighting and candles: important for setting a soothing atmosphere.

- Instructions: people should be encouraged to pray as they feel led or are comfortable. Some may just explore the elements and listen to worship music, but others will want to be guided by instructions. You might include books on prayer here.

- Communion: an area where the elements are provided.

- Prayer wall: a place to post prayer requests and praise reports.

- Worship wall: an area where people can add worshipful thoughts or graffiti.

- Art wall: an area where people can post their prayers in the form of visual art.

- Art supplies: provide all manner of art supplies for guests to use to express their prayers, thoughts and feelings to God visually.

- Journaling desk: a place with a light, computer and/or paper for personal or community journaling or testimonies.

- World map: people can visualize parts of the world to pray for. There might be a community focus on a certain area, or provide small Post-it notes for people to post prayers for certain cities.

- Tactile objects: memorial stones as prayer aids or different symbolic objects to assist in prayer.

- Anointing oil: available to use in praying for the sick in proxy or in personal dedication.

- Sin shredder: an actual paper shredder where people can write down their sins on paper, then shred them.

Prayer, imagination and the culture of your church will lead you in developing your church's prayer room's personality.[15]

PRAYER ROOM IN A BOX

Another idea that can transport the atmosphere of a prayer room anywhere is the "prayer room in a box." It's as simple as filling a couple of plastic tubs with prayer room elements like pillows, lamps, candles, a few prayer prompts, colorful rugs, an MP3 player with soothing music and those sorts of things. Take ten minutes to set the room up before any prayer meeting or appropriate event, and you can create an instant sacred space experience that people will be drawn to.

OUTDOOR SACRED SPACES

The idea of a garden or curated outdoor area as sacred space, a place to meet with God, is as old as the creation of the earth. Adam and Eve talked face to face with God in the garden, expecting him to take walks there in the cool of the day (Gen 3:8). His plan before the fall was that all of us, his children, would spend plenty of time with him in his garden, this sacred space, if not permanently live there. Jesus spent his final hours of freedom meeting his father in a garden space. His body was placed in a tomb in a garden and he appeared to Mary there after the resurrection. The tree of life, which was in the first garden, is also a prominent feature of the garden of glory, where we will again be with God face to face (Rev 22).

A prayer garden or prayer walk on (or off) church property can have a wonderful effect on the congregation. It will enable those who like to work with natural elements to use their creativity and imagination to design and construct it in collaboration with God. It will give those who walk it or spend time in it a space to meet with God that can engage their senses, guiding them along a journey of imagination and connection with God.

> "Solvitur Ambulando: It is solved by walking."
>
> Latin saying, often attributed to Augustine

Infused Arts ministry created a sacred path, about a half-mile mulch trail that goes around the front of the property, weaving in and out of trees and around a field. There are also five prayer gardens along the way, each one very distinct and beautiful and based on a theme chosen by the designer. The designer also created a small devotional of reflections that people take along to help them move into the presence of God. There are little signposts that reflect what's in the booklet, so even if you just drop by from the neighborhood you can enjoy the path.

My pastor, Randy Gooder, is a regular prayer walk user. He finds that thoughts flow more smoothly and he receives from God better when he is moving. He consistently takes the same path. "I have encountered the Lord there so many times that simply stepping on the path brings me to an expectation of encounter. It's like getting into the sauna after a workout. I know what happens in this space—I am enveloped by God."

CREATING SACRED SPACE THROUGH CREATIVE STAGE DESIGN

With the loss of church architecture as a value in much of the Protestant church, buildings became more utilitarian, often with little or no permanent art or symbolism on the platform. The space sometimes feels more sterile and soulless than sacred. This missed opportunity for visual connection has been perplexing for many artists, but it has also opened the door for the phenomenon of creative church stage design. While Catholic, Orthodox and liturgical Protestant churches, especially those with older buildings, were and are known for their beautiful pulpits, Communion tables, altarpieces, stained glass and so on, many newer Protestant churches, particularly larger ones, have embraced stage backdrops and lighting that can change for every sermon series.

Stage design can provide an opportunity for great creativity and impact on the space and the people. It can help tie the theme, elements, graphics and symbolism of a series of messages together. It can evoke an emotion or attitude, such as awe, joy, reverence or warmth. It can help make people feel cared for or valued because you are being intentional about the church environment.

Creating sacred space through imaginative stage design for churches can be much less expensive than you think. Jonathan Malm, who runs ChurchStage DesignIdeas.com, says that almost all the designs on his website can be constructed for under five hundred dollars, with most of these inventive and inspiring treatments coming in well below that. They can also be a lot of fun for the creative makers in your church to design and assemble, and are often made of random materials that most people might not think of. (See "Go-to Materials" in the online resources and extras for this chapter.) When you direct some stage lighting on it the look can become surprisingly dramatic. And the more you utilize stage design the more you can cut costs, as many of the materials like two-by-fours, plastic sheets and fabric can be recycled into new designs.

Tips for starting a stage design plan. In the beginning, especially as the congregation gets used to a designed stage, the pastor can work the designs into his message to help make things feel more congruous.

Kaleb Wilcox, technical arts director at Willow Creek North Shore, advises that if you want to start incorporating stage design into your services, you should start slowly. When his former church in Topeka brought him in to direct tech-

Figure 16.4. An innovative stage design that uses reclaimed pallet wood, from free pallets found at the local recycling center. This was designed by Paul Wingfield and the team at White Flag Christian Church, St. Louis, MO.
Photo: WhiteFlagChurch.org

Figure 16.5. Stage design detail.
Photo: WhiteFlagChurch.org.

nical arts, they had never incorporated real stage lighting, let alone stage design. It would have been a shock to take the congregation from nothing right to an amazing stage and lighting setup. So Kaleb started changing the lighting first, adding color washes on the wall behind the speakers and dimming the lighting during worship. He then introduced stage design during special services like Christmas and Easter. Then he gradually progressed to backdrop designs for sermon series, with lighting to create color and depth. Now, stage design is a regular and expected part of that church. It would seem strange to *not* have it.

Rules of thumb.

- Work backwards from the graphic design of the series. Find out what the branding and the sermon material look like, then take that to the stage and make it cohesive so that the set matches the series.[16]

- Make your stage design an abstract illustration of the sermon series or message instead of a literal interpretation. It will create more visual interest, be less likely to look "cheesy" and keep the cost down. For example, for a series about Jonah, building a boat or a whale may take more stage space, look too much like a prop or look like you are trying too hard. It will also likely cost more than, say, a representational fluid design as a backdrop.[17]

- Avoid using pop culture directly. Don't tie your design to another company or product like a TV show. They could do something offensive and you would be linked to them.[18]

- Find ways to pull your stage designs out into the room. This creates excitement for worship, continuity and crowd engagement.[19]

- You may be on your own when you first start, and it may take a little while to have volunteers catch the vision and start pitching in. But start recruiting people to help right away.

- Build a great stage design team by making sure everyone gets to do a lot of what they like to do best. Partner with people to figure out what that is for each person.[20]

- When working with your team of volunteers, prepare the materials and ideas in advance.[21]

- Share your plans with your team. Kim Miller says, "I'm often temped to keep the plans in my head. Results will multiply, however, when you can physically sketch a plan or picture on paper and explain it to key team players, allowing them to see and contribute more powerfully to the final picture."[22]

Lighting. Lighting can give the design more drama and motion. Jonathan Malm says,

> The biggest expense for a church starting out is going to be the lighting. You'll want to be intentional and think about what lights are going to be

the most useful and versatile for things that you might want to do down the road.

I think for lighting to not be distracting, to not be viewed as manipulating emotions, you have to be intentional about when you use it and when you don't and why you are using it. When you make a change with your lights, you have to think, why is that being done, what is it communicating? If there is no reason to change it, then don't.[23]

Jonathan points out that technology is getting cheaper; LED lighting allows you to change colors instead of having three different lights with three different colors, which helps keep costs down.[24] Also, digital projection is getting much less expensive, so you can use motion backgrounds or static visuals to make engaging and creative backgrounds.

Safety. If you use fabric in the vicinity of heat (lights) or flame (candles), you'll want to make it flame retardant. You can find spray or liquid online, or if you need a certificate to prove that you meet state requirements, you can send your fabric to a company such as F.R.A.P. and they'll treat it and send it back to you with a certificate.[25]

When building, make sure to anchor your elements more securely than what you might think is necessary, especially at first, as you are getting used to how things will work on your stage.

For more information on stage design, see "Starter Stage Designs," at ChurchStageDesignIdeas.com.

ENVIRONMENTAL PROJECTION

The process of projecting large images, such as medieval cathedral architecture, onto the walls of a church sanctuary can be an interesting and effective way to create sacred space with technology. Environmental projection is detailed in chapter thirteen.

Jonathon Malm wraps up this section and chapter nicely,

Some might argue that promoting stage design is leading us into more of a performance-oriented, consumer entertainment direction. That may be true in some cases, but I suspect if that attitude is prevalent in a church, then is it isn't being created by the stage design, the tech team or even the worship team, but comes from top leadership. Certainly we should regularly consider our motivation for anything that we present or any model we follow in the church, because it all comes down to having an authentic heart before God.[26]

See the online resources and extras for this chapter at JScottMcElroy.com/ CCHandbookextras.

NOTES

[1]Duncan Stroik, quoted in Ann Carey, "Church Architect to Speak," *Pittsburgh Catholic*, May 16, 2011, www.pittsburghcatholic.org/newsarticles_more.php?id=3067.

[2]Kim Miller, *Redesigning Churches* (Nashville: Abingdon, 2013), p. 8.

[3]Andy Stanley, *Deep and Wide* (Grand Rapids: Zondervan, 2012), p. 157.

[4]Miller, *Redesigning Churches*, p. 1.

[5]Ibid., p. 21.

[6]Mark Pierson, *The Art of Curating Worship* (Minneapolis: Sparkhouse Press, 2010), p. 7.

[7]Ibid., p. 47.

[8]Ibid., p. 31.

[9]Ibid., p. 32

[10]Ibid., p. 33.

[11]See Leonard Sweet, *Postmodern Pilgrims* (Nashville: Broadman & Holman, 2000).

[12]Adapted from thoughts from the Minnesota Episcopal Environmental Stewardship Commission at www.env-steward.com/reflect/space.htm.

[13]Donald Miller, *Blue Like Jazz* (Nashville: Thomas Nelson, 2003), pp. 120-26.

[14]Pierson, *Art of Curating Worship*, p. 180.

[15]Go to these sites for more prayer room ideas and examples: www.movement.org.uk /blog/still-small-voice-10-creating-prayer-space-some-tips#.UuCxgLQo7IU and http:// hwcprayerroom.wordpress.com/prayer-rooms/prayer-room-instructions/ashes.

[16]Kaleb Wilcox, interview with the author, December 2013.

[17]Ibid.

[18]Jonathan Malm, interview with the author, December 2013.

[19]Kim Miller, interview with the author, December 2013.

[20]Kim Miller, *Redesigning Churches,* p. 26.

[21]Kaleb Wilcox, interview with the author, December 2013.

[22]Kim Miller, *Redesigning Churches,* p. 45.

[23]Jonathan Malm, interview with the author, December 2013.

[24]See more lighting advice in the online resources and extras for this chapter.

[25]Visit www.frapnv.net.

[26]Jonathan Malm, interview with the author, January 2014.

17

Beyond the Church Walls

The artist is thus to be like the Israelite spies in the desert,
bringing back fruit from the promised land to be tasted in advance....
Here is the challenge, I believe, for the Christian artist, in whatever sphere: to tell
the story of the new world so that people can taste it, and want it, even while
acknowledging the reality of the desert in which we presently live.

N. T. WRIGHT,
Sermon at Harvard Memorial Church

IN MANY WAYS THE ARTS are a universal language. They can communicate across cultures, dialects and lifestyles. This makes them uniquely suited for carrying the message of God's love to our communities, countries and the world. May this chapter spark new ideas for the role of the arts in outreach in your life and church.

The existence of arts outreach initiatives at a church can be a sign of a healthy arts ministry and a creative church. As artists grow together in community, becoming more secure in their identity as beloved children of God and as called and empowered collaborators with him, they'll naturally want to share what God has given them, both within the church and beyond the church walls.

TYPES OF ARTS OUTREACH

You'll notice that evangelism is only mentioned in one of the following three categories. Even though leading people to Christ is one of the ultimate goals in arts outreach, the manner in which the arts are used for this makes a difference. Generally, producing art *that is designed to accomplish an evangelistic purpose* can be tricky. What can tend to happen is that the art may have a ring of inauthenticity to it because it is supporting an agenda instead of expressing the heart of the artist. Trying to shoehorn a message into a medium can result in mediocre work, instead of passionate visceral work. All great artists know this, which is why their work must connect with them on a personal level.

> *"If you want to send a message, try Western Union."*
> **Attributed to Frank Capra**

Colin Harbinson, who has seen thousands of people accept Christ through his theatrical productions, says, "For me the bottom line is authenticity. None of us like the bait and switch that we've seen so often taking place in evangelistic approaches. I think if you are going to preach and your ultimate goal is not to share art, but to preach a message that goes beyond that, I think you have to inform people that this is the case."[1] So, instead of trying to create an evangelistic message, if artists collaborate with God to record the personal message that he has implanted in them, the finished work will speak to people in a variety of ways. It takes on a life of its own.

As I mentioned in chapter two, art makes a better portal than a preacher.

> Art has its own ways of "speaking" and "meaning," ... but it's not (necessarily) a good preacher—it by nature is elusive, indirect. The arts should therefore not attempt to evangelize per se, but they can "bear witness" to truth.[2]

More often than not, art and creativity in outreach can provide an entry point into conversation, and then to relationship, and through relationship comes life change.

The following are my interpretation of some types of arts outreach.[3]

Outreach through relational arts ministry. Outreach through relational arts is more or less taking your art to the world and connecting with people through it. You might create the work beforehand or make it while out in the community. But essentially you are putting yourself and your art where people are, so that conversations can start naturally. This doesn't have to be blatantly spiritual or preachy but should be your authentic expression or something God has led you to create.

Two common themes in the examples below are that (a) the leaders saw a need and then looked for a way to meet it, and (b) the ministries helped people discover more about themselves as a way to help them find God.

Bethel Church in Redding, California, has a vibrant relational arts outreach program called City Services. A number of arts programs fall under this banner, and they all include going into the community, sharing art and building relationships. They want to meet real needs in the Redding community. Some of the City Services activities include:

> "A man whose life has been transformed by Christ cannot help but have his worldview show through."
> Attributed to C. S. Lewis

- *Children's drama classes.* A team leads nine-week sessions with elementary children in their schools, providing training in self-expression, confidence building and identity discovery. With arts budget cuts in schools, this program offers a valuable service.

- *Impart Healing Arts.* This team goes into the local hospitals and brings hope and love to patients, family members and staff through art. They use some of the principles of art therapy and seek to bring the power and peace of God to hospital rooms. (By the way, art therapy principles can be effective in a variety of arts outreaches.)[4]

- *Rap and Graffiti Art.* This group takes these art forms to block parties and skateboard parks and ministers to youth and adults though fun and creativity.

- *I Heart Redding.* This team offers free photography to local businesses and assists in social media awareness. They build relationships with various business owners, communicate thankfulness for all that they do to run a great establishment, and promote patronage.

These teams and others that the church supports have seen many relationships built and people healed and saved over the years. Bethel staffs the teams with members of the arts ministry and students from their Bethel School of Supernatural Ministry.

VineArts Boise facilitates art activities for domestic violence victims, women with unplanned pregnancies, local refugees (adults and children), and more. The group will lead these people in art projects that are designed to build self-esteem, identify and overcome lies, and release healing. A number of visitors from these groups have connected with God as a result, and some now regularly attend the VineArts open studio at the church on Wednesdays.

Several times a year the ministry also hosts art and worship events for local Christian universities and parachurch groups, home-based fellowships, youth groups and so on, as requested. They might guide the groups in collaborative art projects, demonstrate creativity or help people identify giftings.

The Sacred Streets project and *common art* examples in this chapter (discussed later) are two models for this style of outreach. Other examples include placing your artwork in mainstream galleries, painting live in public areas, playing music in a non-Christian club, sharing your poetry at open mic, non-Christian venues, and more.

> "I want to suggest to you that the day of the artists has come. That there are things about symbols and the genuine indirectness of art with integrity that can speak into a lost and stuck imagination. We are awakening the imagination of people who have become cynical about the old 'grand stories.' We are sowing the possibility that there might be one which could actually set them free."
>
> Graham Cray, *Art and Soul*

Bridging art and events. These provide a connecting point for people in the community to engage with high-quality redemptive art forms sponsored by the church. This form of outreach is often seen as a way of loving people and serving the community with no strings attached. There will often be no direct Christian message in the art or event. The hope and prayer is that people will sense God's love and want to know more—that the event, service or art form will provide a bridge to a relationship with the church and with God. Grace Community's long-form drama ministry in chapter eleven and some of Bethel's City Services programs fit in this category.

Many churches are looking at the role the arts can play in their efforts to address issues of justice and social concern in the community. These initiatives are often carried out with church sponsorship but no overt evangelistic bent. The arts can shed light on problems in creative ways, draw attention to issues, and facilitate healing and empowerment. Follow the New Renaissance Arts Movement blog at TheNewR.org for more updates on these efforts.

Evangelism with the arts. This is a more straightforward form of evangelism. In this form the medium becomes the vehicle for the message, with the message taking precedence. It's important to be clear about your intention to share the gospel, especially in developed countries that are more sophisticated with the arts, so that people do not feel tricked or manipulated. Examples of evangelism with the arts might be concerts or any art performance where there is a clear gospel message given, or painting/drawing while giving a message of salvation.

Missionaries have used art to convey the gospel to cultures—and still do— because of its ability to speak across language and culture gaps. The Operation Mobilization and Bethel missions stories (discussed later) in this chapter fall into this category, as do arts efforts by organizations like YWAM and the Salvation Army, and Cru with the *Jesus Film.*

Outreach to artists. Outreach to artists involves reaching out to the artists in your community. As I mentioned in chapter two, most artists know there is a spiritual aspect to the creative process, but God is calling them to the joy of personally knowing him and connecting with his creativity.

> "In our life there is a single colour, as on an artist's palette, which provides the meaning of life and art. It is the colour of love."
>
> Marc Chagall

Artists also have a deep longing for supportive community, natural authenticity and people who will speak honestly with them. Jesus, living in and through us, can meet them in these needs.

Elements of some of the examples in this chapter, such as *common art's* ministry to homeless, fall under this type of outreach, as does Grace's long-form dramas described in chapter eleven and some artist-in-residence programs described in chapter eighteen.

Some artists have had bad experiences with religion or the church, having encountered legalistic attitudes or a disdain for the arts. Perhaps we can offer them a way to God through small positive experiences with our churches. Open studio time can be one opportunity to connect with artists, serve them and expose them to loving community. (Open studio is covered in depth in chapter fourteen.)

Ex Creatis arts ministry at Saddleback church often goes on art walks when galleries are open in the Los Angeles area and invites artists to visit their open studio on the church campus. They also go to art colleges and invite students to their art workshops and events.

VineArts also invites the public to their open studio regularly. This is a great venue for artists who are not a part of the church to connect and make art.

VineArts director Jessie Nilo has had scores of conversations with artists who aren't Christians. The ministry will usually ask for a two-dollar donation, and then people get access to materials and supplies in their studio.

EXAMPLES OF ART IN OUTREACH

As I've mentioned several times, it's always best to let arts ministry or creative expression in a church develop organically rather than trying to manufacture a program or project. To paraphrase Fredrick Buechner, look for the places where your church's mission meets an artist's passion. You might think about who the artists are in your congregation and what they are passionate about, then pray about coming alongside them. Of course, there are exceptions to this, such as if through prayer God is leading your church in a certain creative direction, even if there doesn't seem to be a natural path or people there to trail blaze it. He may open doors and bring the right people along as you move forward at his leading. And it's not unusual for artists to need an invitation to step into their creative destiny within the congregation. Artists—and other people—often cannot imagine what moments of joy they'll experience when their gifts and passions collide with God's planned role for them in the body of Christ. Often leaders can help them down that path. That is certainly what happened to me many years ago. I would not be encouraging churches and artists to collaborate with God in their creativity if my pastoral leadership had not invited me into it.

Figure 17.1. Jason Leith sketches a picture for the Sacred Streets project. Photo: Nicole Leever.

Art for the homeless. One of the senior leaders at Saddleback Church was able to recognize the calling on one of their own artists and support him in an exciting project that he could not have accomplished on his own. Jason Leith was still finishing up his art degree at Biola University when he started as the director of Saddle-back's Ex Creatis arts initiative. He wanted to do an ambitious installation for his final project and, knowing it would consume most of his time, asked for time off from his job at Saddleback. Instead, his boss and mentor Jim Dobbs, an artist himself, asked him how the church could help. Could the arts ministry focus their volunteer hours and attention on making his dream project come true? Jason was surprised by the offer and took them up on it.

The project, Sacred Streets, was set up on a vacant lot in Los Angeles's skid row and made international news. Jason spent time walking the streets of the area, meeting people and listening to their stories. Then he began asking if he could draw their portraits. Many agreed, and he says, "The process resulted in people feeling uniquely dignified, heard, and most important, seen. They felt recognized

Figure 17.2. The Sacred Streets gallery was built from found materials. Photo: Nicole Leever.

not only as people in need of food or shelter, but also as aesthetic beings who possess a story to tell. It touched a deep longing among these people who are mostly avoided, overlooked, and invisible to the public eye."[5] All of these portraits were drawn sitting with the subject, face to face, on the streets.[6] Jason made twelve portraits of skid row residents on found objects like beat-up metal sheets, weathered cardboard, tops of rusty barrels and discarded suitcases. He wanted to illustrate hope, restoration and renewal for these outcasts of society.

When he had completed the portraits, volunteers from Saddleback joined him in constructing a gallery on a vacant skid row lot from discarded objects found around the area. There were galleries within walking distance from the site, but these homeless residents wouldn't be welcome in most of them, so they brought the gallery to them.

> They [the homeless] were invited into this beautiful space as a community, to reflect on their lives, their stories. . . . Our opening was hosted by the rescue mission. We did this with all the pomp and circumstance one might expect in an important art opening. The result was something that handing out sandwiches (as helpful as that is) could never have done. There was a lot of emotion, tears—all kinds of responses not typically present in art galleries.[7]

They even invited viewers to respond to the portraits by writing personal notes to the subjects on provided brown paper.

So in the end, the church came alongside the artist, making his passion a reality, and the artist led the church in a beautiful creative expression of care for the homeless in their community.

If you did a project like this you might even consider providing a laminated photograph of each subject's portrait, with a personal message on the back, to

Figure 17.3. Inside the Sacred Streets gallery. Photo: Nicole Leever.

carry with them. See more about the process and details of this project at SacredStreets.org.

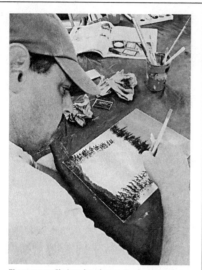

Figure 17.4. Chris, who sleeps on the streets nightly, hard at work on his art in the common art studio. Photo: Heidi Lee.

Art of the homeless. On the other side of the United States, in Boston, Ecclesia Ministries has been quietly reaching out to the homeless through the arts for two decades. Their ministry, *common art*, is hosted by Emmanuel Church in downtown Boston. Each week, they open a space at Emmanuel to provide food, community and an art studio for the homeless. People may come for a meal to enable them to survive another day on the street, but eventually many of them try their hand at making art. It is a form of art therapy, but artist-in-residence Heidi Lee says it's more than that. The program is designed to develop a sense of self-worth in the people who use it.

> When they come to this program, it's run by the homeless; they cook and serve the food and set up and tear down alongside the volunteers and staff. When they start giving in that way they start thinking, maybe I can make something too. And I think the act of creation really helps them to see that there is something really beautiful within them.[8]

Most of these homeless have some sort of mental illness; many are on disability; others can't keep a job because of their struggles. In this highly educated part of the country—home of Harvard, MIT, Tufts and other universities—it's not uncommon to have PhDs among the homeless population.

The *common art* program helps boost self-esteem; it can also inspire a sense of purpose.

> Even if it's not something that is a masterpiece in the beginning, they keep on creating, and they're seeing that, hey, maybe there is something here that

other people can see worth in as well. When they start selling things they get very excited. Then they continue making. We call them "artists" when they see the act of creation as sacred, and see it as a priority in their lives.[9]

Common art doesn't stop at training and encouraging their homeless artists; they also create venues to sell their art.

The gallery is set up every week . . . from 10 to 2 in the middle of workday. . . . It boosts the confidence of the artists by having their artwork up in a gallery. We also have occasional shows on Saturdays where we'll go to a different church or venue.[10]

Some have even been able to make art-making their vocation. "We have several artists who regularly paint at our program, and they sell on the streets almost every day if it's not blizzard conditions. They sustain themselves that way."

Figure 17.5. The *common art* outdoor gallery, where homeless artists sell their work weekly.
Photo: Heidi Lee.

One success story is Laura (not her real name), who has been homeless since she was fourteen, surviving Boston winters for years. She was struggling with her mental illness and Lyme disease and was not able to sustain herself. She came to the program about two years ago and started making art, just doodling. She grew in her ability and started hanging pieces in the *common art* gallery.

> We have this opportunity to display in a café and we asked her to participate in that, she was very hesitant but finally agreed. Her work sold, and she was so encouraged! A year later she built up a group of paintings, and we had a show at another café and she sold several pieces there as well. Since then she's been making art like crazy whenever she's had time. We also helped her find a job, and she was able to find a side porch in someone's home, so she now has some housing and has been able to pick herself up. Her condition has improved quite a bit. She's been selling art at art shows really regularly and sustaining herself through the sales. I think that she really sees herself as an artist. Now she comes in early to the program, stays late and helps clean up. She was kind of reclusive and anti-social before, and now she's very much interactive, positive and enjoying just constantly giving to other people.[11]

Programs like *common art* don't get government funding, so one way churches can help is by contributing.

> You can also invite programs like ours to exhibit at your church because it helps to not just hear about homelessness but to meet the artists themselves. There are some incredible people who are very talented but end up becoming homeless. You realize very quickly when you get to meet these people that there is a very fine line between them and us. We all have the same fears and desire for love.[12]

If there is a ministry like this in your area, you can help by volunteering and encouraging your artists to offer workshops there. You can also provide space for these ministries to operate in your church, or host them. And you could provide gallery space to show the homeless artists' work and have a reception where the congregation can meet them.

If there is no ministry doing this in your area and you feel God calling you to establish one, you might first investigate if an established ministry to the homeless would want to partner with you to do a weekly arts outreach. Of course, anything you do will need take place where the homeless are so that they can easily drop in and take part in the program.

For more information on partnering with a ministry like this, or starting one through your church, visit Ecclesia ministries at ecclesia-ministries.org.

Art in times of tragedy. What is the role of the arts in disastrous times? After the Waldo Canyon fire of 2012 in Colorado Springs, Cindy West Limbrick and her husband, Chuck, were driving around the area looking at the devastation. They saw a home that had completely burned down, but a flowerpot outside it was untouched and full of color. Cindy photographed it and asked herself, *How can we give a little bit of hope from the arts community to the families who lost homes?* In response, the artists Cindy led at Woodman Valley Chapel decided to make custom flowerpots for these families. Someone donated flowerpots from Walmart, and fifty artists joined in to create art on the flowerpots. Then they wrapped each one in paper, put seeds in them and delivered the pots to each family who had lost a home. They called it Beauty for Ashes. "It was a pretty powerful thing for the families in the community and for the artists," Cindy says. "One woman, the president of a neighborhood association, lost over $600,000 worth of art in her home: original, irreplaceable art from Europe. We gave her a flowerpot that an artist had created a beautiful mosaic on, using broken glass. The woman sat and wept over it. Her husband said, 'You have no clue the timing of this piece.'"[13]

"To a social worker the Master said, 'I fear you are doing more harm than good.'
'Why?'
'Because you stress only one of the two imperatives of justice.'
'Namely?'
'The poor have a right to bread.'
'What's the other one?'
'The poor have a right to beauty.'"

Anthony de Mello, excerpted from *Awakening: Conversations with the Masters*

The arts can bring hope and healing when people have suffered loss. Think of the "America: A Tribute to Heroes" broadcast that aired on thirty-five broadcast and cable outlets simultaneously ten days after 9/11, raising $200 million for families of the people lost in the tragedy and soothing the broken spirits of an entire country. There was great spiritual openness after 9/11. I had the privilege of choreographing and producing a synchronized fireworks show set to music to commemorate the tragedy several months later. It was broadcast on mainstream (not Christian) radio and TV and seen live by three-quarters of a million people in my city, and I had the freedom to make it overwhelmingly spiritual. Many told me they felt God's presence during the thirty-minute show, and I'm convinced he touched thousands that night through the art of fireworks choreographed to music.[14]

In chapter sixteen I touched on pop-up sacred spaces. These can be especially meaningful in times of tragedy or community angst. Just a simple setup of a designated space with some seating, a tray of candles, devotional material and peaceful music in a park or anywhere people might gather can be a tangible way to bring peace and bless a community. It can give people a place to pray or process their thoughts or grief. You might even leave it unattended with signs posted to explain what it is. You can also bless the community around your church building by providing an accessible sacred space during this time for drop-in prayer and post that information on local bulletin boards.[15]

Taking personal prayer art to the streets. Carrying the personal prayer art (PPA) concept in chapter ten out into the community can also be a uniquely effective form of outreach. Bethel Church has been using what they call a "treasure hunt" model with art for years.[16] They train a group of three to five people in PPA and either go out and do PPA in public places or ask God to give them pictures before they go out, create them, then ask God to lead them to the people to give them to. The idea is that the people are the treasure, and you are searching for them to bless them with a word of love from God. When this connects, as it often does, it can be miraculous for the person who receives the picture, and an incredible faith builder for the person who made it. People are generally appreciative when you give them free art with a smile. There is rarely a downside. At the very least you get to personally interact with someone, show them you care and bless them with something handmade that they can keep and look back on.

I've heard many wonderful testimonies about this practice, such as the person who prayed for a woman with a broken leg in a hospital and felt led to draw her a picture of a sunset on a beach, specifically in Maui. The woman's eyes filled with tears as she told the artist that she had actually broken her leg on a beach in Maui, which was why she was in the hospital. God was clearly telling her that he saw her, was with her on that beach and cared about her pain. Then there was the homeless traveler that I drew a picture for, who, weeks later when he saw a ministry associate of mine, pulled the picture out of his pocket and declared that he looks at it every day. It was a sketch about his destiny, about how God sees him, instead of where he was living at the time. It had become an icon of hope for him.

Why not take a risk and try this kind of outreach at your church?

Art ministry to the elderly. In chapter two I mentioned employing the arts to reach out to Alzheimer's patients and those in nursing homes or hospice care. Creative stimulation for such patients, like listening to music, dancing, creating or appreciating art, can awaken responses, improve their quality of life and shine God's light in their darkened world. Some studies have shown that after nursing home residents listen to music they become less agitated and aggressive and have fewer hallucinations.[17] "Art is a wonderful activity that taps into imagination," says Dr. Gene Cohen, the director of the Center on Aging, Health & Humanities at George Washington University. "That is one reason there has been increasing attention to art for people with Alzheimer's. Even as memory fades the imagination has the capacity to be robust."[18]

Certainly this type of ministry that brings hope to the broken and forgotten fits within the general calling of the church. Why wouldn't our churches support and invest in organizations that provide this in our communities or create these types of programs where they don't exist?

Sherri was a burned-out professional artist who found healing and a renewed passion for art through her church's arts ministry. She felt God inviting her to bring love to brokenhearted people

Figure 17.6. An elderly artist paints during a Vine Hearts workshop. Photo: Sherri Coffield.

using simple art activities. After overcoming her fears, she began teaching art at a local nursing home and immediately fell in love with her elderly students.

By her third visit Sherri's art students were looking forward to her visits and the opportunities to create were lifting their spirits. The staff began to frame and display the residents' artwork in the hallways. Everyone was happy and proud.

One man, Darrel, hadn't been engaging in any conversation or fun activities with the other residents in over a year, but when he finished a watercolor painting he broke into a huge grin, just repeating, "How about that! I never knew I could do that! How about that!" Darrel passed away not long after that, but for a couple of months he experienced a touch of God's love through Sherri's willingness to reach out.

Sherri has been privileged to see many other stories of people who have been touched by God, encouraged and have accepted Christ through this ministry. And many others are seeing similar fruit.

> "Where there is revelation, explanation becomes superfluous."
> Fredrick Frank,
> *The Zen of Seeing*

If you or your church feels a calling to this type of ministry, the Alzheimer's Association has some practical advice on how to do it. When planning an art activity for someone with middle- to late-stage Alzheimer's, keep these tips in mind:

- Keep the project on an adult level. Avoid anything that might be demeaning or seem childlike.

- Build conversation into the project. Provide encouragement, discuss what the person is creating or reminisce.

- Help the person begin the activity. If the person is painting, you may need to start the brush movement. Most other projects should only require basic instruction and assistance.

- Use safe materials. Avoid toxic substances and sharp tools.

- Allow plenty of time, keeping in mind that the person doesn't have to finish the project in one sitting.[19]

Overseas Creative Missions

As already mentioned, the arts can be a great help in missions because of their unique ability to speak across cultures. In fact, they serve an important role in every culture. Every people group reinforces and passes on its story through the arts, so most cultures can easily relate to the good news story shared through them. This is one of the reasons why a number of missions organizations are using the arts in outreach. They can often gain access where traditional missionaries or evangelists wouldn't be able to.

Perhaps one of the most effective uses of the arts in missions occurred when St. Patrick had the idea to use the art of symbolism to win the Irish to Christ. God inspired him to incorporate traditional Irish ritual into his lessons of Christianity instead of attempting to eradicate native Irish beliefs, specifically combining the symbolism of the cross with the Irish pagan symbol of the sun to create the Celtic cross.[20]

Operation Mobilization (OM) is one of several missions organizations that embrace the arts as a powerful vehicle for sharing God's love. They offer short-term missions opportunities that Christian artists can get involved in through OM Arts International.[21] Here is a quick story of how the arts reached across culture and language barriers to touch lives.

A young artist on mission to Turkey, a Muslim country, was asked to paint a piece for an open-air gallery the team had set up. The gallery's theme was Jesus' statement "I am the door," but instead of a door the artist felt the Holy Spirit inspiring her to paint a lock—a massive, medieval lock—and she did not like how it turned out. She felt she had rendered it poorly and that God probably would not be able to use it. But as an old man strolled through the gallery, he stopped suddenly in front of her painting, seemingly stunned. Seeing his reaction, the artist approached him, and through an interpreter asked him why he was transfixed by the painting. He wept as he told her, "My entire life I have felt locked out from all God had for me. I can see it through the keyhole, but I can't get to it. Can you please tell me, what is the key that will unlock the door of my life, and let me run into the light of God?"

The young woman had the privilege of sharing the love of Christ right there on the sidewalk. The Holy Spirit had used her humble painting to open this man's heart and draw him to the Father heart of God.[22] There are many stories like this that illustrate the power of the arts in outreach.[23] When artists and churches take a risk and create an avenue for God to speak through the arts, beautiful—sometimes miraculous—things will happen.

See the online resources and extras for this chapter at JScottMcElroy.com/ CCHandbookextras.

NOTES

[1]Interview with the author, February 2014.

[2]Colin Harbinson, ed., "Redeeming the Arts," *Creative Spirit Magazine* (Belhaven College, Jackson, MS, 2005), p. 41.

[3]These categories were directly informed by Constantine Campbell's work in *Outreach and the Artist* (Grand Rapids: Zondervan, 2014).

[4]Visit www.arttherapy.org.

[5]Jason Leith, quoted in CIVA's *Seen Magazine* 13, no. 2 (2013): 20.

[6]For more on this ministry, see http://sacredstreets.org/the-artwork/the-process.

[7]Jason Leith, quoted in CIVA's *Seen Magazine* 13, no. 2 (2013): 20.

[8]Heidi Lee, interview with the author, December 2013.

[9]Ibid.

[10]Ibid.

[11]Ibid.

[12]Ibid.

[13]Cindy West Limbrick, interview with the author, December 2013.

[14]J. Scott McElroy, *Finding Divine Inspiration* (Shippensburg, PA: Destiny Image, 2008), pp. 126-29.

[15]Some of these ideas were inspired by Mark Pierson's *The Art of Curating Worship* (Minneapolis: Sparkhouse, 2010).

[16]Detailed in Kevin Dedmon's book, *The Ultimate Treasure Hunt* (Shippensburg, PA: Destiny Image, 2007).

[17]Shari Rudavsky, "Dance, Art Boost Memories for Alzheimer's Patients," *Indianapolis Star*, August 19, 2013, available online at www.usatoday.com/story/news/nation/2013/08/19/health-dance-art-alzheimers/2674973.

[18]Gene Cohen, quoted in Robert Weller, "Art Boosts Alzheimer's Patients' Spirits," *Live Science*, August 3, 2006, www.livescience.com/929-art-boosts-alzheimer-patients-spirits.html.

[19]From www.alz.org/care/alzheimers-dementia-music-art-therapy.asp.

[20]See www.history.com/topics/st-patricks-day/who-was-saint-patrick.

[21]For more information, see http://arts.om.org.

[22]See www.missions-trips-arts-billdrake.blogspot.com/2010/10/lock-and-door.html.

[23]You'll find more stories about the power of the arts in outreach in the online resources and extras.

Your Church as an
Arts Patron, and Working
with Outside Artists

*If you read history you will find that the Christians
who did most for the present world were precisely
those who thought most of the next.*

C. S. LEWIS,
Mere Christianity

*If a patron buys from an artist who needs money, the
patron then makes himself equal to the artist;
he is building art into the world; he creates.*

EZRA POUND, from a letter to
art patron John Quinn, March 1915

IT'S WELL DOCUMENTED THAT the church was once the greatest patron
of the arts. From the iconographers to the monastic illuminators to renaissance artists like Michelangelo and Raphael, the church provided artists with
meaningful work, inspiration and funding.

With the Protestant Reformation the perceived role of the arts in churches
changed for many Christians. Some leaders railed against the possibilities of
idolatry and wasteful spending. But now, things are changing again as more
church leaders are acknowledging that our creative and beautiful God de-

signed us to share in his creativity, and that through this collaboration his love
will be shown to the world.

BECOMING A PATRON OF THE ARTS IN YOUR CITY

So far, we've looked at many different ways that churches can support and
encourage the arts and artists in their communities, ways that will ultimately
lead people to God's love. Here are a few examples of what other churches are
doing to support the arts and share love through them.

Windows of the Soul Chapel at Wheeler Mission. Although not a large
congregation at a couple hundred members, Indy Metro Church in the Mas-
sachusetts Avenue arts district of downtown Indianapolis does more than
their share to support the arts and arts outreach in the area. They host a
monthly art gallery in their rented space, present plays and sponsor arts in-
terns. And in 2011 they funded a large and unique art project, the Windows of
the Soul Chapel at the local homeless shelter, historic Wheeler Mission.

The worn and unappealing chapel was used daily by men in Wheeler's in-
tensive addiction recovery program. The idea was to make it more of an inspiring and beautiful place. The church contacted local artist Steven Kelso,
who is known for creating paintings that look remarkably like stained-glass
windows, and partnered with Wheeler alumni
to commission him to create paintings on the
chapel's stark, white walls.[1]

> "The best way for
> Christians to change
> culture is to make culture."
> Andy Crouch,
> *Culture Making*

The work took over a year and a half to complete, with Kelso pouring his heart and soul
into it. The resulting outcome is jaw dropping.

An eighteen-by-twenty-foot wall is filled with
massive representations of Christ, angels, lions and other Christian symbols
rendered in vibrant colors, making it seem as if light is actually streaming into
the room. It's not often you see this kind of work in an American chapel, let
alone a homeless shelter.

The paintings have had a profound effect on the men who live at Wheeler. Most
are fresh off the streets, just beginning their journey to freedom from addiction. For
these struggling souls to encounter unique and beautiful art, made with them in
mind, is ennobling and inspiring. Some will tell you they've been saved through it.

The Windows of the Soul Chapel is a wonderful example of a local church partnering with an artist to make life better for people of their city. With the lifespan of a piece of art in a setting like this, it could go on influencing beauty-starved pilgrims from the streets for decades.

Figure 18.1. Wheeler Mission Chapel, Indianapolis, in its former blank state. Photo: Steven Kelso.

Figure 18.2. Wheeler Mission Chapel after it was transformed into Windows of the Soul Chapel by artist Steven Kelso. The work was commissioned by Indy Metro Church and the Hebron alumni association. Although it looks like stained glass, it was created with oil paint. Photo: Steven Kelso.

Redeemer Presbyterian / Harrison Center for the Arts. Redeemer Presbyterian Church, also in downtown Indianapolis, has a mission that is being met
through their tenant, the Harrison Center for the Arts. Church member, artist
and Harrison curator Kyle Ragsdale says,

> Redeemer is trying to bring the peace of God and the beauty of God to the
> city. [The church] places a really high value on caring for the city and
> bringing goodness back to the city. If you care for culture, if you care for
> culture makers, that transforms the city. If people in your fellowship can
> feed artists or give them cars or help them have affordable rent, then they
> can have time to make work that changes the work that's in the galleries. So
> it multiplies. It's a much slower process.[2]

Figure 18.3. Detail of a scene in the Windows of the Soul Chapel by Steven Kelso, at Wheeler
Mission Chapel, Indianapolis. Photo: Steven Kelso.

The Harrison is widely regarded as an excellent example of a thriving and
innovative urban art center. They have five galleries and thirty-three artists in
twenty-three spaces, coming from diverse backgrounds and worldviews. They'll
present fun shows and throw huge parties that people can bring their families to
every first Friday of the month. If you were to gallery hop on a First Friday you'd
notice a distinct difference between the atmosphere at the Harrison and any of
the other thirty-five downtown galleries. It's definitely a light in the art scene.

The church owns the building, and they rent to the Harrison Center, which is a separate nonprofit with its own board and executive director. As a non-religious organization, the Harrison Center enjoys partnerships with all kinds of state and city organizations. "We've even seen people in our body that didn't know they had artistic gifts, and after they've been around the art they

Figure 18.4. Artist Quincy Owen's work hanging in the Harrison Center for the Arts main gallery. Photo courtesy of Harrison Center for the Arts.

realize, 'Oh, *I'm* an *artist!*'" Kyle says. "And we've also seen people start coming to art events and then get excited about the church. It's gone both ways, but it's not a + b = c at all. It's just something that we do out of loving the city."[3]

Woodman Valley Chapel Fireside Gallery. Woodman Valley Chapel in Colorado Springs finds that their gallery space has had a significant impact on local mainstream artists. Curator Cindy West Limbrick began a relationship with the Colorado Art Guild years ago because they needed a place to display their biannual art show. There isn't much reasonably priced gallery space that can accommodate large shows in Colorado Springs, so Woodman offered them their Fireside Gallery, which can display eighty to one hundred paintings. The shows each last eight weeks.

"We host a tasteful reception," Cindy says, "and they pay half of that cost. We can't serve wine at the church (because of liability), but we do have smoked salmon and fruit. My whole goal is to just love on the artists. Many don't really understand what the church has a gallery for, what the connection to God is. I'll intentionally open up the doors of the sanctuary and have the stage lit, and I might have an artistic quote up on the screen. It's crazy how it draws them in."

They tell the guild that the art has to be G-rated because there are families coming through on Sundays (the gallery is in the hallways). "The church loves it. It's funny, when there's a new show that goes up, you can tell, because people are late coming into the sanctuary."[4]

> "A hunger for beauty is at its heart a hunger for God."
> Michael Card, *Scribbling in the Sand*

This is an excellent example of how a church can not only provide a space for local artists but also, with four to five thousand people attending the three Sunday services, provide an incredible audience that the guild might not reach anywhere else.

Other patronage ideas. Here are a few more ideas for art patronage that may spark some thoughts for your church:

- Organize prayer support for local artists.
- Buy supplies for artists.
- Buy local artists' work.
- Ask an artist what is on his or her heart to make, and pray about how your church can help make that happen.
- Commission an outdoor mural in a rough part of town.
- Commission art to be displayed at your church.
- Create a scholarship for studio space at local community studio.
- Sponsor a local art contest.
- Sponsor a local art fair.

WORKING WITH OUTSIDE ARTISTS

One of the themes of this book is the importance of encouraging and nurturing artists from within our congregations so that they can step into their identity and exercise their talents in their local church. But there are also times when commissioning an outside artist to make a permanent work of art could be desirable, such as when a master is available and you have the finances to engage him or her. In this situation, there are a number of ways you might work with an outside artist, some of which are covered in chapter fifteen, in

• •

ART FAIRS

An art fair at the church can be another excellent opportunity to support the arts, build community in your arts ministry and showcase your artists' work. Artists can interact while planning and executing the event, and the church community will have the opportunity to see and purchase their work. You might consider presenting a pre-Christmas gift fair. This can provide a real service to the congregation, giving them the opportunity to fill their gift list with original and unique artwork from artists they know.

You might consider doing a benefit for a local charity and splitting the proceeds between the artists and the charity. One note to consider with this option: many artists, especially the accomplished ones, are regularly asked to donate their work for benefit events. Artists are generally generous people and will often acquiesce. But consider that they spend precious energy and resources on their pieces. Materials can be expensive. When asking for artwork to benefit a cause, consider splitting the proceeds with the artist. It will demonstrate that they are appreciated and understood, and then it will be up to them if they want to donate above their split.

• •

the section titled, "Displaying Art in the Sanctuary." The artist may be invited to actually create the work in the space, if that is possible.[5] This allows the congregation to witness the artistic process as it progresses, sparking a sense of excitement and anticipation. Or, more typically, the commissioned artist might spend some time in the space praying and planning, and then create the work in their studio. Catherine Kapikian suggests that there are ways to engage the congregation in that scenario as well:

Ask the artist to visit several times—once during a church lecture series to discuss the body of his or her work, and then again when he or she is crafting the commissioned work to discuss its progress and complexities. These intermediate steps enlighten the community regarding the artist's intent, purpose, and expressive use of vocabulary and its syntax.[6]

A church might even have the artist lead the congregation in a participatory project, which the artist plans, designs and oversees, and the members of the church execute. This can be a delightful and rich community experience.[7]

The art at St. Mary's. One of the more striking examples of new art commissioned in a church is at St. Mary's church in Boise, Idaho. They completed a $4 million renovation to their deteriorating seventy-year-old building in 2008 and were able to add some amazing pieces of original art. Father Thomas Faucher, who grew up in the parish and was influenced by a previous priest who was an art lover, led the effort. He set a goal of raising $400,000 from individual donors specifically for art. This was in addition to, not part of the $4 million budget, a move meant to address the critics who would ask why budgeted money was spent on "frivolous" art. It wasn't; it was all donations.

Figure 18.5. The great door at St. Mary's Church, exterior view. Photo: JSM.

Father Faucher commissioned some master artisans to work on the ambitious projects he envisioned. He contacted Skip Armstrong to fashion the massive carved wood doors to the sanctuary. They stand sixteen feet tall and nine feet wide and weigh about four thousand pounds. On the external side of the doors is a scene taken from chapter 12 of the book of Revelation: the story of the woman clothed with the sun, about to give birth, confronting the seven-headed dragon.

The doors are opened only on the feasts of Christmas, Easter and Pentecost. The artist has said that this is the crowning work of his career, and it's easy to see why.

The second major piece, by internationally known artist Tom Browning, is an oil painting in a triptych style, with an overall size of sixteen feet long and ten feet tall. The painting depicts a life-sized Mary holding the Christ child with nine women of the Old Testament and New Testament around her. It's hung over the altar on the brick back wall of the new sanctuary. The church closes the painting during Lent, encouraging the congregation to fast from the art for a season and then see it again with new eyes.

Father Faucher says that producing this art for the church had a profound effect on the artists. "Tom Browning got a brain tumor

Figure 18.6. The interior view of the great door at St. Mary's features an imaginative scene of Noah's Ark, commissioned by Fr. Faucher (pictured). Photo: JSM.

and almost died not too long after he finished the painting. He was told he could never paint again. But he has since come back to painting, and he credits that to the fact that his painting for us, *The Adoration of Jesus,* was for him a prayer. And he says that that gave him the strength to fight. He says it is still the greatest work he's ever done." He goes on, "The man who did the doors, Skip Armstrong, isn't a Catholic or churchgoer of any kind. He and his girlfriend, Anastasia, had been living together for years and one day he called me to say, 'I can't continue to be somebody who is known for all this religious art and not be

> "If there is one thing I long for above all else, it's that the years to come may see Christianity in this country able again to capture the imagination of our culture."
>
> Rowan Williams, in *Rowan Williams: His Legacy*

married to the woman I'm living with. So we got married last week. You are
going to get a thank-you note from Anastasia.' But he also said, 'You have made
me a believer by having me do all this art.'"[8]

Figure 18.7. St. Mary's altarpiece is closed during Lent. Photo: JSM.

Working with Traveling Artists

Just as guest speakers and missionaries can bring a fresh and important word
to a church, so can visiting artists who from time to time present their art. A
visiting artist can leave behind traces of their creative DNA that can stimulate
new creativity in the church, and they can pick up traces of your creative DNA
and share it with others. God's plan is to raise up artists from inside local
churches who can share in their church's mission and fulfill their role in the
body, but occasionally he will bring in someone from the outside to be a catalyst or add a spark.

Here is a look at some of the art forms that traveling artists practice.

Live painting. Chapter eleven discussed live painting in the church in
depth, including traveling performance painters who create large, exciting
images to music. Often they reproduce predetermined images that they've
painted many times, enabling them to paint very quickly. Generally these professional painters will have an agreement that spells out what they will do and

what your church is responsible for, which often includes providing canvas, paints, and protection for the floor and walls. These professional performances can be a good way to introduce or strengthen an appreciation of the power of art for a church.[9]

Sand art. Live sand art is a simple art form that takes special skill. Its fluid, brown/black and white images can be surprisingly powerful. The artist arranges sand on a backlit glass table that is videotaped from above, so the audience can see the results. The created images flow into each other, often creating a loose story, while music plays.[10]

Pottery. Clay and pottery are referred to in the Bible several times to illustrate spiritual truths. Traveling artists who work with pottery or clay often provide very effective and beautiful presentations. One such artist is master potter Dave Blakeslee, a former pastor. Dave presents a visual parable of God's transformational work in our lives using clay and a potter's wheel. He endeavors to communicate God's intentions to be intimately involved in the shaping of our lives according to his design.

Figure 18.8. Dave Blakeslee creates pottery on stage while he speaks. Photo: Sarah Goetter.

As Dave centers the clay on the wheel, he shares that it is an impressionable yet inert material, therefore requiring the hands of a potter to form it into what he envisions. This requires the clay to yield, in a sense, to the hands of the potter, for it cannot make itself.

Throughout the presentation analogies and metaphors are used to help viewers to identify with the process in a personal way. A potter like Dave can present his art and message during a whole service or a portion of it.[11]

Dance. There are several professional dance companies that tour and present sacred dance in churches. One that is highly regarded is Ad Deum Dance Company, a modern/contemporary dance company based in Houston, Texas, directed by Randall Flinn. Ad Deum doesn't consider what they do religious, liturgical, sacred or praise dance, but rather describes themselves as

"a company of professional dance artists working and serving in their voca-
tional as well as Christian calling." They do this through their commitment to
a biblical worldview of life and artistry. This mandate commissions them to
serve their culture with artistic works that fuse the need for the relevant and
the redemptive to intertwine. Whether presenting in a church or on a mainstream stage, Ad Deum is focused on communicating through the language
of the arts, bathed in the redemptive grace of God, for higher purposes.

The Ad Deum dancers are all practicing Christians, and Flinn says,
"Whether I am creating a biblical story ballet or a comedic dance, I remain
aware of the grace that I have been given to create. Perhaps it's fair to say that
I present both sacred-secular works combined into one."

> "At the back of our brains is a
> blaze of astonishment at our
> own existence. The object of the
> artistic and spiritual life is to dig
> for this sunrise of wonder."
>
> G. K. Chesterton, *Autobiography*

Other traveling artists. Other traveling artists can include those who
present live drama, puppetry, comedy
and, of course, musicians.[12]

One of the wonderful things we can
do as a local congregation is to follow in
Jesus' footsteps by calling people to
their destiny in God, to commission and help empower them to lead a life of
purpose and hope. The church is in a unique position to do this for artists, and
to invite them to share their artistic expressions to inspire others along this
path. In this light, the church's patronage and commissioning of the arts and
artists is a sacred privilege with eternal ramifications. In the next chapter we'll
look at another form of patronage that can have a wonderful impact on the
congregation and the artist: an artist-in-residence program.

*See the online resources and extras for this chapter at JScottMcElroy.com/
CCHandbookextras.*

NOTES

[1]See Steven Kelso's site at http://artisticprophetstudios.com.
[2]Kyle Ragsdale, interview at the Creative Church Conference, Indianapolis, June 2012.
[3]Ibid.
[4]Cindy West Limbrick, interview with the author, January 2014.
[5]Called *in situ*, meaning "in its original place," or "in context."
[6]Catherine Kapikian, *Art in the Service of the Sacred* (Nashville, TN; Abingdon Press,
2006), p. 107.

[7]See chapter seven in Kapikian, *Art in the Service of the Sacred.*

[8]Father Thomas Faucher, interview with the author, January 2014.

[9]See the online resources and extras for this chapter for more on live painters.

[10]See the online resources and extras for this chapter for more on sand artists.

[11]See http://blakesleepottery.blogspot.com.

[12]See the online resources and extras for this chapter for more on traveling artists.

19

Artists-in-Residence
in the Church

It is empowering to the artist to interact with a nurturing community.
Furthermore, artists need space and the church needs the fresh
insight of its artists. Why not risk such a relationship?
Without risk, art and theology will not take us
to an enlarged vision of reality where the
religious imagination can take flight.

CATHERINE KAPIKIAN,
Art in Service of the Sacred

OVER THE LAST SEVERAL DECADES artist-in-residence programs have been growing in popularity around the world. Universities, museums, galleries, studio spaces, theaters, municipalities, festivals and some churches are inviting artists of all types to take time away from their normal environment or daily obligations and create with an institution's or community's support.

These residency programs can provide artists with time for reflection, research, focused production, education or interaction with a community, and they come in myriad variations. Most provide studio space or supplies, and some give the artist a place to stay. Some offer financial support or a stipend; others may expect the artist to raise funding. Some may have a stated purpose or set specific goals for the artist; others may free the artist up to create what he or she wants. Programs may be in urban areas, small towns, national parks or foreign countries. The residency may last for a weekend, a few months, a year or even multiple years.

As we explore ways to integrate creativity into our churches, artist-in-residence programs are a natural fit and offer many mutual benefits. Churches may be able to offer an artist space by turning a seldom-used classroom into a studio. They also may be able to offer them a mix of community support and relationships, discipleship, spiritual growth and inspiration, consistent exposure to a larger audience (the congregation), and a sense of purpose.

In exchange, the artist-in-residence might serve as a creative leader and facilitator for a congregation. They may be the catalyst that releases God's creativity in a church. They can create art to enhance worship, model for the congregation how to connect faith and creativity, lead powerful and innovative art outreaches for the church, draw members into the creative process by having them help design and produce art, and more. In *Music and the Arts in Christian Worship* Catherine Kapikian, who has worked as an artist in many churches, talks about benefits:

> Art and theology are both about the discipline of the imagination. Thus, they have a natural affinity, one with the other, making an advocacy role by the church for artistic expression in process and product a wise investment. In fact, the local parish provides an optimal setting for a resident artist and gives the congregation and artist alike the mutual benefit of each other's imaginings.
>
> The sense of awe and wonder triggered by watching a resident artist work kindles the religious imagination. The presence of grace is experienced when watching an artist transform material and transcend the medium by creating a whole greater than the sum of its parts.
>
> The intermingling of creative processes with religious ideas is productive for the church and empowering for the artist. This mutually beneficial arrangement lifts up the notion that applied creativity is an essential resource for building our world, while the faith of the church lifts up the notion that the capacity to create is a reflection of our being in the divine image.[1]

At the time of this writing there are not many artist-in-residence programs in existence in US churches. In this chapter we'll look at four different examples of those programs and how they work. But first some practical advice.

CULTIVATING AN EFFECTIVE ARTIST-IN-RESIDENCE PROGRAM

In talking with originators, sponsors and artists involved in these artist-in-residence programs, there seem to be some basic truths about how to go about this. As I said there are many variations of artist-in-residence programs, so while the following ideas are true, it's possible to work around each one of them, except the first one.

An artist-in-residence needs a church leader to oversee and/or mentor them who understands what the program is about. Without real connection to the church through a readily available staff member, empowered lay leader or arts committee who believe in the program, an artist-in-residence can end up feeling lost, frustrated and misunderstood. This is the opposite of the effect you want from a good artist-in-residence program, and can actually cause more harm than good to the artist.[2]

The artist needs to understand what the goals of the residency are. There should be a contract that clearly details hours, responsibilities, pay, time frames and program goals. What will the artist-in-residence do? Why are they there? How much will they be paid? How long will the residency last? It's important to spell these things out. Again, Catherine Kapikian has some thoughts about this:

> [Forty] hours per month of working time on behalf of the church is an equitable exchange for a modest salary and in-kind contribution of space and utilities. Give the artist a key and expect him or her to come and go at will, creating in the studio a place where the creative process is given high visibility for the church. A renewal contract or a contract with another artist is a viable option at the end of the first year.[3]

Kapikian also thinks that the congregation and the artist need at least a year together to realize the benefit of each other. You may want look for an artist who is articulate and engaging, like the Ecclesia or Lakeside examples below, or God may lead you to a model where this is not a requirement. If there is leadership qualified to do it, the church may want to try a residency for emerging artists that can be mentored in several areas. There could be a residency program specifically for non-Christian artists as a way to expose them to the faith. Often a residency can be customized to specific artists. The possibilities and variations for residency programs are many and should take into account the artists available and a church's resources and mission.

You'll find two artist-in-residence contract examples and a sample proposal for an artist-in-residence program in the online resources and extras for this chapter.

An artist-in-residence needs space. Scott Erickson, the former artist-in-residence at Ecclesia Church in Houston, says that artists need at least three kinds of space. I've fleshed out his points a bit.

1. *Space to create.* Allow the artist mental, spiritual and emotional space. This can have a profound effect on them and will allow them to create more thoughtful and impactful work for the congregation to enjoy.

2. *A space to work.* The artist needs a place to call their own, where they can be free to flow in the creative process, whether it's a studio, room or designated area. It's good if the artist's studio is accessible at certain times so people can interact with and encourage them so they don't feel isolated. Working live during a Sunday service can also be good, as the congregation gets to be part of the creative process.

3. *A space to show.* Designate a place for the artist to display their work. It needs to be shown at some point in the residency. It's important for the artist's work to become a part of the community's life and experience, and for it to have the opportunity to speak to the community. This will enrich the creative life of the church and encourage the artist to create.[4]

An artist-in-residence needs funding. As a general rule, it is preferable to pay the artist something whenever possible. The examples covered offer some possibilities.

An artist-in-residence may be making a great sacrifice of energy, family time or finances to take part in a residency, and every little bit helps to keep them afloat. Many artists put together several small revenue streams to pay the bills. To add to their income will bless them immensely, and it shows them that you value their time and talent and really are in their corner.

> "God is good but not safe, and the urge for safe art is often a worldly temptation away from goodness."
>
> Ken Myers, *It Was Good: Making Art to the Glory of God*

That said, a program doesn't have to offer an artist money in order for it to be a valuable experience for them. There can be many non-monetary benefits for the artist and for the church. Of course, a congregation must cover the artist's materials when an artist makes a piece for the church, but don't let the inability to pay the artist a stipend or salary necessarily keep you from starting an artist-in-residence program. In fact, you may have opportunities to offer them that they may value more than money.

> "The artist's mission must not be to produce an irrefutable solution to a problem, but to compel us to love life in all its countless and inexhaustible manifestations."
> Leo Tolstoy, letter to Boborykin

POSSIBLE ARTIST-IN-RESIDENCE RESPONSIBILITIES

This list is *not* intended to be used in its entirety in any one situation. An artist-in-residence program should have a good balance between time for the artist to do their work in the studio and the time it takes to fulfill their responsibilities, weighted more toward studio time. It's advisable to let the artist decide on the majority of their responsibilities, based on their skills and interests.

- Teach art technique or education classes.
- Present a gallery show or performance.
- Paint or perform live for services.
- Mentor young artists.
- Be in the studio a designated day so people can drop in and observe.
- Lead a church arts outreach.
- Come to staff meetings.
- Interact with the worship team on ways to integrate art into services.
- Lead a retreat using the arts.
- Interact with the ministries of the church to assist them using the arts.
- Lead a monthly artist community gathering.
- Lead a book study on the arts.
- Donate a painting or work of art to the church.

POSSIBLE THINGS THE CHURCH MAY PROVIDE

Your church may be able to provide more or less of these, depending on your resources.

- A staff contact person or lay leader who is readily available
- Studio space
- Discipleship, mentoring, spiritual training
- Materials and supplies
- A salary or stipend
- Advertising
- A platform during services
- Gallery or exhibit space and/or opportunities to sell work
- A budget for congregational or community projects

ARTIST-IN-RESIDENCE PROGRAM EXAMPLES

Each artist-in-residence program is unique because of its host, environment and the artists involved. The following are four distinctively different examples of artist residencies that have taken place in or around local churches. Take what you can from each one as you construct a unique artist-in-residence program of your own.

Lakeside Church. The program at Lakeside Church, just outside Toronto, aims to support artists as they interact with the local arts community.

Lakeside hosts one artist-in-residence each year over a ten-month period from September to June. The artists they choose only have a few require-ments to meet during their residency, including spending one eight-hour day per week working on their art at the church, connecting with the community through a workshop that they design and lead, and presenting a year-end show of their work at the church. If there are other things the artist wants to do beyond that, creative arts director Chris Deeves will help work out how those

Figure 19.1. New Day, the work of Rachel Albano, artist-in-residence at Lakeside Church. Photo used with permission of the artist.

things fit into the calendar. The artist is also involved in helping select the next artist-in-residence.

In return the church contributes $5,000 in financial support and a studio (in the church basement) if they want it. Deeves says, "We also connect them to the local arts council, get them advertising and other behind-the-scenes things. But they still need to make sure they are promoting their work on their end."[5]

Unlike other church artist-in-residence programs, the Lakeside program doesn't focus on bringing more art and creativity into the church. But it does happen as natural byproduct of the artist's presence. "By having the show and having the workshop here, people naturally start to pick up that we welcome the arts. We like to see that happen but it's not the mission statement of the program."

Keeping the program in line with its mission requires balancing the artist's activities. One artist got too involved in outreach opportunities during his residency and had to scramble to make time for his art, so now Deeves helps artists think through their time and activities.

A recent artist-in-residence, Rachel Albano, is an abstract painter from the area. She reported to and regularly interacted with Chris Deeves. "Just having the wisdom of someone overseeing you and saying 'this is how you do your advertising,' or 'let's run a workshop together' is so encouraging. I'm a stay-at-home mom at this point, so for me to have monetary support to take a full day off just to paint every week was amazing." She's also grateful that the residency was open to an artist with her style of expression. "The point of my year here was to kind of make abstract art accessible. Often people find it elitist and really hard to grasp. Abstract art is about emotion and texture and color and form, and I want to give people tools to not feel afraid of approaching abstract art."

Though there is still plenty of room for growth in the program, Lakeside's vision is clear and they want to leave a lasting legacy. "This is not just sort of a yearlong 'you make work for us and we don't care what you do after that' thing. We're trying to set the artists up so they succeed in our local arts community or even broader, beyond the residency. We want to help them create and sustain."[6]

Ecclesia Church. Scott Erickson can paint really fast, and he does it extremely well, often live on stage while a speaker is speaking. Erickson has developed a reputation for creating vivid paintings that illustrate or complement the speaker's content, and it's a talent that's put him in demand for conferences and events. But there was a point where this itinerate painter focused his skills on one particular church as its artist-in-residence.

Ecclesia Church is set in the urban Neartown area of Houston. Pastor Chris Seay is a noted author and speaker, and the church has a remarkable openness to the people that live in that urban area and to the raw creativity that seems to thrive there. Chris and Scott met and worked together—speaking and painting—at a couple of conferences. "During the second one we worked together maybe five days and Chris said, 'Man, I just really love what you do. You should come down and visit the church.'" During that visit Chris offered Scott a job as artist-in-residence, inviting him to "Just come paint here, be a part of our community and do whatever the Holy Spirit tells you to do."

Scott moved his family to Houston and became a paid part-time staff member of the church (the pastor and worship leader were part-time as well), essentially creating his own artist-in-residence job description. From 2009 to 2012 he led monthly artist gatherings, did creative projects with the community, painted in the church studio and dove into live painting like never before. He usually

Figure 19.2. Painted live by Scott Erickson during the Sunday service at Ecclesia Church, Houston, TX, while he was the artist-in-residence. Photo used with permission of the artist.

painted live during all of Ecclesia's five Sunday services, sometimes producing five different paintings on a weekend, each in under an hour. He would discuss with the speaker what the topic was for the coming Sunday, then he would pray beforehand that God would give him an image to paint, and he always got one (more about Scott's process in chapter eleven).

It didn't take long for the practice of live painting during every service to become part of the church's culture. "When I first starting doing this people were like, 'Oh that's really neat, that's cool,' kind of like churchy entertainment. Then maybe the sixth or seventh time they'd go, 'Wow, I actually learned from this thing.' The painting, then, is no longer a novelty act but something that enables the community to grow closer to God, just like corporate singing or corporate prayer. It's there as another layer to everything."[7] He saw clear effects from creating this visual culture in the church. "The children's director pulled me aside and said, 'I just want you to know that all the kids have adopted your symbology. Whenever we have them do art projects, they all draw houses and trees, birds and water and all these symbols that you use. They use your visual language to describe ideas of faith.' I think that's amazing, because if you look in Protestantism our religious symbolism for ideas is limited. These kids were expanding their visual connection with their faith."

At Ecclesia, Scott saw his job as advancing a visual culture in the church. "So everything we did as a church—our teachings, our learning, our experiences, our prayers, our sorrows, our joys, our accomplishments, our failures. . . . I was there to make sure that there was some kind of visualization of that story."[8]

Scott sold a lot of the paintings he made to church members, but since he was paid staff he wanted to put the money back into the arts fund. It enabled them to buy computers, studio equipment and supplies to further the arts in the church. He figures there are three hundred to four hundred of his art works in homes and businesses around Houston and loves the fact that people probably say, "Oh, this is from church."

One of the keys to helping an artist thrive in an intense artist-in-residence program like this is to provide the artist a team that can care for them spiritually, emotionally and mentally. Painting during services—especially five services—can be exceptionally draining. You want to set up boundaries, accountability and care so that the artist doesn't burn out. You want this to be a refreshing experience for the congregation and the artist.[9]

The Church Studios. In 2004 a group of eight to ten Philadelphia artists who had been engaged in community together for four years decided to look for a space where they could work together as well. "We were all in our midtwenties right after college, just trying to grind it out and figure out how to be better artists," says Dayton Castleman, one of the founders of the group. All artists of faith, the group connected spiritually as well as artistically, praying for each other and exploring how their faith informed their work. "We thought, 'You know, the only thing that would be better is if we could work together too.' So we prayed about possibly splitting the cost of a large studio space."[10]

Dayton grew up in the Presbyterian Church so he decided to look into local churches, knowing that with declining attendance there might be some unused or underused Presbyterian buildings in central Philadelphia. A visit to the PCUSA website turned up Olivet Covenant Presbyterian Church in central Philly, a historic church that had about a sixty-member congregation but was still operating in an old thirty-thousand-square-foot building. He visited

Figure 19.3. An artist's studio at the Church Studios. Photo used with permission of the Church Studios.

and discovered that there were actually two floors of unused space that could work for artists' studios. "So I told them, 'I have an idea for what you can do with this. You can meet a felt need of some believing people and basically consider it a ministry of your church.'" After talking with local leadership (Presbyterian congregations don't own their buildings) the church agreed to let the artists use the space—for free—and the Church Studios were born. "There were ten initial studios, I think, housing twelve artists. We had kind of an open-door policy and the idea was that it was a laboratory as well as a studio space."

The building was erected in 1895, and the space the studios occupy was constructed in a unique educational-style architecture from that time. Two stories of side-by-side rooms surround a large central area, and all their doors open out to it. One hundred–some years later this design was a dream come true for a community of artists who wanted to work together.

Eventually some of the artists started paying a small token rent, even though the church didn't request it. Keith Crowley, one of the current leaders of the artist community says, "There is also a four-hour-a-month chore system we have to help with the maintenance of the building and serving (the church's) needs with basic house matters." They clean the upstairs floors and keep those nice, and when it snows they shovel the sidewalks and the parking lot. "This wasn't something they asked us to do, but we wanted to. Now it's become something that they are depending upon, especially as their numbers haven't grown, and they've factored it into their budget. We also do a once-a-year benefit auction where we contribute our works and the proceeds of the auction go to the church."

Over the years there have been dozens of artists-in-residence at the Church Studios. They don't really have an application process; each one has been invited by the community because their work and their values seem to "fit." The church's willingness to open their unused space to these artists, even though

Figure 19.4. The Church Studios common area, with artist studios around the perimeter. Photo used with permission of the Church Studios.

many in the congregation are older and don't have an appreciation for contemporary art, has been a remarkable gift that's allowed talent and lives to flourish.[11]

Imago Dei Arts. Imago Dei Church in Portland reflects the personality of its city with a strong connection to the arts. They invest in artists in a number of ways, including pastoral leadership and mentoring from worship and arts pastor Paul Ramey and his team of lay leaders. They provide exhibit space in their building and in an off-site gallery, and an artist-in-residence program that includes five fine artists.

Imago's artist-in-residence program is fairly unstructured, with a few expectations, the most important being that each artist is asked to create art for a series at the church at some point in time, usually once a year. They may choose whether they want to make work for the church lobby, art that will be shown on the screen during services, or do something live on stage during a service. With the Imago community's enthusiasm for the arts, it's not unusual for the artists to go beyond their yearly commitment and volunteer to create art for a few events or sermon series.

The artists have a key to the Imago Arts studio space and can come and go 24/7. There is no required amount of time they need to be there and no time limit either, so you may find an artist working on a project or preparing for a gallery show at any hour of the day.

The residencies rotate, but there is no set length of time they last. It's just at the discretion of leadership. Artists sign a contract so that expectations are clear, and they pay a small fee of $250 a year for upkeep of the building. Paul says, "It's just a way for them to go, 'I paid for this; I've got some skin in the game here.'"[12] A deacon in the church, one of the lay arts leaders, oversees the program and connects with the artists, building community with occasional

Figure 19:5. The five artist-in-residence studios at Imago Dei are connected so that artists can work in community. Photo: Erik Railton.

book studies and inclusion in regular artist gatherings and retreats. "We want to unleash them so that they feel loved, poured into, pastored, and then free to bring their gift to the table," Ramey says.

The artists-in-residence are not paid by the church, but when they create art for a sermon series all the materials and cost are covered. The work done by these artists is high quality, and it's not uncommon for it to sell.

The resident artist contributions are significant in the life of the church, sometimes affecting the direction of the community. One artist, Stephan Wolf, created woodcarvings, then made relief prints of them on paper and canvas to be used during an Advent series. "As we started seeing some of his pieces they were so compelling that they affected what [pastor] Rick [McKinley] did with his series." It was one

> *"Artists are interpreters for us of richness and meaning. Artists can reinforce a healthy sense of God's grandeur and nearness."*
>
> **Sandra Bowden**

of many examples of the partnership of spoken message and art creating a powerful experience for the Imago Dei congregation.[13]

WHAT DREAMS MAY COME

An artist-in-residence program can offer a congregation and an artist the chance to dream together. The chance to mix the artist's imagination with the church's dreams for their community give both material form and offer a glimpse of our destiny in Christ. It's the opportunity to create something beautiful and unique for that congregation, releasing joy in the artist and the people as gifts are shared and enjoyed for the benefit of all, the way it should be in the body of Christ.

See the online resources and extras for this chapter at JScottMcElroy.com/ CCHandbookextras.

NOTES

[1]Catherine Kapikian, "The Artist-in-Residence in the Local Congregation," *Music and the Arts in Christian Worship, Complete Library of Christian Worship IV*, ed. Robert Webber (Nashville, TN: Star Song, 1994), pp. 652-53.

[2]For more on how an arts committee can work, see Kapikian, *Music and the Arts.*

[3]Ibid.

[4]From Scott Erickson's website: scotterricksonart.com.

[5]Quotes in this section are from interviews with the author in December 2013.

[6]For more info contact Chris Deeves: cdeeves@lakesidechurch.ca.

[7]Quotes in this section are from interviews with the author in December 2013 and January 2014.

[8]Quotes in this section from interviews with the author in January 2014.

[9]Scott blogged about his experience at artist-in-residence at CreateVisualCulture.com. For more information, see ScottEricksonArt.com and EcclesiaHouston.org.

[10]Quotes in this section are from interviews with the author in December 2013 and January 2014.

[11]To contact the Church Art Studios, go to olivetcovenant.com/Artist_In_Residence .html. Also search for "The Church Studios" on Facebook.

[12]Quotes in this section are from an interview with the author in February 2014.

[13]For more information, see imagodeicommunity.com/arts.

20

Working Around Barriers to the Arts and Creativity in Your Church

Love recognizes no barriers. It jumps hurdles, leaps fences,
penetrates walls to arrive at its destination full of hope.

MAYA ANGELOU,
Maya's Facebook page

Consider it pure joy, my brothers and sisters, whenever you face
trials of many kinds, because you know that the testing
of your faith produces perseverance. Let perseverance
finish its work so that you may be mature
and complete, not lacking anything.

JAMES 1:2-4

THERE ARE STILL MANY CHURCHES and church leaders who are wary of embracing the arts. This chapter addresses some concerns and objections, as well as the legitimate difficulties that come with working with artists and the arts in the church.

GENERAL DIFFICULTIES AND BARRIERS TO THE ARTS IN THE CHURCH

Barrier: Pastors and leaders who don't understand the arts. Some pastors, particularly the older generation, don't "get" the arts' spiritual significance.

Many Christians just weren't taught to appreciate or understand the arts.

Work around: Approach leaders slowly and respectfully, educating yourself on their objections, and speak to those when it's appropriate. Graciously explain some things about art and artists if you notice a leader who doesn't understand. A large part of what you're doing is educating your leaders so they can relax and benefit from the art too.

Cindy West Limbrick also suggests that you might make a questionnaire that asks leaders about their good experiences with the arts. Questions such as "What is your favorite movie and why?" (story and film), "Is there a song that brings back good memories?" (sound and rhyme), "How do you feel when you see the American flag?" (design and symbolism), "What is your favorite picture of your mom or dad?" (image and photography), "Do you have a favorite Van Gogh painting and why?" (visual art and color). With these types of questions you can point out the power of the arts by highlighting their reactions, and connect them with how God wants to move through the arts to touch people for his kingdom. Point out that their reactions to the questions affirm this reality. Of course, do it gently and humbly.

Another thing you might do is invite pastoral leadership to observe the creative process or artists at work. This can have a real effect on them as they sense the atmosphere, the presence of the Holy Spirit and people's lives being touched in real time.

Also see "Developing a Theology for the Arts" in chapter three.

Barrier: Ignorance of the arts in churches. Christians (especially Protestants) sometimes have a hard time valuing the arts as a legitimate ministry because they haven't been educated in how to understand or appreciate the arts. Dr. Colin Harbinson, in his DVD *Stone by Stone,* talks about how this can hinder the arts and creativity in churches, highlighting three areas where there can be fear:

- *Fear of emotion.* Art is often created through deep emotion, and that can make people uncomfortable.

- *Fear of ambiguity.* Many Christians are used to the three-point sermon, so abstract ideas can cause consternation. But, in fact, Jesus often taught in abstract, not easily understood, forms.

- *Fear of metaphor and symbol.* For some, the arts may seem too mystical.

However, the Bible is full of story, symbol, ritual, rites, metaphor and mystery.[1]

Work around: This lack of understanding and fear can be addressed with education and exposure to the arts and artists. If they can see the positive effect of the arts on faith, and in services, this will help as well. Some of the interactive arts projects in chapter ten can help with that.

> "The barriers are not erected which can say to aspiring talents and industry, 'Thus far and no farther.'"
> Ludwig van Beethoven

Barrier: Personal salvation focus. Salvation is key. A personal relationship with Jesus is indispensable. But to focus singularly on salvation is "doorway" theology. "You must be born again" is the doorway into the relationship, not the relationship itself. The relationship includes restoration, the kingdom of God, the incarnation. Doorway theology produces doorway art, which is sometimes preachy or simplistic.

Work around: Help people embrace a kingdom worldview where God reigns over every aspect of life.

Barrier: Churches that don't bring the arts into services or don't allow art on the stage. Some churches or denominations are hesitant about bringing the arts into their services. Some will allow it in the building but not on the platform. This may be due to denominational policy or church leaders' personal preferences.

Work around: Look for ways to do arts ministry outside of services. This book is full of inspiring and effective examples of arts ministries that have a huge impact on their congregations this way. Stay faithful and bring this barrier to God in prayer. He may surprise you with an open door.

PASTORAL FEARS

The arts often release a new way of thinking and doing things in the church. Pastors may have concerns about this. (Much of the material under this heading is adapted from the thoughts of Dave Blakeslee, an artist and former pastor.)

Barrier: Potential negative reactions from the congregation. The pastor may think, *How much heat am I going to have to take from the membership when this drama or dance or gallery is over?*

Work around: Make sure that the leadership has a good idea of the projects and performances you are doing in services before you do them. See the detailed description of including pastors in the gallery jury process in chapter fifteen.

Barrier: *Can I trust these artists?* As an artist or arts leader functioning in the church, you will begin to captivate the hearts of the people of the church. The pastor needs to know that you are in this for the glory of God, not your own exaltation. He needs to know and be comfortable with you.

Work around: The art ministry should have an overseer on staff and a liaison that can allay pastoral fears and advocate for the arts ministry. I address this in chapter seven.

Barrier: *Can we afford this?* Pastors may be thinking, *Do I have the space, money and leadership for the arts?*

Work around: In chapter three I offer a path to envisioning arts ministry and putting a plan together, which can help address these questions. I talk about how arts ministry can be done with a small budget, if necessary, in chapter four. Eventually, after they see how the arts enhance the church community, leaders may conclude that they can't afford *not* to have arts ministry at the church.

Barrier: *What if our church becomes filled with bad art?* It's true, there has been a lot of mediocre Christian art made in the past. It's understandable that a pastor could become concerned that embracing the arts and creativity might mean the church walls could become covered with poor-quality art and the congregation subjected to amateurish performances.

Work around: Set up some standards on the quality of work that can be showcased in the church. I touch on this in chapter fifteen. I also deal with how to have standards but still be inclusive of all levels of creativity in chapter six. God is honored when we give our very best for his glory, but he also invites us to "make a joyful noise" and become like little children. So there is always a tension between excellence and childlikeness in the kingdom and in kingdom creativity. But it's a tension worth maintaining.

We can't address here all the barriers to the arts that may arise.[2] You may deal with some that are unique to your church. But through prayer, patience and God-inspired creativity, barriers to the arts and creativity can be overcome. And if any remain, rest assured that God can give you the creativity to thrive within them. Even more than you do, he wants to see the arts and creativity flourish in and through the church so that his love can be known in the world.

See the online resources and extras for this chapter at JScottMcElroy.com/ CCHandbookextras.

NOTES

[1] Colin Harbinson's DVD series, *Stone by Stone,* is available at www.colinharbinson.com /order.

[2] More barriers are addressed in the online resources and extras for this chapter.

Conclusion

I BELIEVE AS INDIVIDUAL CHRISTIANS and as part of the body of Christ we are on a creative journey that will never end. In one of his final talks, Dallas Willard said, "The glory of our future is continuing creativity in the life of God."[1] We might as well start practicing now! In fact, pursuing creative collaboration with God reveals his coming kingdom to the earth.

Ten points I hope you'll take away from this book:

- We cannot separate God from creativity. He invented it and he defines it. If we want to be like him we must embrace it.

- As his children, made in his image, we are all inherently creative, even if we are not artists.

- God longs to collaborate creatively with each of us, whether in artistic expression or daily decisions, whether intentionally sharing his love or just living our lives. Pursuing this collaboration releases joy in us and others.

- The body of Christ will not reach maturity until we encourage development of all the gifts, including those that artists carry and release.

- Christian community is a place where creative gifts can and should thrive.

- Properly discipled and encouraged, the artists in your church will help lead your congregation into its creative destiny.

- Your church can already begin embracing and practicing creativity and the arts with the people you have in your congregation and the resources you have available.

- There is room for all levels of artistic skill and creative exploration in a creative church.

- Creativity and the arts were *designed* to glorify God. In the church they help us to love people more effectively, worship God more completely and facilitate the maturity of the body of Christ.

- Creativity and the arts are the some of the largest untapped resources available to the church for our mission to share God's love with the world.

No two creative churches will look exactly alike. Most already include music and media, but many will want to develop an artists' community as a foundation for their arts ministry and growth in other mediums. Some may eventually put an additional emphasis on drama, others on a gallery. Some may have live visual art on stage for every service; others may focus on creative workshops and classes. Some may develop dance, others a regular open studio. Some will thrive at doing outreach through the arts; others may be able to practice a mix of several art forms. As you seek God, he will show you the unique ways he wants to bring creativity to life in your congregation. It's a journey that leads to joy and fulfillment. It's a true honor that the *Creative Church Handbook* and its resources can be a part of it.

May his kingdom come and his will be done, in and through *your* creative church.

NOTES

[1] From a talk at the Talbot School of Theology faculty retreat in La Quinta, California, on September 16, 2011.

Acknowledgments

I WANT TO ACKNOWLEDGE THE CREATOR of the universe, my constant friend, who never gives up on me, for compelling me to write this book. I'm continually amazed that he drew me into collaboration with him and encouraged me relentlessly through the long process of writing it. He is always merciful and faithful.

Jessie Nilo, my friend and director of VineArts Boise, had a major influence on the content of this book. She and I began as coauthors, but as schedules and focuses changed, so did our roles. In the end, Jessie contributed greatly to the effort and shaped the thoughts in a number of sections. Without her input and contributions, this book wouldn't be nearly as rich and comprehensive.

My wife, Danielle, read and critiqued every word of the manuscript, transcribed dozens of interviews and supported me through months of working seven days a week on the content. God has truly blessed me with her love and partnership!

My daughter, Hailee, has supported me in speaking engagements across the country; my son, Kaia, has sacrificed time with me and been an encouragement during the writing process; and my amazing mother, Carol, has—as always—been a wonderful cheerleader.

Thanks to my agent, Amanda Luedeke, with MacGregor Literary, for working with me to create a solid proposal, and then shepherding the project to IVP.

Thanks to David Zimmerman for taking an interest in bringing the book to IVP.

Thank you to the dedicated prayer team who prayed daily for this project as I wrote: S. Randall Gooder, Sean Tienharra, Gaylene Golden, Annette Jurecki, Pricilla Poindexter, Connie Kottmann, Damilola Opedun, Dean and

Judi Estes, Lisa Marten, Susie McElroy, Carol McElroy and Marco Ray.

Thanks to the prayer supporters who have been praying with me over every aspect of the ministry for many years: Eric and Meredith Poland, Jeff Sparks, Wendy Weeks, A. J. Corrales, Becky Pico, Bryan Meyers, Steve Freeman, Annie Gonzales, Cathy Feeman, Cathy Howie, Colleen Clifford, Alyee Willets, Ann Williams, Dan and Marsha Kiel, Danny Wright, Dave Noel, Don Renollet, Eddie Mathews, Elizabeth Harriman, Geoff Wybrow, Holly Worrick, Jacqueline Furness, Jane Gooder, Jessie Nilo, Joy Herpel, Johnathan Thomas, Jim Komaskinski, Judy Gilbert, Karen Griffen, Keith and Marcia Calhoun, Matt Guilford, Mitch Malloy, Nathan Tobey, Robbie Hunt, Selah Cohen, Steve Sargent, Sherri Coffield and Tammy Morton.

To those who helped transcribe the many hours of interviews—Tammy Morton, Holly Worrick, Lisa Marten, Sherri Coffield, Dottie Olin, Nancy Kirby and Marcia Calhoun—thank you!

Thanks to all the arts leaders who so willingly gave their time to share what God is doing through the arts in their sphere of influence: David Arcos, Scott Erickson, Amena Brown, Nick Benoit, Theresa Dedmon, Cindy West Limbrick, Paul Ramey, Paul LeFeber, Rodney Schwartz, Ann Williams, Cyndee Buck, Roy Cochran, Tom Clark, Jason Leith, Liz Hetzel, Jim Dobbs, Chris Deeves, Rachael Albano, Dayton Castleman, Keith Crowley, Dave Blakeslee, Aaron Story, Steve Kelso, deAnn Roe, Gilly Sakakini, Fr. Faucher, Heidi Lee, Jason Tennehouse, Jeff Unruh, Darren Wilson, Jill Cardwell, Jonathan Malm, Kaleb Wilcox, Keith Braebender, Kim Miller, Luann Jennings, Marianne Lettieri, Randall Flinn, Jason Moore, Tim Gagnon, Tina Colon Williams, Bryn Gillette, Matt Tommey, Colin Harbinson and others. And a special thank you to Manuel Luz for contributing his thoughts on developing a theology of the arts.

Thanks to Theresa Demon for her friendship and for offering her home as one of my final writing spaces for this work.

Thanks to Indy Vineyard Church, the Up and Out Kinship and IVAC for their support, camaraderie and encouragement.

Appendix

Resources and Extras

THE ARTS AND CREATIVITY in the church is a very broad topic, and there is so much more to say than will fit within the pages of this book. So I am providing you with expanded resources and extras online. You'll find additional material for every chapter: more examples, expanded information and specific details, helpful documents, listings and links to more resources, all complimentary with the purchase of this book.

Simply visit JScottMcElroy.com/CCHandbookextras.

Important online resources include:

Chapter 3: Envisioning the Arts and Creativity in Your Church
- A worksheet for envisioning the arts and creativity in your church
- Seven arts ministries and their vision/mission statements
- More information on the design team concept

Chapter 4: How to Launch an Arts Ministry in Your Church
- The pastors' and leaders' guide to starting an arts ministry in your church
- An arts survey for determining what your arts ministry could focus on

Chapter 5: Inspiring, Empowering and Leading Artists in the Church
- Lists of important books for personal and community book studies

Chapter 6: Crafting a Creative Arts Community

- Creative exercises for your arts community
- A testimony survey from Bethel Church
- Creative meeting icebreakers
- Churches with creative communities

Chapter 7: Structure for Arts Ministry

- A detailed arts ministry budget from VineArts
- How to approach your pastor about arts ministry

Chapter 8: Building a Creative Congregation

- Expanded details, ideas and information for building a creative congregation

Chapter 9: Applications for the Arts and Creativity in Sermons

- Additional applications for sermons

Chapter 10: Five Interactive Art Projects for Churches

- Many more complete art projects for churches, with photos

Chapter 11: Live Art in the Church

- Details on the processes of live painters, including Bryn Gillette's process of painting live with oils and eliminating turpentine fumes
- Thoughts on pricing paintings
- Helpful details on art tables
- What is prophetic art?
- Testimonies on the effect of live art in the church

Chapter 12: Dance in the Church

- More details and examples of dance in the church

Chapter 13: Media, Film and Video

- Tips from professionals on shooting video for your church
- Links to technical experts and sites

- Details about environmental projection
- Links to media sermon illustration
- More about church graphics and design teams
- Resources for backgrounds

Chapter 14: Creating an Art Studio and Workshops to Foster Creativity

- More about church arts studios
- Workshop ideas and examples

Chapter 15: Displaying Art in Your Church

- A VineArts gallery brochure and artwork release forms
- More church gallery examples
- A ministry vision worksheet for galleries

Chapter 16: Creating Sacred Space Experiences

- Complete description of "The Well" sacred space experience
- Advice on go-to material for church stage design
- Lighting advice

Chapter 17: Beyond the Church Walls

- More church outreach ideas

Chapter 18: Your Church as an Arts Patron, and Working with Outside Artists

- Specific info on traveling artists who can perform at your church

Chapter 19: Artists-in-Residence in the Church

- Two artist-in-residence contract examples
- A sample proposal for an artist-in-residence program

Chapter 20: Working Around Barriers to the Arts and Creativity in Your Church

- More discussion of additional barriers and solutions

IVP PRAXIS

EQUIPPING LEADERS FOR MINISTRY

"...TO EQUIP HIS PEOPLE FOR WORKS OF SERVICE,

SO THAT THE BODY OF CHRIST MAY BE BUILT UP."

EPHESIANS 4:12

God has called us to ministry. But it's not enough to have a vision for ministry if you don't have the practical skills for it. Nor is it enough to do the work of ministry if what you do is headed in the wrong direction. We need both vision *and* expertise for effective ministry. We need *praxis*.

Praxis puts theory into practice. It brings cutting-edge ministry expertise from visionary practitioners. You'll find sound biblical and theological foundations for ministry in the real world, with concrete examples for effective action and pastoral ministry. Praxis books are more than the "how to"—they're also the "why to." And because *being* is every bit as important as *doing*, Praxis attends to the inner life of the leader as well as the outer work of ministry. Feed your soul, and feed your ministry.

If you are called to ministry, you know you can't do it on your own. Let Praxis provide the companions you need to equip God's people for life in the kingdom.

www.ivpress.com/praxis